THE POLITICAL PHILOSOPHY
OF NEEDS

This ambitious and lively book argues for a rehabilitation of the concept of 'human needs' as central to politics and political theory. Contemporary political philosophy has focused on issues of justice and welfare to the exclusion of the important issues of political participation, democratic sovereignty and the satisfaction of human needs, and this has had a deleterious effect on political practice. Lawrence Hamilton develops a compelling positive conception of human needs: the evaluation of needs must be located within a more general analysis of institutions, but can in turn help to justify forms of coercive authority that are directed towards the transformation of political and social institutions and practices. His argument is animated throughout by provocative and original discussions of topics such as autonomy, recognition, rights, civil society, liberalism and democracy, and will interest a wide range of readers in political and social philosophy, political theory, law, development and policy.

Lawrence A. Hamilton is Mellon Research Fellow at Clare Hall, Cambridge and Senior Lecturer in the Political Science Programme, Faculty of Human Sciences, University of Natal, Durban, South Africa. He has published a number of journal articles.

THE POLITICAL
PHILOSOPHY OF NEEDS

LAWRENCE A. HAMILTON

Clare Hall, Cambridge
University of Natal, Durban, South Africa

 CAMBRIDGE
UNIVERSITY PRESS

PUBLISHED BY THE PRESS SYNDICATE OF THE UNIVERSITY OF CAMBRIDGE
The Pitt Building, Trumpington Street, Cambridge CB2 1RP, United Kingdom

CAMBRIDGE UNIVERSITY PRESS
The Edinburgh Building, Cambridge, CB2 2RU, UK
40 West 20th Street, New York, NY 10011–4211, USA
477 Williamstown Road, Port Melbourne, VIC 3207, Australia
Ruiz de Alarcón 13, 28014 Madrid, Spain
Dock House, The Waterfront, Cape Town 8001, South Africa

http://www.cambridge.org

First published 2003

Printed in the United Kingdom at the University Press, Cambridge

Typeface Adobe Garamond 11/12.5 pt.   *System* LATEX 2$_\varepsilon$ [TB]

A catalogue record for this book is available from the British Library

Library of Congress Cataloguing in Publication data
Hamilton, Lawrence A., 1972–
The political philosophy of needs / Lawrence A. Hamilton.
p.   cm.
Includes bibliographical references and index.
ISBN 0 521 82782 5
1. Common good.   2. Public interest.   3. Basic needs.   4. Civil society.
5. Democracy.   6. Political participation.   1. Title.
JC330.15.H36   2003   320′01′1 – dc21   2003043811

ISBN 0 521 82782 5 hardback

You invent luxury
I invent humiliation
You invent love
                I invent solitude
You invent the law
And I invent obedience
You invent God
And I invent faith
You invent work
And I invent hands
You invent weight
And I invent a back
You invent another life
And I invent resignation
You invent sin
And I **remain** in Hell
So help me God
                    —Tom Zé and
            Odair Cabesa de Poeta

Contents

vii

Preface

This book is about human needs and politics. These are vast, complex areas of human action, interaction, conflict and value, and the reader may wonder why I chose to tackle both topics and not one or the other. The reason is simple. Quite early on I realised that both needs and politics have to be understood in their unexpurgated historical, causal, cognitive and normative contexts, and an understanding of one involves an understanding of the other. I do not profess to have got very far in either task, or in my related task of developing proposals for the evaluation of needs and institutions. That is for the reader to judge. However, the fact that I take this view about how to understand needs and politics explains why I cover two big topics in one relatively small book, and why I hope this contribution to political philosophy may also be of use to moral and legal philosophers, political scientists, economists, sociologists and policy-makers.

What I know about politics and political philosophy in general is, amongst other things, the fruit of many conversations and arguments with a number of people. It gives me great pleasure to single out and thank a few of them. One person in particular has pride of place: Raymond Geuss, my teacher and friend. Raymond was my original thesis supervisor, and I would like to thank him for his constant intellectual inspiration, guidance and discussion, and for his ability simultaneously to encourage freedom over ideas while demanding strict control over delivery. I am deeply grateful to Lisa Brown for many years of creative stimulation, and for providing invaluable criticism of my work at every stage of its development. She found things to discuss and correct on every page of a number of 'final' drafts. I am indebted to Amartya Sen, John Dunn, Stephanie Blankenburg, Ze'ev Emmerich and Geoffrey Hawthorn, all of whom provided searching criticism and patient guidance in reading and commenting on earlier draft chapters and sections. I thank two anonymous readers for Cambridge University Press and my original thesis examiners, Andrew Gamble and David Runciman, for their careful reading of the manuscript and for crucial suggestions. I owe particular thanks to David Bilchitz, Lucy Delap, Des Gasper, Freddy Hamilton, Jeesoon Hong, Istvan Hont, Jaeho Kang, Andy Kuper, Melissa Lane, Clive Lawson, Tanni Mukhopadyay, Glen Rangwala, Sanjay Ruparelia, Morag Patrick and Andrea Sangiovanni for reading, criticising and discussing parts of the manuscript with care and fervour. Final thanks go to my parents: pillars of support and founts of knowledge for longer than I can remember. Although I have sometimes been unable or too pigheaded to follow all advice and criticism, all these people have provided invaluable help and stimulus. None of them, however, should be construed as responsible for any of the remaining mistakes and deficiencies in what follows.

I would like to acknowledge the generosity of the Cambridge Commonwealth Trust and the Cambridge Political Economy Society Trust for funding my doctoral research. I am particularly indebted to Clare Hall, Cambridge, for electing me as their Mellon Research Fellow, thereby providing me with financial support and an excellent environment to continue my research. I am very grateful to Cambridge University Press, and in particular Hilary Gaskin, for making the arduous task of transforming a manuscript into a book seem simple.

The final section of the second chapter is an abridged and modified version of my article, 'A Theory of True Interests in the Work of Amartya Sen', *Government and Opposition*, 34. 4 (1999). The first three sections of the third chapter are an extended and developed version of my article, '"Civil Society": Critique and Alternative', in *Global Civil Society and Its Limits*, edited by S. Halperin and G. Laxer (London: Palgrave, 2003).

I would like to thank Tom Zé for permission to reprint several lines of the song lyrics from his track 'Ui ! (Você Inventa)'. I have been aided in my translation by the translation found in *The Best of Tom Zé* (Milwaukee, WI: Luaka Bop, Inc., 1990).

Introduction

Modern moral, legal, economic and political thought is characterised by an unwarranted glorification of the virtues of justice and welfare at the expense of political participation, democratic sovereignty, and the satisfaction of human needs. This characteristic of contemporary thought is closely associated with the current predominance of very abstract and theoretical approaches to politics as opposed to practical forms of political philosophy: moral principles and technical formulae are developed in lieu of an understanding of politics as collective evaluation and decision as determined by the need to act. For example, Kantian rights theory and prevalent forms of utilitarianism adopt opposing political philosophies that reduce politics to either the security of individual human rights or the aggregation of individual preferences. This has the effect of prioritising and sanctifying individual rights on the one hand, and individual preferences on the other. By contrast, in practice, politics is characterised by the constant accommodation of rights and preferences within a larger framework of collective human action. And this practical accommodation is normally based in considerations of human needs. The prevalent exclusive focus on justice and welfare provides little scope for understanding these central elements of politics. Thus it impoverishes our understanding of liberal democratic politics, and stifles practical proposals for transforming that politics.

In order to overcome these problems I develop and defend an approach to theorising and practising politics that is based on a political understanding and conception of human needs. I propose an account of the normative and causal properties of needs, and advance a framework for the political evaluation of needs. This constitutes a needs-based conceptual framework for critically assessing political institutions and public policy, and a broad, speculative outline for a radically new kind of coercive authority. This conception of human needs delivers a means of overcoming the limitations that derive from taking the concepts of rights and utilitarian preferences as the only two relevant variables in politics. Within the contemporary legal and political framework rights are legally, coercively enforceable entitlements that are conceived as being objective, abstract and universal. Preferences, on the other hand, are construed as avowed human wants that are subjective and particular to context, agent and time. They complement one another in theory and practice: rights set the legal structure within which preferences are allegedly given free play. This contingent coupling of rights and preferences, or what I call the rights-preferences couple, constitutes the predominant theoretical *and* practical *framework* for politics today. In other words, what I call the rights-preferences couple is a characterisation not of liberal political theory alone but rather of the relationship and edifice of liberal theory and liberal democratic practice. I argue that this theory and practice together form a loose package of institutions and practices that tend to reinforce and legitimise one another.

The rights-preferences couple is normally justified by historical precedent *and* in terms of its alleged universal efficiency in guaranteeing certain valued political objectives (sometimes with the support of a normative moral theory). In other words, it is defended because of how well it fits into and functions within modern politics of a particular pedigree, about which more below. I reject both of these two main justifying claims, the claims based on historical precedent and universal efficiency; but, before I explain why, it is important to note that I am *not* claiming that rights are useless or proposing that they be completely scrapped. They have a role, especially with regard to issues of efficiency surrounding personal property ownership and exchange. I am claiming, though, that it would be more theoretically and practically felicitous to reduce their significance and scope by understanding them within, or at least as secondary to, a theoretical conception that better articulates the larger material and ethical concerns of practical politics. One possible candidate is the political philosophy of needs developed in this book.

I   LIBERALISM'S RIGHTS-PREFERENCES COUPLE

It has become customary amongst the more acute analysts of rights to make a strict distinction between positive, legal rights and natural or human rights; or, in other words, between those rights specified within particular civil codes and those rights whose grounds hold 'by nature' or those rights applicable to all human beings. Jeremy Bentham is a famous modern example, although there have been others since. In making the distinction he dismissed natural rights as 'nonsense upon stilts'.[1] The distinction is

---

[1] J. Bentham, *Anarchical Fallacies*, in J. Waldron (ed.), *'Nonsense Upon Stilts': Bentham, Burke, and Marx on the Rights of Man* (London: Methuen, 1987), p. 53.

real and important, but it can sometimes cloud the fact that even the most basic of legal rights, like certain civil liberties, are constitutive parts of civil codes that have historical and ideological links to broader philosophies of rights. The link may be opaque in the most pared-down of civil codes, but it has become more obvious where legal rights have been expanded beyond civil liberties to include 'social', 'welfare', and 'labour' rights. And it is manifest in those systems of law that have incorporated the doctrine of human rights into their civil codes, something common to countries as constitutionally diverse as Britain and South Africa. In the contemporary world, the doctrine of human rights is in the process of changing from being a set of moral demands erratically upheld by international law to a central element or supplement of civil codes. Hence, in what follows, I do not always stick to the distinction between natural and legal rights. When I do not specify the kinds of rights I am talking about, I mean rights as they are encountered within modern *liberal* discourse and political practice; that is, as part of an overarching political philosophy and practice founded on individual rights justified by nature, reason or extant civil code.[2]

A political philosophy founded on rights is illusory, and in practice it often acts counter to some of its own intended goals. This is the case because thinking about modern politics in terms of rights is a crude means of political explanation or ethical assessment and proposal, not least of all because rights, I claim, are in fact retrospective and impede change and evaluation. This is partly due to the fact that rights are *meta*-political: they naturalise and hierarchise political and ethical means and ends prior to any contextual political process of evaluation. They are the outcome of an attempt to provide secure conditions for a particular kind of political rule and order, but when stipulated in the form of rights these conditions depoliticise politics. They entrench the status quo and undermine the need for political participation. But this rigidity and inherent conservatism is also due to the fact that rights have their historical source in, and have developed alongside, institutions and practices that are ill suited to modern

---

[2] A distinction of some kind is still important: one way of proceeding might be to begin with a more general distinction between rights as they appear within particular civil codes and those found in philosophies of rights, rather than the customary one between legal and natural rights. One could then move on to make distinctions between the various theories of rights and investigate their overlap with, and influences upon, particular civil codes. This is no simple task. Modern (broadly) liberal political philosophy now parades a varied array of rights theories. Just for starters, there is a distinction between 'will' or 'choice' theories of rights and 'interest' or 'welfare' theories of rights. For examples of the former see W. Hohfeld, *Fundamental Legal Conceptions as Applied in Judicial Reasoning* (Westport, CT: Greenwood Press, 1978); and H. L. A. Hart, 'Are There Any Natural Rights?', *The Philosophical Review*, 64. 2 (April 1955), pp. 175–9. And for examples of the latter, see J. Raz, *The Morality of Freedom* (Oxford: Oxford University Press, 1986); J. Feinberg, *Rights, Justice and the Bounds of Liberty* (Princeton: Princeton University Press, 1980).

politics, for example, the institutions and practices of the seventeenth- and eighteenth-century European occupation, exploitation and enslavement of non-European (and non-Christian) land and peoples. The forerunners of modern liberal rights-discourse and the modern notion of human rights, the natural rights theories of early modern Europe, in their Grotian, Hobbesian and Lockean forms, provided the overarching ideological framework that legitimised the colonial exploits of countries like Spain, France, Holland and England. As in the case of modern human rights and the discourse of globalisation, natural rights were both a universal moral guide for how isolated sovereign agents should treat the inhabitants of the 'new world' and a means to guide imperial powers and sovereign individual *conquistadores* in their colonial land grab.[3] Moreover, this intellectual history suggests that the origin of the modern notions of individual rights, autonomy and sovereignty is the outcome of an analogy between the sovereign state in a condition of perpetual war (in a state of nature) and the condition of the modern individual.[4] The fact that the mainstays of western freedom, and individual autonomy (or sovereignty), are supported by an analogy forged in an era of colonial violence and exploitation casts serious doubt on the suitability and significance of the analogy and its concomitant notion of individual rights for contemporary political understanding and prescription. However, in order to provide a full defence of these claims concerning rights, I would require (at least) an account of the social, historical and ideological links between these antecedent institutions, practices and ideas and the present predominance of rights-discourse. That long and complicated history will not be recounted here.[5] But if that historical record is

[3] The difference between natural rights and human rights is that natural law draws on the idea of a single deity (Christian God) as the creator of general, universal *static* laws of human nature and reason, an idea that ultimately depends on the claim that this deity can 'enforce' these natural, pre- or meta-political rights. Without recourse to God, human rights must create its own secular (human) version – we have rights by virtue of being human and once we institute a global, legal order we have a kind of Global God. Witness the current 'globalisation' debate and the willingness of western powers to 'defend' human rights as they intervene in the internal affairs of other countries of whose regimes they disapprove. Thus this difference between natural and human rights is in fact immaterial; monotheistic imperialism lives on healthy and secure. See my 'Needs, States, and Markets: democratic sovereignty against imperialism', *Theoria*, 102 (December 2003). For the significance of colonial conquest in the political theories of Grotius, Hobbes and Locke, see R. Tuck, *The Rights of War and Peace: Political Thought and the International Order from Grotius to Kant* (Oxford: Oxford University Press, 1999); D. Armitage, *The Ideological Origins of the British Empire* (Cambridge: Cambridge University Press, 2000).

[4] Tuck, *War and Peace*.

[5] For more on this particular intellectual and political history, see Tuck, *War and Peace*; A. Pagden, *Lords of All the World: Ideologies of Empire in Spain, Britain and France c.1500–c.1800* (New Haven and London: Yale University Press, 1995). And for the contemporary importance of the early modern period, see R. Tuck, *Natural Rights Theories: Their origin and development* (Cambridge: Cambridge

correct, the first claim – historical precedence – in the usual defence of the rights-preferences couple is very seriously challenged. This is the claim that, based on its allegedly long and creditable pedigree in the history of western political thought and politics, the rights-preferences couple is the natural basic category to use in understanding politics.

If the historical argument I have given is not persuasive enough, there are two more related and important historical facts that together throw doubt on the claim of historical precedence. The first is that rights-discourse antedated by several centuries anything that could be called 'liberalism' in its modern theory and practice. The relationship between rights and liberalism is a purely contingent one. Second, the idea that a whole series of rights could be the free-standing and universal framework for politics is a very recent idea that arose partly from the fact that today's rights were developed under the aegis of, and are now irrevocably linked to, the relatively efficient operation of a legal apparatus (of the kind that has developed in western European countries in the past hundred years or so).[6] That is, in contrast to the lean moral philosophy of natural rights, the modern legal and political practices and theories surrounding rights are now able to justify rights without much recourse to nature (or God).[7] It is under these modern procedural constraints that rights in the form of privileges have become rights as the *objective* property of political subjects who are *universally* equal before the law.[8] Hence, modern rights are *not* free-standing, self-evident, universally accepted material requirements or moral elements of universal human nature or existence. Rather, I suggest, the ascription of rights to individuals is better seen as dependent on a wider social framework and certain extant kinds of political formations.

As regards the second claim in the usual defence of the rights-preferences couple, the universal efficiency justification, it is argued that a properly instituted and enforced objective rights structure guarantees human life and

University Press, 1979); A. S. Brett, *Liberty, Right and Nature: Individual rights in later scholastic thought* (Cambridge: Cambridge University Press, 1997); R. Dagger, 'Rights', in T. Ball, J. Farr and R. L. Hanson (eds.), *Political Innovation and Conceptual Change* (Cambridge: Cambridge University Press, 1989); J. Finnis, *Natural Law and Natural Rights* (Oxford: Clarendon Press, 1980).

6 R. Geuss, *History and Illusion in Politics* (Cambridge: Cambridge University Press, 2001).

7 I say without *much* recourse to nature (or God) because within this literature and practice, and within liberalism more generally, the idea of natural human rights is understood as a legitimate and legitimising given. For examples, see R. Dworkin, *Taking Rights Seriously* (London: Duckworth, 1977, repr. 1991), p. vi; J. Rawls, *A Theory of Justice* (Oxford: Oxford University Press, 1973), pp. 28, 30–3, 505n; Rawls, *Political Liberalism* (New York: Columbia University Press, 1996), pp. xliv–xlviii, 6, 16, 77, 108–9n, 180.

8 For an account of the historical transformations of privileges into rights, see M. Mann, *The Sources of Social Power*, 2 vols. (Cambridge: Cambridge University Press, 1986–92); J. A. Hall, *Powers and Liberties: The Causes and Consequences of the Rise of the West* (Oxford: Basil Blackwell, 1984).

liberty, and provides equal 'freedom' for all with regard to their preferences and choices.[9] This is an appealing image of politics in which rights act as safeguards or guarantees that the state must honour: at least in theory, it escapes the uncertainties of consequentialist ethics and practices. But this claim lacks empirical support on three separate fronts. First, an abstract, universal code of rights often inhibits the attainment of the valued ideals and guarantees found within particular civil codes. There are a number of cases in which these rights *weaken* the civil liberties embedded in the legal system of a society. For instance, the suspension in Northern Ireland of trial by jury in terrorism cases is a classic example of how civil liberties can be suspended under the auspices of arguments concerning the state's obligation to secure the lives (natural right) of its citizens.[10]

The second front on which the universal efficiency claim lacks empirical support is that the enforcement of rights is *de facto* too fragile and distorted to achieve the goal of guaranteeing human life and liberty. The supposed inviolability and unconditionality of rights are constantly belied by the actual practice of their enforcement, determined as it is by conditions that cannot be forced to fit the rigid framework of objective, legal rights. Think how often actual individuals' rights are overridden by their governments. The right to life is weak in the face of capital punishment; the right to freedom of movement is restricted by incarceration and national boundaries; and no state on the globe would allow free movement around, and information about, its army bases.[11] But even if we discount these 'special' cases, rights have become so prolific in practice that not only have they lost any significant relationship to institutional or individual responsibility, but also their proliferation entrenches an already over-legalistic approach to political evaluation. Rights proliferation creates increased conflicts over rights, and the resolution of these conflicts reduces political evaluation

---

[9] E.g. Rawls, *Political Liberalism*, pp. xli, xlviii. In Rawls' case, as with many liberals, another condition is the provision of 'all-purpose means' ('primary goods' or 'basic needs') to make effective use of these rights (p. 6). See chapter 1, section 5, and chapter 4, section 4, for why it is misguided to understand the necessary conditions for freedom in terms of 'all-purpose means'.

[10] The British government at the time justified this move by arguing that trial by jury was setting free too many 'terrorists' and thereby endangering the population. There was no consideration at all of weighing up other outcomes against that risk, for example the consequence of removing an important instance of citizen participation in the structures of government (which is the underlying reason Britain has trial by jury), because rights trumped any consequentialist considerations. R. Tuck, 'The Dangers of Natural Rights', *Harvard Journal of Law & Public Policy*, 20. 13 (1997), pp. 683–93. As Tuck notes, this kind of justification and move is reminiscent of Hobbes' absolutist account, which is not the kind of association that would please modern liberal theorists, politicians and commentators – the cheerleaders of 'democracy'.

[11] Geuss, *History and Illusion in Politics*, p. 148.

to the legal adjudication of *individual* rights claims.[12] This kind of evaluation occurs within unelected administrative bodies rather than elected institutions and is therefore neither political nor accountable. Thus rights-based politics reinforces judicial sovereignty and makes a mockery of the idea of accountability. These consequences of the legalisation of politics reduce rather than enhance equality of freedom over preferences and choice because they make one's freedom dependent on one's educational and financial ability to access legal advice and support. And they tend to create the illusion of political power while undermining real individual political agency. When we defend our rights we naturally feel better about our power within the existing political framework, but this diverts our attention away from evaluating the way our governments govern, and the broader political questions of who is governing whom and how. This legalisation of politics under the auspices of rights is no accident, for rights create problems not because of their individualistic character so much as their jural character. They conceive of persons as legal rather than political agents.

An objective rights structure therefore does not provide equal 'freedom' for all with regard to their preferences and choices. This problem is reinforced by the third manner in which the claim concerning the universal efficiency justification lacks empirical support. In practice, rights are associated with the unconditional prioritisation of an individual's preferences, independent of any assessment of the material conditions under which the preferences were formed or of the effects on the lives of other individuals on satisfying the avowed preferences. In other words, rights-based political theory and practice provides the conditions for the theoretical defence of, and practical dependence on, avowed and unevaluated individual preferences. More specifically, this theory and practice engenders and legitimises the *idea* of the inviolability of utilitarian preferences. And thinking about politics in utilitarian terms generally provides a ready, though artificially restricted, means of defending the prioritisation of preferences: preferences are deemed important for reasons that relate to their epistemological importance in *calculating* individual welfare or as a consequence of the moral imperative to respect individuals' judgement about the 'good life' and how it relates to the living of their lives. Both of these concerns are important and retain a place in my account of needs. However, in their present rights-preferences mould they tend to generate the *unconditional* prioritisation of subjective preferences despite the acknowledged fact that preferences are determined (at least in part) by sources beyond the individuals who avow

[12] R. A. Primus, *The American Language of Rights* (Cambridge: Cambridge University Press, 1999).

them. Amongst other things, this *a priori* principle of priority excludes any systematic political process of evaluation or transformation of preferences, that is, any account of how preferences are and ought to be transformed. And this indiscriminate exclusion impoverishes our understanding of and control over the institutions and practices that do in fact determine, influence and transform our preferences, for example, existing state institutions and practices such as constitutions, legal practices and welfare provision, and extant market-related institutions and practices, such as consumption practices.

These problems emerge because preference-based political theory tends to reinforce subjectivist understandings of politics. In artificially isolating individual concerns and preferences, it engenders the idea that preferences are unaffected by larger societal structures, and that the satisfaction of individual preferences has little effect beyond the individual concerned. Moreover, it tends to exclude from political analysis and politics the evaluation of objective human goods. Hence, preference-based political theory not only generates acknowledged difficulties in specifying how preferences should be aggregated in social decision contexts,[13] it also undermines the political significance of objective human goods. And a political philosophy founded on the aggregation of human preferences only reinforces (and sometimes even disguises) these shortcomings.

In sum, the rights-preferences couple is either too abstracted from normal human motivation for action, or too subjective and particular in its analysis of how human drives, preferences and attitudes relate to human goods and the means to their attainment. It bifurcates and impoverishes political theory; and theorists who adopt it tend to exclude a large domain of modern politics. This domain, arguably the central domain of politics, is concerned with the urgent distribution of resources and requirements for human functioning under conditions of non-agreement. Concomitantly, any attempted *analysis* of this domain in terms of rights or preferences

---

[13] These difficulties have been the objects of intense theoretical study and debate, the original modern account of which is Arrow's General Impossibility Theorem: K. J. Arrow, *Social Choice and Individual Values*, 2nd edn (New Haven: Yale University Press, 1963 [1st edn 1952]). But Sen provides the best introduction to the context and formal elements of the theory: A. K. Sen, *Collective Choice and Social Welfare* (San Francisco: Holden-Day, 1970). The problems concerning social choice have their basis in utilitarian-inspired philosophies of economics, like those developed by Walras and Pareto, which turned on the impossibility of making interpersonal comparisons of manifest preferences. As Tuck notes, in 'The Dangers of Natural Rights', p. 690, this rests on a scepticism about whether anything worthwhile can be said about the mental processes that might underlie manifest preferences, a scepticism with its origins in the work of Hobbes. The notion of 'revealed preference' simply systematised this basic thought. For more on these issues, see my discussion of Davidson's response to the problem in chapter 2, section 5.

results in a tendency to underplay the motivational and conflictual elements of everyday politics.

2 BEYOND THE RIGHTS-PREFERENCES COUPLE

The political philosophy of needs I develop here elucidates and rehabilitates a concern with this rejected domain of politics. This political philosophy stresses the central significance of conflict and evaluation in politics, especially conflict over power and value and the evaluation of needs and institutions. It develops and defends a method of political evaluation that connects avowed preferences with more objective and often divisive human concerns and interests. And it shows why these conflicts cannot be resolved or overcome by means of theoretical, *meta*-political diktat. Rather they are inherently practical problems that require contextual evaluative and ultimately coercive 'resolution' within specified structures of authority and participation. Thus the political philosophy of needs proposed here involves a conception of needs and a specification of these need-disclosing structures. This conception of needs is at once more motivational than the current conception of rights and more objective than the prevalent utilitarian conception of preference, but it is developed within a framework that proposes constant recourse to individual preferences. It clarifies why preferences are indispensable in the everyday evaluation of needs and why they have ontological and epistemological significance, and it clears a path between the abstract objectivity of rights on one side and the particular subjectivity of preferences on the other. Furthermore, in retaining a significant motivational element, this approach to needs provides an improved means of capturing some of the claims people bring to the political arena, and of understanding and explaining a common language of politics. For it is an empirical fact that the terms 'need' and 'needs' are constantly employed in practical politics: the notion of need is a mainstay in policy-oriented discourse, analysis and legislation.[14]

---

[14] I have chosen four random everyday examples. (a) According to Senator George Mitchell in a speech on Northern Ireland (2/12/1998), 'Peace and stability are the minimum needs for a caring society.' (b) As current Mayor of London, Ken Livingstone believes he 'would be bringing the needs of Londoners to the government' (Channel 4 News, 15/11/1999). (c) For Thabo Mbeki, the South African President at the time of writing, 'The question is: Do we as political leaders have the will to permit the fundamental national imperative of addressing the people's needs to take precedence over narrow partisan interests?'. Mbeki speech, Budget vote, National Assembly, Cape Town, 6 June 1995, in T. Mbeki, *Africa: The Time Has Come* (Cape Town/Johannesburg: Tafelburg/Mafube, 1998), p. 144. (d) Clause 2 of the 1978 Transport Act (of Parliament) requires County Councils in England and Wales to review existing services 'in relation to need' – the White Paper, *Transport Policy 1977 Cmnd. 6836*, 'lays it down as one objective of official policy to "meet social needs by

There is, therefore, an urgent practical imperative for theorists to clarify what people feel and mean when they use the concept of need and related terms and concepts in modern politics. However, most recent attempts at theoretical elucidation have struggled against a common misperception that need-based political theory *necessarily* provides theoretical support for the overriding of people's preferences because it tends to condone paternalist politics and *dirigisme*.[15] This has been reinforced not only by the history of Soviet communism, which in practice lived up to its billing as the 'dictatorship over needs',[16] but also by an unhelpful polarisation that has taken place in the broadly liberal theoretical analysis of needs. On one side, theorists tend to stick devotedly to the rights-preferences couple, ruling out of court any mention of needs. At the other extreme, most modern theorists who have been concerned with needs have developed static, purely normative conceptions that conceive of needs as universal basic requirements of human existence that 'ought' to be met by the state and whose evaluation can safely ignore preferences and the evaluation of how needs are formed.[17] This theoretical disregard for preferences has created a strong association between the concept of need and paternalism (about which more below).

Yet the common idea of a stark theoretical *impasse* or dichotomy with regard to needs, especially with regard to how Marxism and liberalism conceive of needs, shrouds a greater degree of intricacy and overlap. Although liberal theorists are avowed devotees of the rights-preferences couple, in practice liberalism employs needs at every level of policy and politics.[18] Since the theoretical problems inherent in the aggregation of individuals' preferences for social policy are also practical ones, policy-makers and politicians have no option but to make constant recourse to the notion of need. In any case, as is discussed below, needs creep in even at the level of theory, though admittedly in a warped form. Liberal theorists like Rawls and Dworkin tend to champion the priority of individual preference while at the same time developing theoretical systems that attempt to provide the *conditions for* the heeding of 'freely' formed preferences. Their theoretical

---

securing a reasonable level of mobility"'. D. Wiggins, 'Claims of Need', in *Needs, Values, Truth: Essays in the Philosophy of Value*, 3rd edn (Oxford: Clarendon Press, 1998), p. 4n.

[15] For an example of the misperception concerning *dirigisme*, see A. Flew, *The Politics of Procrustes* (London: Temple Smith, 1981), pp. 115–18.

[16] F. Fehér, A. Heller and G. Márkus, *The Dictatorship Over Needs* (Oxford: Basil Blackwell, 1983).

[17] Rather than give a selective list of the theorists I have in mind here, I refer the reader to chapter 1.

[18] Wiggins captures the situation with aplomb: 'In practice — and to an extent that could not be predicted or even suspected on the basis of an examination of present day political theory — the political-cum-administrative process as we know it in Europe and North America could scarcely continue (could scarcely even conclude an argument) without constant recourse to the idea of need.' Wiggins, 'Claims of Need', p. 4.

blueprints rest on notions such as 'primary goods as citizens' needs' and 'resource equality'.[19] At the other extreme, western Marxism has tended to denigrate concrete, allegedly universalising, issues like needs. Hence, there is a revealing similarity between liberal and Marxist theory: they have both strayed too far away from the reality of everyday politics. But they have done so for different reasons. Liberal theory has done so as a result of a relatively recent neo-Kantian turn (in both its Rawlsian and Habermasian moulds). Marxist theory has suffered from its own history, as it were, to the extent that it now tends to prefer theoretical deconstruction to the concrete concerns of practical politics. Witness some of its postmodern progeny. And where it has been more concrete it has failed to give clear practical means of discriminating between the diverse goals, needs, rights, preferences and claims that characterise modern politics. One of my main claims is that the philosophy of needs defended here more accurately explains the realities of modern (liberal democratic) politics as well as re-orienting critical political theory towards the basic issues of power, necessity and ethical aspiration that drive daily politics. Consequently, this approach is better positioned to engender certain kinds of political transformations. I attempt to show that if needs are properly understood, not only are the perceptions regarding the necessary relationship between the concept of need and paternalism erroneous, but also that need-based political theory and practice can overcome the inadequacies of the rights-preferences couple.

3   THE FORM AND OUTLINE OF THE ARGUMENT

In the first two chapters I explain the nature of contemporary needs that lies behind the *prima facie* ambiguity of need claims and statements, and provide an understanding of the mechanisms through which different types of need are formed in contemporary society.[20] The first chapter begins by

---

[19] Rawls, *Theory of Justice*, pp. 276f.; *Political Liberalism*, pp. 178–90. However, as will be discussed in chapters 1 and 4, Rawls' conception of needs is a good example of a purely normative approach to needs that (ironically) undermines political participation and the importance of preferences therein.

[20] The contemporary society with which I am immediately concerned is early twenty-first-century Europe, its present ideological dependants, and those countries with an historical connection to Europe developed out of colonialism. This does not mean that I do not think (and hope) that what I propose could be extended beyond these confines to incorporate the entire globe, but that would require a necessarily too large diversion to ensure that the concept of need does not break down in the process of translation. It does not seem too much to presume that the concept, as understood here, has life beyond its English-speaking origins, whether in this exact form or assimilated within cousin concepts. I can vouch that it stretches at least into Spanish, Portuguese, French and German. But that is not much, although thanks to colonialism and imperialism (if I can be forgiven the expression) it is quite far afield.

proposing an heuristic categorisation of need, and describes and analyses the nature of the needs that constitute each category. It pays particular attention to two kinds of *general* needs, what I call vital needs and agency needs. Vital needs are defined as the necessary conditions for minimal human functioning. Agency needs, at least the ones I discuss, 'intersubjective recognition', 'active and creative expression', and 'autonomy', are the necessary conditions for individual and political agency that is characteristic of full human functioning. These are human needs, but human beings do not necessarily (or even normally) feel needs in this general form. *Felt human needs* are normally *particular* in form and are defined as strong motivational forces that take the form of physically felt lack or emotional and ethical aspiration, *and which have direct causal relation to and consequences for human functioning*. The chapter ends with a discussion of the nature of needs that specifies precisely how my approach to needs is distinct from other needs-based political philosophies, for example, modern universalist and relativist approaches to needs and Marx's groundbreaking conceptions of needs.

The second chapter provides a causal analysis of how *particular* needs and wants, or in other words socially interpreted necessities and socially legitimised preferences, are generated and legitimated and analyses how this affects the perception and cognition of vital and agency needs. It focuses on the determinants of normative and causal power relations, and the extant practices and institutions of need recognition and satisfaction. Finally, the link between need and interest is clarified, and an intentionally contextual political concept – true interest – is developed using my account of need coupled with a critical analysis of Amartya Sen's 'capability approach'.

Hence, in my account, needs are defined ultimately in terms of human functioning, not in terms of lack. (I use the idea of lack only for one part of felt needs.) But, in contrast to other theorists who think about politics in terms of human functioning, for example Martha Nussbaum, I do not develop a full *list* of general conditions or general human needs (whose satisfaction constitutes full human functioning). Complete lists of general human needs are archetypal examples of the dictatorship of theory: they are *meta*-political naturalisations of historically contingent human means and ends because they entrench a single moment in a dynamic process. They disregard two facts. (1) A need-based frame of reference in practice is not normally a general (theoretical) frame of reference, but rather a particular one concerned with responding to or changing a particular context. And the substance of these frames of reference is the existing discourses and objects of need and want and the spectrum of desires, not the theoretical needs stipulated by philosophers. (2) Alongside other institutions and practices, existing particular frames of reference influence the content and form of any extant theoretical, general frame of reference. To think otherwise is to make the erroneous assumption that the conceptual and moral world can be isolated from all material and ideological influences. However, it does not follow from this that philosophy or theory cannot be used to elucidate and understand the process of need formation and provision. The general needs that I specify within my approach are part of a conceptual framework for understanding how needs are generated and evaluated within existing societal mechanisms. In contrast to other theories or philosophies they are few in number and highly generalised. The understanding that emerges can be and is used to form a critical frame of reference in different contexts, but I stress that the evaluation of particular needs can and must only be attempted *in situ*, for reasons that relate to the importance of contextual political participation in the evaluation of needs. However, the objectivity of the critical frame of reference developed here is important because it is developed as a means of influencing or transforming the content of any actual empirical framework. The fact that this is not a relativist account of need is also important because a number of determinants of need formation and provision are not restricted to specific contexts. More exactly, there exist institutions and practices that take the same form and produce the same consequences right across the globe; and there are others that, despite being situated in a specific geographical area, causally affect need generation and satisfaction across the globe. Moreover, there is no moral or political reason to restrict our concern with the 'needs of others' to those 'others' within our own context.[21]

For obvious reasons, then, the normativity of need is a central concern of this study. My analysis of the nature of need and my discussion of an *array* of ineluctable vital and agency needs simultaneously emphasise the political character of need *and* negate the possibility of grounding political analysis on a single moral foundation. In contradistinction to the work of Rawls and other proponents of the relatively recent neo-Kantian turn in modern

---

[21] G. Brock (ed.), *Necessary Goods: Our Responsibilities to Meet Others' Needs* (Oxford: Rowman and Littlefield, 1998). However, in contrast to the contributors in this volume, I take this moral philosophical issue to be secondary to the main task of understanding the *political* force and significance of human needs. We may have a moral responsibility to meet the needs of others, but whether we do or not is not going to depend on *a priori* reasoning or individual moral responsibility, but on how needs are perceived and evaluated, and whether we can create institutions that encourage the articulation, recognition, evaluation and satisfaction of (evaluated) needs. Moreover, the evaluation and resources required are of a scale and significance that makes meeting needs primarily a political rather than a moral question.

liberalism, this approach questions the relevance of the quest to identify a fundamental *universal* principle with which to ground political theory. In fact, if my views about the nature of need are correct, the premise and the main conclusions of this prevalent rights-based discourse are false: needs are many in number, mostly strongly felt, often contradictory, and normally specific to (or at least modified by) subject and context. It is an empirical fact that consensus or agreement over them in practice is the exception rather than the rule. Hence, my approach also implicitly rejects the now massive theoretical field of Habermas-inspired discourse ethics and analysis, and its political theoretical offshoot, deliberative democracy. To see need in its full density, force and contentiousness is to see how discourse ethics and deliberative democracy exclude the core of practical politics: felt needs, expressed need-claims and the disputes to which these give rise. Thus, as a model of any kind, this Habermasian theoretical template (which, like Rawls' account, is heavily indebted to Kant) is too wide of the empirical mark to offer much assistance to actual politics.

Consequently, when I use the notion of 'normativity' it is not in the same way as many contemporary thinkers, especially those within the Kantian fold. There is a broad and a narrow sense of normativity. In the broad sense a normative claim or theory is understood as being an evaluative claim or theory as opposed to a descriptive one, where there is not necessarily any further analysis concerning obligation or enforcement: it encompasses a wide range of 'oughts' and 'shoulds' (even those applicable to the evaluation of things like apples). The narrow sense maintains that the normativity of a claim or theory is determined by whether or not it incorporates a claim that there is an absolute moral obligation (often on some particular agent) that X should come about. This is the Kantian and particularly Christian moral usage. I maintain, however, that there is a large and fruitful area of normativity that lies between these two extremes, one aspect of which is the sense of normativity I entertain in relation to need: in short, what ought to be done in any specific context to ensure individual full human functioning and the good life. This, I claim, captures the nature of the kind of normativity that is relevant to politics and political action; rather than beginning from a politically unrealistic, narrow moral notion of normativity, it starts broadly and then works (in context) to narrow the issues down to a number of preferred possibilities. I argue that this understanding of normativity is intimately related to my understanding of politics and to what it is that distinguishes a political theory of need from an apolitical one. If nothing else, politics is an activity defined by some notion of collective choice among differentially assessed paths, where the assessment is in terms of evaluated goods and any significant action in the light of the choice will ultimately involve coercion.[22] I will argue that there are various different actual and possible paths or trajectories down which the development of needs can progress, which I call 'need trajectories', and that some of these can be evaluated as 'better' (in a sense that I will specify) than others. Hence a political theory of needs is one that sees needs as variable in dimension depending on the state of politics, often with a concomitant claim that political action has some hope of influencing the trajectory of needs.

The normativity of need is a central concern of this work for another related reason. Need is a good example of a concept in political, economic and social theory that can easily be misunderstood in merely descriptive terms despite its manifest normative content. An intentionally normative stance is an important move in preventing this slip into the illusion of 'pure description'. There are a number of reasons why 'pure description' is common, one of which is the obstinacy of positivism, but the real ideological basis lies in the link between utilitarianism and the discipline of economics. The legacy of utilitarianism has provided sturdy theoretical support for both the drive to aggregate preferences and the philosophical underpinning to modern neo-classical economic science – the human science that has greatest impact on policy. At its base, as an approach to morality, utilitarianism is subject-relative; it treats pleasure or desire-satisfaction as the sole element in human good, and evaluates actions dependent on their consequences on human welfare determined by individual avowal (preference) alone. Therefore, the value of an act or institution is determined by how much pleasure it produces and this is ascertained by an analysis of preferences alone. These assumptions still underpin most mainstream economic theory, especially econometric (microeconomic) modelling. This is the case because individuals' preferences are relatively easily accessible and the notion of utility is theoretically specific and minimal. The introduction of a normatively and ethically explicit notion of human need complicates the evaluative process at both levels. As will be shown, an evaluation based on need requires more

---

[22] This accords with Weber's important observation that modern societies are characterised by a distinction between the sphere of administration (the postal services, the inland revenue) and the sphere of *politics* strictly so called, in which people are called to make decisions about which values and paths of development they are going to pursue and what forms of collective coercion they are going to accept. M. Weber, *Economy and Society*, ed. G. Roth and C. Wittich (Berkeley: University of California Press, 1978).

participative control on the part of the individuals concerned and the out-come is not a simple formula, but rather a rich account of the physical and mental conditions of individuals (or, where necessary, representative individuals of societal groups) and their quality of life. But, as I argue, it is a mistake to think that the attribution of needs involves more athletic epistemological claims than is the case with the attribution of preferences.

In contrast to utilitarian approaches to value, my account of need implies that value is not determined by pleasure alone but by the (positive or negative) effects of a specific act or institution on the meeting of vital needs and the development of agency needs, as specified here. Hence, this approach to need provides both an alternative means of understanding value and a framework for the evaluative process. The development of this alternative evaluative framework is begun in chapter 3. The chapter starts with an analysis of freedom and rights based on a critique of the recent renaissance in the use and understanding of the concept of 'civil society'. 'Civil society' has been prioritised in theory and practice as an 'arena' within which citizens can and do evaluate their needs and rights free from relations of power. I argue that the concept of civil society is premised on an unrealistic notion of freedom that creates the illusion of an arena of 'free' deliberation separate from relations of power and, therefore, develops a distorted conception of rights. Thus, political theory that adopts this concept actively blocks critical political understanding and distorts the evaluation of how needs are formed and met. The chapter then defends the first part of an alternative approach to understanding how needs and true interests are and could be evaluated, which is rooted in the analysis of need formation developed in the second chapter. I define three main concepts – 'practice', 'institution', and 'role' – and defend the claim that a political economy and sociology that pivot on the use of these concepts in a given concrete context, coupled with an analysis of true interest within an elaborate and frequent census, are an improved means of evaluating need-claims and engendering the meeting of needs. The concept of 'true interest' can then be fully defined: if something is in A's true interest, it designates a particular post-reflective and role-dependent vital or agency need of A in the here and now, or a satisfier thereof that can be justified causally as a means of meeting A's vital needs and developing A's agency needs. The 'truth' in true interests is contextual in two ways. First, given the nature of needs, the evaluation of true interests must make constant recourse to subjectively felt needs and preferences. Second, I reject the assumption that there is or could be an ultimate 'view from nowhere', or universal 'God's eye view'.[23] The evaluation and meeting of true interests is a necessarily incomplete, constant practical process and thus there is a premium on contextual political participation.

It does not follow from the fact that the evaluation of true interests is a necessarily incomplete, practical process that the conditions under which individuals evaluate their true interests cannot be improved. True interest evaluation is dependent on a number of variables that relate to the development and satisfaction of needs, the configuration of institutions and roles, and the distribution of normative power. I show how the configuration of institutions and roles might be transformed in order to ensure the more efficient meeting of particular vital needs *and* the improved development of agency needs and thereby the improved evaluation of true interests. This analysis involves the explanation and defence of what I call 'institutional consequentialism'. I argue that institutions can be evaluated in terms of five measures that relate to their effects on meeting vital needs, on the individual perception of needs and true interests, and on the 'naturalisation' of pathological roles. This consequentialism is *not* a kind of utilitarianism. The evaluation and meeting of needs is not the same as the gratification of subjective preferences or desire, but if it is to be true to the nature of need it must incorporate a rich analysis of preferences and it is at base consequentialist.

In chapter 4, I argue that a coercive authority is a precondition if these evaluative goals are to obtain. This is the case not only because there is always the possibility that some groups might vehemently defend the criticised institutions and roles, but also because there is a need for an ultimate evaluator of possible trajectories of need. In other words, there is a practical imperative for there to be a single agent that can use its authority to decide when to act upon the outcome of the proposed method of need evaluation and what action to take in the light of that outcome. I maintain that the modern state is the coercive authority that has the *potential* to meet these conditions, but it will fulfil this potential *if and only if* it institutionalises successfully this need-based and institution-directed dynamic approach to constant transformation. This is the case because the state would gain the authority to resolve conflicts over institutions, roles and need trajectories when it successfully institutionalises this process. I analyse the nature and functions of the modern state, arguing that at least in one sense its legitimacy

---

[23] The rejection of an ultimate 'view from nowhere' and a universal 'God's eye view' has its source in Nietzsche's account of objectivity and truth. For further discussion and references, see the end of chapter 2.

(and authority) are determined already by how well it carries out its functions as ultimate need evaluator and ultimate guarantor for the meeting of
valued needs.[24] However, in order for the modern state to become the kind
of need-disclosing state envisaged here it would have to become a radically
new kind of political authority. I call this radically new kind of authority,
the state of needs. But it does not follow from this understanding that the
state of needs could be or ought to be the actual provider for the valued
needs; under certain conditions and in some areas the market might do
a more efficient job.[25] I then provide a modest, speculative institutional
proposal for how citizens might efficiently evaluate and communicate their
interests and needs to the state of needs and have greater control over
the periodic requirement to choose between possible need trajectories. I
confine my proposal to institutions related to the required political participation and related constitutional safeguards. Built into this proposal is
an account of how citizens might evaluate their government's mechanisms
of evaluation and transformation. The argument ends with a discussion
of legitimacy and paternalism in the light of my proposal for the state of
needs. The political philosophy of needs advanced in this book includes a
number of safeguards against paternalist politics and one of its goals is to
generate strict anti-paternalism with regard to needs. However, in contrast
to liberalism's principled allergy to all forms of paternalism, which marks a
failure to acknowledge the reality of human dependence, my account analyses different kinds of paternalism and thus permits the identification of
forms of paternalism that are not only benign, but also necessary to human
functioning.[26]

In contrast to both Hegel and Marx's positions, the state of needs in
my proposal is not understood teleologically either as the apotheosis of a
society's *Sittlichkeit* or as that thing which necessarily needs to be overcome
to reach real communism; in other words, it does not require the kind
of metaphysics that underpin these kinds of 'leap[s] to the kingdom of

---

[24] States in practice are also simply structures of domination. This empirical fact (along with facts
obtainable through an analysis of international capitalism) helps explain why existing legitimate
states facilitate the meeting of needs to widely varying degrees of proficiency. Moreover, states
have to meet certain requirements in order to continue to exist as states. It is important to keep
these different facts and considerations in balance while attempting to understand the state. J. Dunn,
The Cunning of Unreason: Making Sense of Politics (London: HarperCollins, 2000), p. 78.

[25] The complex issues surrounding the provision for needs are discussed at the end of chapter 4, but
only relatively cursorily. I will develop this in a work provisionally entitled *States and Markets of
Needs*.

[26] I am indebted to an anonymous Cambridge University Press reader for criticisms and suggestions
on the topic of paternalism. I have taken the liberty of lifting some phrases verbatim from her or
his report.

freedom'.[27] It is a main claim of this account that evaluating and attending to need will continue to be a *political* problem, requiring a coercive authority understood in *functional* terms. I develop a practically applicable conceptual and evaluative apparatus that develops out of my account of true interest evaluation, but it does not follow from this that the concept of true interest somehow resolves once and for all the constant political problem of need; nor do I think the concept of need can be replaced by the concept of interest. Not only are the concepts of need and true interest inseparable — the one is necessary for the conceptual existence of the other — but also the choice over the trajectories of need remains a fundamental procedure. And, of course, it is needs not interests that are constantly formed, satisfied and left unsatisfied.

Moreover, as is evident in my discussion of true interests, I reject the kind of universalism that either defends or assumes a 'view from nowhere', which in most cases emerges from at least an implicit belief in a universal 'God's eye view'. This kind of universalism is all too common in political philosophy and theory, and, as I will argue, it normally rests on misguided assumptions about impartiality that tend to impoverish practical politics, political participation and evaluation. For example, the well-intentioned impulses to provide full theoretical lists of human needs or theoretical blueprints for elaborate institutional design undermine rather than facilitate political understanding, guidance and agency.[28] In the kind of political philosophy I develop, theory and theoretical proposal are envisaged as a kind of filter that works to undermine needs, interests, institutions and roles that are counterproductive to the meeting of vital and agency needs, while providing theoretical support for true interests and certain kinds of need trajectories, and their associated institutions and roles. This does *not*,

---

[27] A. Walicki, *Marxism and the Leap to the Kingdom of Freedom: The Rise and Fall of the Communist Utopia* (Stanford: Stanford University Press, 1995).

[28] For example, Rawls argues that 'we must find some point of view, removed from and not distorted by the particular features and circumstances of the all-encompassing background framework, from which a fair agreement between persons regarded as free and equal can be reached'. Rawls, *Political Liberalism*, p. 23. This point of view, Rawls claims, is the original position (with the features he calls the 'veil of ignorance', p. 23). The significance of the notion of the 'original position' as a 'device of representation' (p. 24) is a disputed point amongst commentators, but it is beyond dispute that it reveals the intuition of ('God's eye view') impartiality that underpins Rawls' political liberalism: he claims that we can 'enter this position at any time simply by reasoning for principles of justice in accordance with the enumerated restrictions on information' (p. 27). As is argued below, in chapter 2, section 3, the idea that citizens can perform this kind of 'role playing' (p. 27) or 'reasonable' impartiality with regard to their individual material, political and ethical interests (p. xliv) asks too much of human beings, and it does so because it rests on a misconstrual of needs and interests. In *Theory of Justice* Rawls calls this sharing a 'common standpoint'. Rawls, *Theory of Justice*, pp. 526–7. See chapter 1, section 5, for a discussion of various other examples of 'God's eye view' universalism.

however, restrict theory to pure critique. The kind of political philosophy defended here is intended as a means of guiding political action and choice. It is concerned with truth and truths, especially with regard to the history and extant forms of human needs, institutions and practices; and it discusses objective human goods and develops practically applicable conceptual and institutional proposals. But the result is not a universal theoretical blueprint for action and institutional construction. Any theoretical proposals within my speculative account of the state of needs, say, are intended merely as modest guidelines that will only take their full, developed form in the practical context of their application. It follows from this approach to political philosophy, therefore, that in order to get some grasp of how theoretical guidelines might influence contextual practice theorists must descend from the 'heights' of theory and attempt to experiment with their proposals in a particular concrete context. In the main conclusion, therefore, I provide an example of how an existing institutional arrangement might be transformed in line with my understanding of needs and my speculative proposal for transforming one institution — the constitution. It is no accident that the example I have chosen, the South African Constitution of 1996, is heavily influenced by the main hegemonic blueprint of *meta*-political theoretical dictatorship: the human rights discourse.[29]

Consequently, I would hope that this work be read as a political demand on two related fronts: first, a demand on modern states in general, and the South African state in particular, to transform their political, legal, economic and social institutions and practices in tune with human needs, or, in other words, to become states of needs; second, a demand on political philosophy and theory to start thinking in terms of needs rather than rights, or at least to refrain from providing a 'God's eye view' of the world. One serious impediment to both tasks is the predominance of monotheism. Hence, maybe the first task is to undermine monotheism. That is obviously not attempted here, but this political philosophy of needs is a theoretical intervention into the practice of politics, which holds firm to the belief that political philosophy cannot and should not try to replace politics or act like a non-existent God.

[29] J. Dugard, 'International Law and the South African Constitution', *European Journal of International Law*, 8. 1 (1997).

CHAPTER I

The nature of needs

Think of the statement, 'I need a car'. Do I need the car for transport or social esteem, or a combination of the two? Are there other forms of transport? Could a car justifiably be called a necessary condition for human functioning? In contemporary society I experience my need for a car as a felt impulse or drive, and I relate it to more general needs, aspirations and goals; that is, the drive and goal aspects of this particular need are very much constitutive of the need itself. And my drive to have a car might be justifiable as a need because of the present state of public transport. I might really need a car in order to get to work, which is an important part of a good life. However, the present state of public transport might be the consequence, among other things, of the general acceptance and legitimation of the unanalysed transformation of a specific luxury item of social esteem from a want into a need:[1] my felt need for cars may actually act against the meeting of my need for mobility as it justifies the degeneration of public transport. In other words, a particular car may satisfy my felt need (for a combination of mobility and social esteem), but fail to properly satisfy my need for mobility. And in making me feel like I have satisfied my need for mobility, it may *prevent* me from identifying and thus satisfying my need for mobility. Moreover, given that car use contributes to the degradation of the planetary environment, the satisfaction of my need for a car leaves other needs of mine unmet, or distorts my functioning in other less easily discernible ways. Thus the satisfaction of a felt need of mine may actually fail to satisfy that and other needs of mine; that is, it may inhibit or distort my human functioning.

A common response to this kind of reasoning is that needs are therefore not related to human functioning, for if they were I would be faced with the paradox that a need of mine is not one of my needs. However, this

---

[1] T. Veblen, *The Theory of the Leisure Class* (Boston: Houghton Mifflin, 1973 [1899]), in which he provides an analysis of how luxury items are transformed from indicators of 'taste' to the basic necessities of modern life, especially within the norm-creating 'luxury' or 'leisure' classes.

assumes that because needs tend to be subjective and felt, all felt needs are (justifiable) needs. Is this a correct assumption? Can it explain the everyday normative distinction between needs and other felt desires such as wants? What of the insight that needs are socially generated? Are human needs the needs that are felt by humans, human goals and aspirations, or the objective requirements for human functioning? If needs are, for example, associated with subjectively felt wants and goals as well as with objective human functioning as distinct from wants, how can they be a separate category in politics and political philosophy?

Contemporary need theorists do not adequately answer these questions. In many cases, they do not even ask them. I will argue that this is because they think of needs as subjective or objective *means* to other goods, goals or ends, such as freedom over preferences, choice, or the good life, whose *lack* of satisfaction creates subjective or objective *harm*. This is a seriously flawed definitional triumvirate of means, lack and harm, and it is a contingent outcome of the fact that in modern discourse human needs are forced to fit the theoretical straitjacket of the rights-preferences couple. In the most developed and systematic accounts, needs are understood as normative underpinnings for rights, or in other words conditions upon which rights can be used by all to secure the freedom to form and act upon their individual preferences and 'life plans'.

I provide an account of the nature of need that does not resort to this definitional triumvirate or subordinate human needs to rights. Instead, my account defines general needs in terms of full human functioning; provides a means of understanding the causal determinants of felt particular needs; and then develops an account of how these needs and determinants affect the perception and interpretation of the general needs, and thus how they shape human functioning. This provides a means of identifying and evaluating the nature of needs that lies behind the *prima facie* ambiguity of needs and rights claims and statements. In this chapter I focus on various need forms followed by a substantive analysis and defence of these different forms. I begin by proposing a tripartite categorisation of needs. In the subsequent three sections of the chapter I provide a substantive analysis of the needs that constitute each category. Then, in the final section, I distinguish my understanding of the nature of needs from other modern approaches to needs, and identify the similarities and differences between my account and that developed by Marx. This enables me to develop a short account of why my categorisation of needs enables a *political* conception of needs. I end the section with a summary of my understanding of the nature of needs.

I   NEED CATEGORIES

The categories I propose below are not lists of human needs. Rather, they constitute a map of the different *forms* needs take; that is, the different ways in which they are (can be) felt, cognised and conceptualised. Thus they are categories of different *kinds* of need, where differentiation between the categories occurs on two planes: with regard to the manner in which the component needs are manifested, and the felicitousness of the distinctions for grasping the need generation dynamic as a whole. In other words, they are distinguished for reasons of ontological accuracy and cognitive and evaluative (and thus heuristic) aptitude. I propose general vital and agency needs, but they are not intended as actual conditions or normative underpinnings to practical tools such as rights. Rather, they are *more* general and as such are posited as starting points for contextual interpretation and understanding of the generation and evaluation of felt needs (and rights), the subject of subsequent chapters. Thus this categorisation is intended as a means to facilitate thinking about needs in their different forms. This approach to understanding needs engenders the evaluation of particular needs in terms of the environment of need generation as a whole. *There is no dualistic distinction between 'social' and 'physical' necessity and the boundaries between the following categories are necessarily porous.* As introduced here, the categories constitute an outline that is subsequently developed and discussed. Moreover, as discussed in chapter 2, the causal inter-relationship between needs means that in reality these categories are not as rigid and distinct as may seem the case at first.

Category A: Vital Needs These needs are the *general* ineluctable needs that are unproblematically associated with individual 'health'. A non-exhaustive list of examples might be the need for adequate shelter, sufficient clothing, the required daily calorific intake, periodic rest, exercise, and social entertainment.[2] These needs are experienced both as felt drives and general goals in the form of conditions for minimal human functioning.

Category B: Particular Social Needs This category covers a broad spectrum of largely uncontested *particular* needs that are felt in everyday experience. More exactly, they are the *particular contingent manifestations* of needs that are the focus of public policy, and those that are perceived and felt as needs, as ineluctable, and yet are seen to be of private concern. In other words, the actual needs brought to light in three different ways: by bald need-claims,

---

[2] Cf. D. Braybrooke, *Meeting Needs* (Princeton: Princeton University Press, 1987), p. 36; L. Doyal and I. Gough, *A Theory of Human Need* (London: Macmillan, 1991), pp. 56–9. See section 5 below for why these theories of needs are otherwise problematic.

for example, the need for an efficient train service; by the content of public –
state or otherwise – provision, for example, the need for a television, as discussed below; and by patterns of consumption and production, for example,
the need for a car.

Category C: Agency Needs These needs are the *general* ethical and political objectives of individuals and groups. Examples are autonomy (as
a goal rather than moral premise), which in common parlance is called
'control over one's life'; intersubjective recognition; and active and creative expression.[3] Agency needs can be experienced in their general form as
aspirations, or in their particular form as expressions and manifestations of
the general form of these needs, determined by time, locale and scope.

This fact about the experience of agency needs provides conditions for
negative and positive possibilities. First, it is easier to engender criticism
of particular expressions of agency needs if these particular expressions are
interpreted as such, as particular manifestations of more general needs,
than if they are interpreted as 'universal' human needs. This is a positive
consequence in itself; but, moreover, it tends to undermine the (often)
naturalised mould of extant moral discourse, thereby generating both a
general motivation for change and imaginative forays into possible alternatives. The second point is the negative scenario: the fact that the general
form is normally mediated by particular manifestations also provides ample
room for harmful misinterpretation and misrepresentation of the agency
needs themselves, as well as misidentification of other needs as examples
of agency needs. As will be argued, the contingent fact that members of
a society, or societal group, do not individually perceive one or any of
these needs does not mean that they cannot come to do so or that these
needs are not needs of theirs. And this categorisation does not mean that
all needs manifest these different forms at different points in time, or that
they pass through historical stages in which these forms have differentiating
influence. All it holds is that everyday desires, impulses and ethical concerns emerge out of or take the form of one of these need forms, and that
the political evaluation of everyday needs is only 'political' when it intentionally sets out to grasp how the particular need satisfiers impinge upon
the perception of needs. Hence, this categorisation is not only distinctive

---

[3] There are of course general means to improved agency need development that could be categorised
as agency needs, for instance a safe environment (security) and involvement in meaningful work.
However, I do not include the means in this category for two reasons. First, if thought of as means,
they only display causal significance as, or in the form of, actual particular needs within specific
contexts of causality. And, second, if taken to be general needs, they are (arguably) component parts
of, rather than means to, the broader agency needs. I define what I mean by 'meaningful work' in
section 4 below.

because it categorises needs according to their 'forms', it also clarifies how the needs that constitute the three categories are all *experienceable* as impulses or are all cognisable as *functional sine qua non* by single human beings.

An analysis of needs based on forms of needs and particular and general needs provides a means of understanding how concepts and material reality interact, and how this process occurs with regard to the concept of needs and thus affects the nature of needs. It identifies the causal significance of ideas and values *and* material reality and necessity. It is distinct from Kantian approaches, which use the inherent normativity of needs to claim that the concept of need is most clearly understood if de-linked from the material reality of needs (about which more below), as well as devoutly materialist conceptions, which normally snort at the significance of ideas and concepts. Ideas are a kind of activity that affects political and economic orders, change and policy, just as these orders, changes and policy affect ideas; that is, the causality is bi-directional: ideas and material reality interact causally on one another. The ideas are usually more general values, goals and means, whereas the material reality is constituted by particular instances of these values, goals and means and their satisfiers.

As Hegel argues, these particular and general (or in his terminology, 'universal') phenomena are not always separate, distinct and unrelated; some are inter-related moments of one and the same concept. These moments, he argues, are instances of the movement and interaction between the universal, the particular and the individual; and thus the nature of a concept is constituted by these particular and universal moments.[4] As Hegel argues in the *Philosophy of Right*, in the case of needs these moments constitute the different forms needs take, either particular or universal.[5] And

---

[4] G. W. F. Hegel, *The Science of Logic*, trans. A. V. Miller, (London: Allen and Unwin, 1969), pp. 600–1; 613. Hegel, *The Logic of Hegel*, trans. W. Wallace (Oxford: Clarendon Press, 1892), §§ 163–5. My conceptual approach to needs draws on the logic and political philosophy of Hegel, but the terminology of particular and general is derived from Marx. Hegel contrasts the particular (and the concrete) with the universal. I prefer the Marxian terminology for reasons discussed above and because, as will become clear in section 5, the notion of 'universal needs' carries with it a great deal of problematic conceptual baggage.

[5] As has been well documented, Hegel's *System of Ethical Life and First Philosophy of Spirit*, written between 1802 and 1803, is an early embryonic attempt to provide what is later elaborated in the *Philosophy of Right*. The former gives a more explicit account of his treatment of need but it is in the latter that the discussion of need is placed within the full context of his mature speculative political philosophy. Hegel, *System of Ethical Life and First Philosophy of Spirit*, trans. H. S. Harris and T. M. Knox (Albany, NY: State University of New York, 1979); Hegel, *Elements of the Philosophy of Right*, ed. A. W. Wood, and trans. H. B. Nisbet (Cambridge: Cambridge University Press, 1991). The emphasis on form is crucial throughout his philosophy. I. Fraser, *Hegel and Marx: The concept of need* (Edinburgh: Edinburgh University Press, 1998).

these forms are developmentally interconnected, even dependent on one another. Human beings begin by having to satisfy their 'natural needs' in order to exist. These needs are universal, but the form they take is particular and immediate; that is, they relate to the 'subjective' or 'contingent' need of a specific individual, to how they are subjectively experienced. Through the development of the means of meeting these needs, which involves the deferral of gratification and the development and division of labour, an interdependent 'system of needs' arises: what Hegel calls '*bürgerliche Gesellschaft*' ('civil society'). Needs develop to the extent that man is now concerned with a 'necessity imposed by himself alone'[6] (§ 194). These needs are universal because they are experienced by all, and because everyone becomes aware of that fact. Hence, natural needs have moved from a universal form, to a particular form, and back to a universal. However, according to Hegel, this universal form is characterised by instrumental individual action directed at meeting particular individual needs. And since these needs can be multiplied and divided they can be created not so much by those who experience them directly as by those who seek to profit from their emergence (§ 190; § 191A). This leads to the polarisation of 'civil society' between an unemployed rabble (*Pöbel*), whose members lose self-respect and the ability to acquire skills and education, and wealth and luxury characterised by whim and fancy (§ 195; §§ 240–1; § 245). Hegel argues that these needs must, therefore, be re-universalised by institutions that intermediate between 'civil society' and the state: the 'police' (§§ 231ff.) and the 'corporations' (§§ 250ff.). Thus, for Hegel, the development of human needs is characterised by the inter-relation between universal and particular needs, which affects not merely the means of satisfying needs, or need satisfiers, but also the (human) nature of individuals.

Thus a (universal) concept for Hegel is not simply a generalisation of a collection of particulars.[7] A concept does not separate the universal and the particular, but rather moves between and encapsulates these different forms. Given this and the fact that the world is constantly changing, it

---

[6] Hegel refers to these developed needs as 'social needs' and defines them 'as a combination of immediate or natural needs and the spiritual needs' (§ 194). These social needs emerge when isolated abstract needs are made concrete through the '*quality of being recognized*', through the realisation of the impact of conventions on needs (§ 192). Cf. my analysis below of particular social needs.

[7] Thus, what political economists like Smith and Ricardo took to be the finite, mutually exclusive character of phenomena from which could be produced valid inductive generalisations, Hegel approaches as an instance of a movement and an interaction between the universal, the particular, and the individual. According to Hegel, the final goal of the political economists is the mechanical explanation of the arbitrary satisfaction of 'certain universal needs, such as food, drink, clothing, etc.' in a particular society (§ 189).

follows that concepts change as they encapsulate the particular and universal. Moreover, in the process they act upon the world. Hegel's conceptual approach to needs creates a means of grasping how the concept of need emerges out of a response to both material necessity and imaginative forays into new ideas and ethical concerns, and subsequently acts back upon the material world.[8] The extant concept and definition of needs determines how humans interpret material reality, and therefore how they act to conserve or transform that reality; and material reality determines the practical form, significance and applicability of new or transformed concepts.[9] Thus, thinking of needs in terms of particular and general needs provides a good means of understanding the main determinants of these bi-directional causal mechanisms in the context of needs. It highlights the fact that a particular form of a general need (as part of the extant concept of need) might be the result of an environment of other particular, contingent forms of needs and wants, and, therefore, that a given need might not be a 'natural necessity' even if it is commonly thought to be one. This is an important theme throughout this book.

2 VITAL NEEDS

Greek, Roman and Christian thought tended to think of needs as the limited, natural, universal and fixed necessities of human life. For example, for Plato and Aristotle, needs were the three basic necessities, sustenance (food and water), shelter and clothing, and these were the concern of the household, or *oikos* (*oikonomike*, or 'household management', being the source of the term 'economics'). Desiring above and beyond these needs was both distinct in kind – it was the domain of luxury wants – and dangerous – it was liable to lead to the corruption of the virtues

---

[8] It is thus a significant advance on earlier philosophy. In the *Logic*, Hegel notes the inadequacies of both empiricism and Kant's philosophy. Empiricism made the important shift of moving away from abstractions and focusing on the world but it takes the phenomena it finds completely uncritically, thereby not seeing the relationship between the universal and the particular. Kant, on the other hand, restored the dialectic but saw contradiction and antinomy as evidence of our trying to comprehend something that is beyond our experience. His approach was, therefore, purely negative; its goal was the clarification of reason to free it from 'errors'. Hegel, *The Logic of Hegel*, § 9, § 38, § 38R, § 48A, § 81A; and *The Science of Logic*, pp. 28–9, 56.

[9] For this reason, as with other concepts, the nature and significance of the concept of needs is only fully appreciated if it is taken to be both a term of its time and a significant determinant of its age; that is, it is best understood contextually. In contrast to ahistorical analytical political philosophy, I maintain that a politically constructive conception is developed best when it first attempts to understand both the history and the contemporary meaning of a concept. For a similar approach to understanding political concepts see the various contributions to T. Ball, J. Farr and R. L. Hanson (eds.), *Political Innovation and Conceptual Change*; and A. O. Hirschman, *The Passions and the Interests: Political Arguments for Capitalism before Its Triumph* (Princeton: Princeton University Press, 1997 [1977]).

of temperance and courage. The proper and noble concerns of politics and philosophy, Justice and Truth, were understood as distinct from the potentially problematic need-based concerns of the household.[10] Later, Hume and Smith moved needs and wants to the centre stage of politics. Smith in particular undermines the link between virtuous action and good consequences; that is, he argues that desire driven by luxury wants can have the unintended consequence of meeting one or more of our basic needs. But he still confines needs to the domain of three or four natural, unchanging, basic material requirements, thereby retaining a strict distinction between needs and wants.[11]

My category of vital needs is not equivalent to these conceptions of needs in which the concept of needs is restricted to three or four basic, fixed, physical necessities of life. It may include these needs, but it also includes other needs that are not strictly physical or biological; and it is only the first of three categories whose boundaries are necessarily porous. Similarly, my category of vital needs includes but is not identical to the group of needs with which welfare (development) economic research into 'basic' needs concerns itself; that is, as understood here vital needs are not a

---

[10] Plato, *Republic*, trans. and intro. D. Lee (Harmondsworth: Penguin, 1974), 369c, 372e, 373d, 590b; Aristotle, *The Politics*, ed. S. Everson (Cambridge: Cambridge University Press, 1988), 1252b, 1258a, 1330b; Aristotle, *The Nicomachean Ethics*, trans. and intro. D. Ross (Oxford: Oxford University Press, 1980); Aristotle, *Eudemian Ethics: books I, II and VIII*, trans. M. Woods (Oxford: Clarendon Press, 1992), 1221a.

   The Romans attempted to institutionalise the 'policing' of the desires (via sumptuary taxes) and Roman thought reiterated the Greek arguments concerning the corrupting effect of luxurious desire on the virtues. This was most clearly evident in later Roman moralists (chiefly the Stoics), who were heavily influential on early Christian thought. But unlike Aristotle's conception of virtue as a mean, Christian thought, for example Augustine's analysis, has no room for mediation or compromise: the relationship between virtue and vice is conceptualised as one of conflict, which occurs within the soul of each individual. Luxury is associated with lechery and is drawn within the catalogue of the seven deadly sins. Augustine, *The City of God against the Pagans*, ed. R. W. Dyson (Cambridge: Cambridge University Press, 1998). Thus Christian thought began the process of individualisation and individual responsibility for the 'policing' of felt desires that now predominates in western thought and practice, the legacy of which undermines real political thought and action. For a full discussion of the Roman and Christian contributions, see C. J. Berry, *The Idea of Luxury* (Cambridge: Cambridge University Press, 1994), chs 3 and 4.

[11] David Hume, *Political Essays*, ed. K. Haakonssen (Cambridge: Cambridge University Press, 1994), esp. 'Of Luxury' and 'Of Commerce'; Adam Smith, *An Inquiry into the Nature and Causes of the Wealth of Nations*, ed. A. S. Skinner and R. Meek (Indianapolis: Liberty Classics, 1981), pp. 22–3, 25, 37, 181, 341, 712, 870; Smith, *The Theory of Moral Sentiments*, 6th edn (1790), ed. A. Macfie and D. Steuart (Indianapolis: Liberty Classics, 1982), pp. 50, 60; Smith, *Lectures on Jurisprudence*, ed. R. Meek, D. Raphael and P. Stein (Indianapolis: Liberty Classics, 1982), p. 488; I. Hont and M. Ignatieff, 'Needs and justice in the *Wealth of Nations*: an introductory essay', in Hont and Ignatieff (eds.), *Wealth and Virtue* (Cambridge: Cambridge University Press, 1983); Hirschman, *Passions and Interests*; Berry, *Luxury*.

descriptive list of 'basic' universal needs.[12] In the basic needs approach, needs are unproblematically and unpolitically understood as 'physical' conditions for human functioning. Thus, needs are interpreted as extra-political facts to be objectively observed and verified, and from which universal and unchanging laws of human nature are induced. And this is pivotal in their being adopted by these kinds of approaches as the basic conditions upon which to judge the welfare of individuals. The assumption seems to be that what makes them necessary conditions for human existence is that they are instinctual (and genetic) parts of our actual biology.

In contradistinction, as understood here vital needs are necessary conditions for human existence that are not necessarily determined by genetic or biological necessity. For, although there is little doubt that these kinds of needs are rooted in our biology, the road from some possible original human biology through history and culture (and historical and cultural particular manifestation of needs) to their present forms is a long and winding one. For example, my need to watch the television after work can be felt fiercely as a drive, as fiercely as my need to eat is at that time, but it seems to have very little to do with my genetic make-up. Rather, it has more to do with a generally felt, and generally agreed upon as important, need for social entertainment. The fact that this need is now often mediated through the television does not make it any less of a drive. Had I lived in a different time or place, I might have been able to join in the nightly hallucinogen-inspired communal dance of my 'people'. The fact that those halcyon days are (mostly) past does not make my felt need to engage in, say, the 'communal' activity of television viewing any less of a drive.

Besides this general point, there are two specific reasons to doubt the validity of the assumption that vital needs are instinctual or determined by biological necessity, which help to elucidate the historical and normative nature of even the most basic or vital of needs. First, the needs that constitute the category display different degrees of necessity – their 'vitalness' is not strictly uniform. This makes the notion of 'vital' (needs) a little ambiguous. There are some needs, for example oxygen and water, that are essentially vital in the pure sense of being necessary for *vita*, or life. And there are others like

---

[12] Examples of welfarist approaches include F. Stewart, *Basic Needs in Developing Countries* (Baltimore: Johns Hopkins University Press, 1985); P. Dasgupta, *An Inquiry into Well-Being and Destitution* (Oxford: Clarendon Press, 1993); B. Wisner, *Power and Need in Africa: Basic Human Needs and Development Policies* (London: Earthscan, 1988). For a critique of mainstream welfare economics, which does not make the same mistakes, see T. Lawson, *Economics and Reality* (London and New York: Routledge, 1997), esp. pp. 278–80.

adequate shelter without which *in extremis* humans can and do exist. The
term 'vital needs' is intended here to capture a relatively open continuum
of all these kinds of health needs. Hence, those needs like oxygen and
water that are literally immediate matters of life or death would be found
at the extreme left of the continuum. Then, somewhere in the middle
of the continuum, would be the needs required for continued existence,
though not necessarily 'healthy' functioning. Examples might be basic food
rations and minimal protection from the elements; in other words those
things required to sustain life, which are not necessarily sufficient to sustain
(or provide the conditions for) ongoing basic life. The validity of this
distinction between what is required to sustain life and what is required for
ongoing basic life is corroborated, for example, by the fact that a woman
on starvation rations can continue to live in a stable state, but that state will
usually be characterised by the cessation of normal menstruation.[13] Needs
that create the conditions (and along with the others are the necessary
requirements) for ongoing minimal functioning are situated further along
the continuum to the right: for example, requirements such as clothing,
shelter, and the time for, and ability to, exercise and participate in social
entertainment. This is the first reason why vital needs are not understood
as necessarily 'instinctual': they are situated on an open-ended continuum,
which cannot incorporate a strict biological or physical determinism nor
any categorical distinction between 'social' and 'physical' needs. (This latter
point is reinforced in the next section, and at greater length in chapter 2,
where I analyse how luxuries and wants become part of the vital need
continuum over time.)

The second reason for questioning the necessarily 'instinctual' nature of
vital needs, especially if 'instinctual' connotes that the needs are necessarily
experienced as need-drives (or impulses) by living human beings, is that
many vital needs are not felt directly by the individual even where and
when they have to be met urgently. For example, humans have a need for
periodic exercise but particular individuals may never feel this need for a
number of reasons. I will discuss two.

First, a western workaholic might never give herself the time for exercise
despite the fact that she is aware of the need; that is, she might *know* about
the need but never actually *feel* the drive to attend to it, never feel that she
needs to exercise. The fact that she might not experience the need in this

---

[13] This example illuminates another distinction, that between the vital needs of individuals and those
of human groups. If the group is on stable starvation rations perhaps no individual will die, but if
the women stop menstruating the group will die out.

sense does not mean it is not a need of hers.[14] It is an empirical fact that an individual's knowledge about some of her needs does not necessarily translate into reasons for action (motivation) and/or action itself towards meeting them. Frequently, individuals do not need to be given extra information about needs but they do need to be given the opportunity to act upon both public information concerning needs and their own particular experiential knowledge of their own situation and needs.

Second, on the other hand, a Zulu goat-herd might be meeting his need for periodic exercise every day as he walks for miles behind his goats, but he does so as an unintended consequence of the one means he has to meet other (more immediate) vital needs, for example, his need for food. Here again, the fact that he does not experience the need does not mean it is not a need of his. And, as these two examples show, this is the case – that the need is a need experienced or not – whether or not the need is being met or attended to at the same level or not. Hence vital needs are necessary conditions for everyday minimal human functioning whether they are felt as ineluctable – experienced as a condition that if left unattended will impair human functioning – or remain unfelt, *and* whether they are being met or not. Needless to note, depending on the position of the need on the vital need continuum, the meeting of a need can wane – even stop – for some time before functioning becomes impaired.

Finally, my account of vital needs is distinct from the earlier approaches and the contemporary basic needs analyses because for them human needs constitute one single homogeneous set confined to the physical requirements of life. In contrast, my category of vital needs is only one of three categories whose constitutive needs are causally inter-related. Particular social needs are major determining factors within these causal relations and mechanisms.

3 PARTICULAR SOCIAL NEEDS

Particular social needs are 'social' in as much as all particular needs are social: they all arise within a social context. This fact leads some modern political theorists (mistakenly) to associate the 'social' with discursive and consensual interaction. They then construct idealisations that exclude actual power relations, arguing that needs acquire a special 'social' dimension

---

[14] Nor does this mean that she ought to exercise as her contemporaries do. The statement, 'she has a need for periodic exercise' says nothing about the form her exercise should or might take, although the form of extant exercise might be an interesting part of an answer to why she fails to actually exercise.

when they are generated (and satisfied) in an apparently 'discursive' environment under conditions of relatively equal power relations or just and equal distribution of knowledge. In political theory this is achieved either via an artificial mechanism based on a kind of hypothetical pre-societal contract, for example Rawls' 'original position', or through an idealised rationalisation of actual political discourse, evidenced in Habermas' Discourse Ethics, about which more below.

At the level of applied political theory, this kind of apparently discursive social environment is given concrete manifestation using the concept of 'civil society', a full discussion of which appears in chapter 3; while in economic theory this type of idealisation is articulated in terms of supply, demand and a construction of human rationality commonly known as *homo economicus*, where bargaining power and interpretive normative power are sanitised out of the equation in order to render the latter – an equation – possible.[15] Supply is depicted as responding to demand within a stylised environment in which the interpretation of needs, the expression of demand, and the response of supply remain undistorted by either disparities in bargaining power or an unequal environment of value generation, amongst other variables. In all three cases, the attempt to answer the (allegedly) empirically verifiable question of whether or not an environment is free of domination or power relations presupposes a number of empirical and theoretical concerns that remain unresolved; for instance, whether the idea of need generation and evaluation (and discourse) in a power-free environment is a realistic assumption and possibility, and whether it is a desirable possibility. These concerns are discussed in their own right in chapter 3, but I am making what seems to me to be a realistic assumption: the social environment is the archetypal locale of unequal distribution of bargaining power and normative power.[16] If this is the case, it seems highly unlikely that particular social needs would display discursive or consensual characteristics or potentials.

The needs that constitute category B (particular social needs) are of pivotal epistemological and ontological importance, but they have received insufficient theoretical attention. The extant matrices of particular social needs provide the most manifest interpretive framework within which actual individuals and groups interpret their own everyday needs; and

---

[15] I use the notion of idealisation rather than abstraction because abstraction *per se* is not necessarily problematic. Furthermore, it is (arguably) unavoidable, at least at the level of theory. See O. O'Neill, *Towards Justice and Virtue: A constructive account of practical reasoning* (Cambridge: Cambridge University Press, 1996), pp. 39–44, 62–9; and Z. Emmerich, 'The Form and Force of an Argument' (unpublished paper, Cambridge 2001) – an excellent criticism of O'Neill's account.

[16] I discuss and define normative power in chapter 2, section 2.

they are the first point of entry into, or initial evaluative framework for, an analysis of how vital and agency needs are being interpreted by these individuals. They provide evidence for otherwise hidden power relations and (apparently) unconnected accumulations of power and its consequences. In the case of hidden power relations, and by way of example, even though the affairs of the 'family' (or 'union') are normally 'privatised' in modern liberal democracies, the social needs they generate are 'public' signs of their 'private' power relations. The needs that are generated are normally satisfied in one form or another outside the family, and any power differentials tend to become revealed by the nature and distribution of these needs. Certain kinds of consumption patterns and the need for certain kinds of services can provide important insight into the origin and structure of these contingently more inaccessible environs of need generation. Consequently, criticism can and does find evidence for the distorted interpretation of both vital and agency needs.

Category B is the broadest of the three categories. It is constituted by particular needs whether they are interpreted (presently and contingently) as having private or public sources and consequences. More specifically, this includes the actual content of public provision, in the form of welfare state provision or supererogatory charity, and the kinds of needs that emerge from the extant patterns of consumption and production. Simplifying somewhat, I am going to assume that there are two kinds of needs under consideration here. I call them *public ineluctable needs*, and *private ineluctable needs*. Public ineluctable needs are on the sturdier epistemic (and therefore evaluative) footing because they are needs that have become generally accepted by the society concerned as requiring the state (or other public body or act) for them to be adequately (and fairly) met. For example, in Britain this would include those needs that are included as basic necessities, which it is argued are coverable by the monetary resources provided by the social security package. The social security package is presently in the form of housing benefit, that is, adequate shelter and water; and basic income to cover necessities like food, heating and entertainment (i.e. enough over one year to pay one's television licence), and transport. These needs are particular needs that have become legitimised as the minimum requirements for meeting vital needs as well as some very basic means for the development of agency needs. It is an empirical fact that in Britain they are not even adequate for the former.[17] I call these needs *public ineluctable needs* not because

---

[17] Despite the intermittent use of 'need' rhetoric by British governments, the social security package is determined by what the government can afford, rather than perceived vital need. This is corroborated

they display any inherent publicness or ineluctability, but because of the empirical manner in which they become legitimised: they are the needs that, at the extreme point of contextual public ineluctability, are interpreted as necessities. They are, therefore, normally felt as ineluctable, but this is not a necessary or sufficient condition of their being ineluctable. *Hence, what for most theorists has come to define the idea of needs – the content of welfare provision – is only a subset of one of my three kinds of need.*[18]

Private ineluctable needs do not display the same epistemic qualities as public ineluctable needs, but they are just as important here. In everyday experience they are simultaneously thought of both as means to the meeting of vital needs and agency needs and as ends or goals in themselves. For example, a need for a new car is often (1) a means to improving the purchaser's mobility (dependent on various empirical givens like the state of public transport provision and policy in the context concerned); and (2) the attainment or development of the goal of status and esteem. Furthermore, although these kinds of needs are interpreted as necessities of a kind, they are understood as being of private concern. Is this because they are thought to have only private consequences? Or because they allegedly come from individual private passions and ambitions? Or simply because they are costly necessities, beyond the reach of public provision, and are in fact resourced from private sources? Obviously, these questions demand empirical answers that relate to the legitimising ideologies of the existing private ineluctable needs. I cannot provide an empirical analysis here, but a theoretical sketch of how particular need generation affects the perception especially of agency needs will involve an evaluation of this subgroup of needs, and must incorporate an account of their structures of legitimation. This evaluative exercise demands justification in the everyday and policy-oriented context, and leads to analysis of vital and agency needs. This occurs because private ineluctable needs are always particular needs, which require legitimation with reference to more general goals, such as vital and agency needs. For example, I will justify my need for a new car

by a recent comment made by the current Chancellor, Gordon Brown MP, while being interviewed by Alya Din, a 22-year-old New Deal trainee: '**AD**: Well, what I mean is, when you set the amount, how did you decide that £56 [a week on the New Deal] was enough? . . . **GB**: Well, I think that it's what we could afford as a government, but obviously you will want to move on and get a job and then get a better income. You've got to see it as a start.' *What If . . .?* (London: Short Books, 2000), pp. 79–80, cited from N. Sagovsky, 'Who Needs What? Minimum Income Standards and the Ethics of Adequacy' (unpublished paper given at St Edmund's College, Cambridge, April 2000), p. 1.

[18] For an example of an analysis of needs (or 'vulnerabilities') in terms of the welfare state see R. Goodin, 'Vulnerabilities and Responsibilities: An Ethical Defense of the Welfare State', in G. Brock (ed.), *Necessary Goods: Our Responsibilities to Meet Others' Needs* (Oxford: Rowman and Littlefield, 1998).

via my belief that my new car will not only be an improved means for me to meet my vital needs – it will get me to work faster and more safely – but will also enhance my 'freedom' and provide me with social recognition and respect, even 'creative expression'. Consequently, unlike the first kind of particular social need (public ineluctable needs) and obviously unlike vital needs, these needs are always felt as drives or impulses; and in worst case scenarios they are experienced in the form of addiction. As will be argued in chapter 2, they are therefore of significant causal importance within the mechanisms that distort the perception of agency needs.

4 AGENCY NEEDS

Agency needs are *general* ethical and political objectives that relate to human functioning and the performance of valued social tasks within valued social roles. They are evident in everyday practical claims-making as well as theoretical work, such as moral, social and political theory and philosophy and the human sciences more generally. These needs are experienced in the general form depicted here, as general aspirational objectives, but they are *normally* experienced as particular manifestations of these general goals or the means to their achievement. However, unlike particular social needs that are satisfied in a more or less uncomplicated sensory way, in practice agency needs are not ever fully 'satisfied', at least not by a single satisfier or by a single moment of completion once and for all. Agency needs are developed and met, and in the process they help enable individual full human functioning. They are called 'agency' needs because they are ongoing aspirations whose *development* increases an agent's 'causal power' to carry out intended actions, particularly those that relate to the meeting and evaluating of needs generally.[19] And if the particular manifestations of agency needs are being met they provide the feelings of safety, self-esteem, *confidence* (and courage) that provide individuals with the ability to function fully, individually and politically. Agency needs, at least the *general* ones I discuss, 'intersubjective recognition', 'active and creative expression'

---

[19] Thus I use the notion of 'meeting' the particular manifestations of agency needs, and I discuss general agency needs in terms of their 'development' as *general* objectives. In contrast, since *general vital* needs are more static than agency needs, and unlike particular social needs must be constantly 'satisfied', and are therefore in a sense never 'satisfied', I speak of general vital needs being met rather than developed or satisfied; *particular* vital needs are, of course, 'satisfied'. For more on intention, agency and causal power, see D. Davidson, 'Agency' and 'Freedom to Act', in *Essays on Actions and Events* (Oxford: Clarendon Press, 1980). In subsequent chapters I elaborate more fully on how particular vital and agency needs are generated and changed and how this affects the interpretation and nature of general vital and agency needs.

and 'autonomy', are so called because they are one of the necessary conditions for the individual and political agency that is characteristic of full
human functioning and that enables the participant evaluation of everyday
needs.

Thus met agency needs do not exhaustively constitute full human functioning. There exist other component parts of full human functioning, such
as met vital needs, and context-dependent needs and activities, including
the need for intimacy and the individual and political participation in the
evaluation of needs. Even with regard to vital and agency needs, the particular form full human functioning takes depends on both the context and
the individual concerned. In any case, full human functioning is not a final
or single state of the mind or body. Thus by definition I cannot provide
a full and positive definition for full human functioning. But since, for
reasons discussed below, these other constitutive elements are enabled by
met agency needs, I can elaborate on some of the conditions for full human
functioning. (1) Individuals must be able to meet their vital needs, or have
their vital needs met, to provide for minimal functioning without undue
worry and exhaustion. (2) Individuals must be provided with the opportunity to carry out successfully the social tasks constitutive of the four main
social roles – carer, householder, worker, citizen.[20] (3) Individuals must be
provided with the opportunities to fill the four main social roles, should
they wish, as these give them a kind of parity (and depth) of perspective
from which to evaluate the social roles themselves and the development of
their agency needs. (Extant social roles must be understood as susceptible
to criticism: what it means to be a citizen or worker is not self-evident and
demands empirical and normative analysis.) (4) Individuals must also be
given parity of opportunity to meet their *particular* agency needs.

Two central claims of mine follow from the fact that agency needs are
often felt in the form of particular social needs and constitute one of the
necessary elements of full human functioning; claims, I argue, that are best
defended using my categorisation of need. First, particular needs that can
otherwise seem unconnected due to historical separation, differing cultural
interpretation or intentional and unintentional disfigurement, are often
interconnected attempts to meet the same general ethical and political objectives, or agency needs. Second, the development of agency needs provides
constantly improving means for individuals to have their need-claims heard
and their everyday needs heeded, and – where appropriate – met.

---

[20] Cf. Braybrooke, *Meeting Needs*, pp. 48–9, 200. See below, chapter 3, section 3, for the argument
concerning roles.

The latter point highlights *why* the agency needs discussed here are also the *general* ethical and political objectives of this project as a whole: as they are developed, they enhance the individual's ability to become more actively involved in the everyday evaluation and meeting of needs. This is the first of the three reasons for the special and prolonged attention given to agency needs in this approach to need. The second reason is that the concepts of 'autonomy' and 'recognition', which are forms of two of the three agency needs, have become theoretical linchpins of modern political thought; and my conceptions of both concepts are distinct from the mainstream analyses in two different ways respectively. I do not analyse each concept as if it were the only significant theoretical issue, moral foundation or practical concern. I conceive of each respective notion as one amongst a number of other equally important agency needs and vital needs. And I emphasise more than usual the empirical forms which individual experiences of these agency needs take. Thus, for example, the conception of autonomy developed here is at odds with the now fashionable neo-Kantian conception of autonomy on two counts. (1) It begins from an empirical understanding of how autonomy is actually experienced; and (2) it does not conceive of autonomy as a moral premise, but rather as a kind of ethical goal determined by various conditions that relate to other agency needs and human vital needs. As regards recognition, I emphasise that recognition is only *one* of a number of agency and vital needs, and I develop a more 'active' account of recognition than is usual. This stresses the material basis to the intersubjective process of recognition – the importance of meaningful work, social roles and 'active and creative expression'.[21] Thus I begin with an analysis of intersubjective recognition, followed by a discussion of active and creative expression, and end with an analysis of autonomy itself. Active and creative expression constitutes the main causal link between intersubjective recognition and autonomy.

The third reason for the prolonged attempt to give a clear understanding of agency needs (and their relationship with the other need categories and with wants) is the concern of the second chapter. Agency needs are constant general goals, but the nature and form of the goals can be transformed through time and across space depending upon how their particular

[21] In doing so, I criticise the common tendency to assimilate recognition with identity and 'identity politics'. Some theorists argue that the concepts of 'autonomy' and 'identity' are the mainstays of different kinds of political understanding. I am less sure that there is as much difference as they make out. I maintain that the modern phenomena of ethnicity, nationalism, cultural integrity and theoretical accounts of 'identity politics' are simply the flip side of the now hegemonically fashionable neo-Kantian liberalism and its assumptions concerning autonomy, choice and an unencumbered liberal self.

manifestations are interpreted and legitimated in everyday experience. Consequently, the determinants of their particular manifestations are of significant political import.

Intersubjective recognition

There is a great deal of theoretical debate as to the definition and understanding of recognition.[22] Despite much discord there is also general agreement that at an abstract level recognition is a developmental process of individualisation of oneself (and the other) via an intersubjective process that involves at least two people and a significant object in the material world. In Hegel, the common figure in many strands of recognition analysis, the 'significant object in the material world' is the products of an individual's labour; that is, what makes an object significant is the fact that it is the material result of an individual's use of both his powers and the material world to create an object in the material world. In Hegel's work, both in the earlier *Jena Lectures*, through the *Phenomenology of Spirit* and into the *Philosophy of Right*, recognition involves a process of externalising one's powers in the world, having one's powers recognised by another through the medium of the created object, and accepting one's separateness from the other and the material world via the ability wilfully to hand over (alienate) the object from oneself. This process involves both the experience of the other's esteem as she recognises you through the object, and a self-realisation of one's own limitations and frailties made manifest in the interdependence created by the division of labour.[23] This is a fundamental human agency need whose development will only obtain under certain

[22] In his paper for a recognition conference at the Institut Français, London, 3–4 June 2000, S. Grosz discussed ten different definitions of recognition in the psychoanalytic and political literature.

[23] Hegel, 'Jena Lectures on the Philosophy of Spirit', in *Hegel and the Human Spirit: A Translation of the Jena Lectures on the Philosophy of Spirit (1805–6) with Commentary*, ed. and trans. L. Rauch (Detroit: Wayne State University Press, 1983); *Hegel's Phenomenology of Spirit*, trans. A. V. Miller, with analysis and foreword by J. N. Findlay (Oxford: Oxford University Press, 1977), pp. 104–19; and *Philosophy of Right*, §§ 41–71. There are a number of unresolved concerns over the interpretation of these ideas, especially as regards the account of Lordship and Bondage in the *Phenomenology of Spirit*. Kojève defends an existential reading of this process of recognition that takes Hegel to be making universal claims about ongoing processes within human consciousness. A. Kojève, *Introduction to the Reading of Hegel*, trans. J. Nichols (New York: Basic Books, 1969). Honneth, however, argues that the analysis of recognition in the *Phenomenology of Spirit* marks an authoritarian turn, and that Hegel's original intersubjective recognition analysis is to be found in the earlier Jena period. A. Honneth, *The Struggle for Recognition: The Moral Grammar of Social Conflicts* (Cambridge: Polity Press, 1995). I maintain that in his account of Lordship and Bondage, Hegel is analysing an historical moment through which human consciousness passed as a consequence of (and alongside) other historical and structural conditions, including particular kinds of production relations. But in taking this view, I do not think that Hegel's interpretation of the problem of recognition can be relegated to the past. It is still a human need to which we aspire, but one that has moved with history beyond its crude beginnings in Hegel's analysis of recognition under conditions of slavery.

conditions. As will be argued, these conditions themselves only obtain when disparities in attending to vital need are reduced to a minimum; in other words, if they are kept below a specified threshold on a continuum of increasing disparities. Furthermore, this approach to meeting vital need will only arise given certain kinds of institutional arrangements, as discussed in subsequent chapters. This is the case because the process of intersubjective recognition involves the ability of individuals to produce things in the world through which they can inter*act* with others. Hence, recognition must be a process with a material basis; it is not just a psychological process between two (or more) Cartesian subjects. (For Hegel this process is both a condition for and a constitutive part of our 'absolute need' to be reconciled to our contemporary world.[24])

There is another more recent approach to recognition that has its origins in the psychoanalytic work of Donald Winnicott and Melanie Klein (with its source in Freud). I cannot go into this here, suffice to say, though, that it is also developmental, but does not involve any of the connotations of work, production or creative expression that are arguably central to the Hegelian conception. In this psychoanalytic rendition, recognition is understood as the process of individuation of the child, involving a similar triadic structure to Hegel's conception but one that is confined to the mother, the child, and the breast (the object).[25]

Honneth develops the notion of recognition in a more sociological manner that conceives of recognition beyond the triadic formulation common in the psychoanalytic tradition. In Honneth's account of the 'struggle for recognition', there are three modes of recognition: emotional support; cognitive respect; and social esteem. And these three *modes* of recognition have three corresponding *forms* of recognition: love/friendship; rights; and solidarity.[26] In Hegel these kinds of recognition occur within different environs – the family, civil society and the state – although Hegel does not describe the process explicitly in terms of recognition in his later writings. Honneth's account of recognition in terms of love, rights and solidarity is highly significant for two main reasons. First, in contrast to the psychoanalytic formulation, his more sociological conception of recognition locates recognition in all spheres of human interaction. Second, it provides a more structural and political account of conditions for recognition.

---

[24] M. Hardimon, *Hegel's Social Philosophy: The project of reconciliation* (Cambridge: Cambridge University Press, 1994).

[25] But see the recent move beyond this triad to a quadratic formulation; a process of recognition in the child which also involves siblings and peers. J. Mitchell, *Mad Men & Medusas: Reclaiming Hysteria and the Effect of Sibling Relations on the Human Condition* (London: Allen Lane and Penguin, 2000).

[26] Honneth, *The Struggle for Recognition*, ch. 5, esp. p. 129.

There are, however, two aspects of recognition – the significance of work as an instance of creative expression and the issue of role relativity – that are left untreated by Honneth. These two aspects of recognition highlight how I can be recognised in all Honneth's senses and still feel far from empowered to act or make need-claims. First, I can be recognised in Honneth's ways without actually being actively employed in interactive roles with other people in which my individuality is recognised via my creative products or via my contribution to the meeting of other people's needs. That is, I can be in a loving personal relationship within a society that provides me with a catalogue of rights, and be employed in a solidarity-enhancing job, but my work might obstruct or distort intersubjective recognition. This occurs if my work does *not* include either of the two characteristics which, I maintain, constitute 'meaningful work': work which requires active and creative expression or work in which I am functionally significant, in the sense of having an indispensable role in a combined effort to produce goods and services which meet other people's valued needs.[27] And if my work (assuming I have work) is non-meaningful it will restrict me from becoming a properly active member in the material-based intersubjective process of recognition; in other words, I will be under- or mis-recognised. Consequently, although some kinds of recognition, like love or emotional support, are important initiating conditions,[28] others enhance the individual ability to understand and have the self-esteem to make specific claims; in other words, they enhance agency in the broad sense. One of these is the kind of self-esteem that comes from being involved in meaningful work. Hence, being involved in meaningful work is not a means to recognition nor an agency need in its own right; it is in fact constitutive of the agency need of intersubjective recognition and the agency need for active and creative expression, as defined below.

The second aspect of recognition that is left untreated by Honneth relates to a specific point about recognition and roles. The closest Honneth comes to including an account of roles in his analysis of recognition occurs when he argues for a kind of parity in social esteem. However, he fails to specify social esteem and leaves open the possibility of a subjectivist understanding of it; that is, an understanding that defines social esteem purely

---

[27] For more on the second characteristic, see Braybrooke, 'Work: A Cultural Ideal Ever More in Jeopardy', in *Moral Objectives, Rules, and the Forms of Social Change* (Toronto and London: Toronto University Press, 1998), pp. 85–112 (p. 89).

[28] It does not follow from this criticism of Honneth that I underrate the importance of love or the need for intimacy. For an erudite analysis of love as a fundamental force in the development of human individuality, see J. Lear, *Love and Its Place in Nature: A Philosophical Interpretation of Freudian Psychoanalysis* (New Haven: Yale University Press, 1990).

in terms of feelings of social esteem. This will not necessarily engender the improvement of recognition conditions because individuals may feel recognised even in objectively adverse conditions. For example, as is discussed fully in chapter 3, I could feel recognised and respected and have comparatively rich self-worth, but if my reference points are tightly restricted and my recognition partners are very like me in that they fill similar roles, I may feel this way even when and where my agency need for recognition remains starkly undeveloped. I maintain, therefore, that it is preferable to define intersubjective recognition as the ongoing intersubjective process of acknowledgement of equivalent status under specified conditions: apart from the above-discussed conditions concerning a minimum of disparities in meeting vital need and involvement in meaningful work, parity in the kind and distribution of roles is a prerequisite for this process of recognising equivalent status. Roles are important because they are the framework for an individual's various evaluative reference points concerning the state of his recognition. Roles, that is, do not simply cover positions at work, but include the various positions or functions people have in different locales, for example, at work, in the household, and as a citizen. In sum, these two criticisms of Honneth's account of recognition highlight that, as a consequence of recognition's inherent intersubjectivity and materiality, the greater the material inequalities in the ability to meet vital needs and fill social roles the more possibility there is for distortion in the process of recognition.[29]

Intersubjective recognition is only one of a number of human agency needs. It is a necessary but not sufficient condition for the kind of individual self-worth required for the making and defence of need-claims (i.e. for agency) because there are other necessary conditions – the other vital and agency needs. However, in the everyday experience and practical interpretation of recognition, a feeling of self-worth and significant agency can be produced by forms of recognition that for whatever reason are not instances of intersubjective recognition. That is, warped or incomplete forms of recognition that would otherwise not amount to necessary conditions for agency can actually enhance agency in particular contexts, even to the degree that they become *interpreted theoretically* as *sufficient* conditions for agency. Think, for example, of the historically all too common celebrations of racial or national identity and supremacy. Need-claims that depend upon

---

[29] For more on the connection between distribution and recognition, see N. Fraser, 'From Redistribution to Recognition? Dilemmas of Justice in a "Post-Socialist" Age', in *Justice Interruptus* (London and New York: Routledge, 1997). In general there is a dearth of causal analysis on the connection between recognition and material conditions. I provide a causal account in chapter 2.

or relate to these kinds of warped recognition display evidence of extensive self-worth, and they emerge as a matter of empirical fact even under conditions of stark non-recognition and material and role disparity. But they are either highly role-relative or contingently restricted to a single group, class or 'race' for reasons that are ultimately not based on intersubjective recognition. However, because instances of non- or mis-recognition can provide the kind of self-worth that enhances agency, an over-subjectivised theoretical standpoint can easily offer warped analyses of recognition. The contemporary emphasis on 'identity politics' that transforms the politics of recognition into the recognition of identity and difference is a good example of theoretical confusion fuelled by an over-subjectivised position.[30] These approaches normally make two fundamental mistakes. First, they imply that the need for recognition crosses unproblematically from the individual case to the group case. This is an erroneous and dangerous theoretical move. The tendency to think of cultural identity as sacrosanct, and therefore deserving of recognition, is premised on a conservative notion common in communitarian discourse that the subject and her wants and needs are embedded in the cement of her own culture.[31] This theoretical claim does not stand up to many empirical examples to the contrary. Furthermore, it is an empirical fact that the recognition of a group's identity may often entail the endorsement of institutions and practices of non- or mis-recognition.

---

[30] A purely subjectivist approach to recognition and its relationship to self-worth and esteem is complicated by the fact that respect creates the same feelings but can be the result of acts and institutions that pay no regard to recognising the other in terms of the other's products and powers. For example, the kind of recognition for the Portuguese *conquistador* in sixteenth-century Portugal – for, amongst other things, his 'bravery' and 'courage' in 'educating' and 'saving' (from eternal damnation) the African and Brazilian 'natives' – emerges either out of a lack of knowledge about the actual events or as a result of non-recognition of the exotic 'other'. Contrast this with the recognition enjoyed by Sebastiao Salgado today for his photographic portrayal of the plight and misery of the descendants of some of the survivors of these early 'educating' massacres. It is possible to indicate substantively that there is a fundamental difference between the nature of the activity involved in these two examples. The sixteenth-century act or practice involves respecting acts, practices and institutions that fail to recognise the different 'other': the pre-colonial African and South American resident. The twenty-first-century case involves respecting a creative attempt to recognise this same 'other' as worthy of the same kind of recognition (though not *necessarily* the same degree) that we feel for Salgado ourselves. For examples of colonial acts and attitudes in Brazil, Africa and Australia, see G. Freyre, *The Masters and the Slaves*, trans. S. Putnam (New York: Knopf, 1963); R. Davenport and C. Saunders (eds.), *South Africa: A Modern History*, 5th edn (London: Macmillan, 2000); M. Newitt, *A History of Mozambique* (London: Hurst, 1995); M. Kneale, *The English Passengers* (London: Penguin, 2001).

[31] This is evident in Charles Taylor's work, for example, 'The Politics of Recognition', in A. Gutmann (ed.), *Multiculturalism: Examining the politics of recognition* (Princeton: Princeton University Press, 1994).

The second mistake made by approaches that over-emphasise identity is a failure to note the all-important point that empirical claims for recognition of difference are often claims for relatively equal treatment with regard to meeting needs generally and vital needs specifically.[32] For example, when a black Briton takes up a particular issue, say the recent Stephen Lawrence case, and demands that the oppressed position of black Britons be recognised and institutionally remedied, the claim is not (normally) made so as to reinforce black identity *per se*, and least of all to reinforce racist conceptions of difference.[33] Rather, a claim is being made about the empirical condition of the institutions and practices of modern Britain, and the claim is (normally implicitly) legitimised via the individual agency need for recognition. The kind of recognition being sought is intrinsically related to two different kinds of concerns that connect causally to recognition: (1) as a relational concern (often expressed in terms of equality of recognition) over disparities between the recognition and respect shown to others (non-blacks) and that shown to blacks; (2) in terms of more general concerns such as the consequences this lack of recognition will have upon black people's quality of life and material well-being – their self-respect, self-esteem, freedom and so on. The interpretation of the claim for improved recognition of black people in Britain as a claim that emerges out of concern for a particular group's (or culture's) identity and survival creates a pernicious imbalance in understanding the bald claim. In summary, recognition interpreted as recognition of identity both reifies identity and displaces other (often related) claims that centre on resources for the meeting of vital needs.[34] As will be further developed in chapter 3, the theorisation of these kinds of practical acts (where by 'act' I include 'speech act') in terms of identity and difference actually results in a trend towards conformity rather than difference because it tends to reify strategic moves (means) aimed at broader goals.

---

[32] It could be argued that the case of Quebec is an example of the opposite; that is, an example of claims for *special* treatment based on arguments for cultural integrity. It is not inconsequential that the theoretical defence of 'identity politics' makes constant recourse to the example of Quebec.

[33] There is also the important point that our identities are not singular. They are composed of a variety of (sometimes contradictory) elements. M. Bull, 'Slavery and the Multiple Self', *New Left Review*, 231 (Sept./Oct. 1998); K. A. Appiah, 'Race, Culture, Identity: Misunderstood Connections', in K. A. Appiah and A. Gutmann (eds.), *Color Consciousness: The Political Morality of Race* (Princeton: Princeton University Press, 1996); A. K. Sen, *Reason Before Identity* (Oxford: Oxford University Press, 1999); chapter 3, section 1 below. For a subtle analysis of the Stephen Lawrence case, see M. Patrick, 'Liberalism, Rights, and Recognition', *Philosophy and Social Criticism*, 26 (2000).

[34] N. Fraser, 'Rethinking Recognition', *New Left Review*, 3 (May/June 2000).

Active and creative expression

This is the most commonsensical of the three agency needs. It is important in itself, and is also one of the two defining features of meaningful work, which in the previous section was shown to be a central component of the process of intersubjective recognition. And, as will be argued below, it is also a highly significant determinant of the agency need for autonomy. By active and creative expression I do not mean, or at least not only, the kind of exclusively creative activity carried out by various kinds of artists. Nor, obviously, does the expression concerned have to be both active and creative, although creativity often involves activity and vice versa. Think of musical expression, dance and football. Active and creative expression is an agency need because it is distinct both from consumption to satisfy need or want directly, and the mechanical application of a learnt routine. It is characterised by the need for thoughtful and novel application in the process of creation or action; and it involves the setting and meeting of goals (or at least the meeting of goals set by others) that require planning, responsibility and the expectation of certain desired or needed outcomes. Successful active and creative expression is usually characterised by a sense of achievement and accomplishment rather than satisfaction *per se*. If it is characterised by any satisfaction at all, the satisfaction normally takes the form of what might be called delayed gratification. Furthermore, active and creative expression usually involves a material product of sorts that is consumed or enjoyed (or at least experienced) by other members of an individual's society.

Since the process of intersubjective recognition rests on an essentially material base, the kind of interaction with the material world that is characteristic of active and creative expression is indispensable to the process of recognition. But this does not mean that types of work that do not include active and creative expression are not meaningful; recall that there is another kind of meaningful work, involvement in production and services that meet people's needs, that may not necessarily be an example of active and creative expression. Hence, active and creative expression does not equate to work and is not the only factor that distinguishes meaningful work from non-meaningful work. Moreover, an emphasis on creative and active expression is not the consequence of what might be called a 'productivist ethics', for many of the most important instances of active and creative expression are in fact restricted by stoic hard work and puritanical application to tasks. Finally, although all the agency needs are given the same ontological, epistemological and ethical importance, active and creative expression is causally significant because it links intersubjective recognition with autonomy. The process of individuation that is characteristic of autonomy is not only dependent on the non-distorted meeting of people's vital needs but also requires marks of individual endeavour that characterise active and creative expression.

Autonomy

Autonomy as understood here is not equivalent to the now prevalent Kantian conception of autonomy as a necessary moral premise (or imperative) for human existence – as an *a priori* condition of the ability humans have to believe, cognise and choose. I maintain that it is better to think about autonomy as a goal, as the ever-shifting individual aspiration and objective to have greater control over everyday decision-making. This is distinct from the Kantian conception in three important ways. First, as with the other agency needs, autonomy is conceived as only one agency need among others. It is *not* given moral, ontological or metaphysical priority. Second, this conceptualisation of autonomy is more concerned with the actual empirical experience of autonomy than Kant's *a priori* account. Autonomy, like the other agency needs, can be experienced in the particular, and it is important to note that particular manifestations of autonomy are not usually expressed as autonomy. Individuals do not normally feel the need to be autonomous as such, or feel that they have satisfied their need for autonomy, or that they have now gained autonomy, though they often feel that (now that something objective has changed, like their income) they have *more* control over their immediate world and their immediate choices. This leads into the third difference. In contradistinction to the Kantian conception, I maintain that autonomy is a question of the *degree of acquired level of power*. Understood empirically and practically, autonomy is not normally a binary issue of being free or unfree in Kantian moral terms, and it is not a fixed state of the mind or of material existence, but individuals can feel *more* or *less* autonomous. Hence, autonomy pivots on the power to accomplish plans and tasks and the strength and means to make and defend need-claims; and in everyday experience there is no particular need or satisfier for autonomy.

Obviously, a neo-Kantian critic would be unhappy with this account of autonomy. He would probably argue that I need to provide a single specified normative ground, or foundation, for my discussion of agency needs and that there is no better candidate than autonomy. However, I would argue that the contemporary tendency within political philosophy to require (allegedly) solid *a priori* foundations for normative claims under the guiding light of Kant's moral philosophy, which especially of late are discussed in terms of either rational discourse or rational pre-societal contracts, is nothing more than a vogue. Furthermore, it is the result of a kind of implicit religious (especially Christian) reaction brought on by discontent with the general growth in scepticism over fixed moral foundations. The approach proposed here is, by contrast, assertively non-foundational in its analysis of needs and its understanding of ethics and politics generally, and in its conceptualisation of autonomy in particular. Put brutally, it seems a little spurious to give theoretical priority to autonomy as the normative foundation of human existence when (as far as records go) hardly ever is it given absolute priority on the ground by individuals or policy. The history of human morality and need satisfaction is characterised by a number of (sometimes competing) different demands that emerge out of necessity and morality, and the need for autonomy ranks alongside other important ethical, political and material concerns. Therefore, autonomy is misconstrued if it is understood as the foundational concept of political theory, not only because it is just one of a number of other concerns, but also because it is experienced in practice not as freedom or its lack (unfreedom) but in terms of degrees of power and control. And as a question of degree, it depends on the state of the other agency needs and whether vital needs are met or not, both in the individual concerned and in others.

It is for these reasons that my approach to autonomy begins from the socially embedded and thus socialised individual – who might not embody anything like the kind of Kantian autonomy assumed by many contemporary thinkers – and it takes the goal (the ever-shifting posts) to be increasing individuation.[35] Contrary to common prejudice as well as the work of communitarian theorists such as Taylor and MacIntyre, I maintain that autonomy (and individuation) understood as a goal alongside the recognition and active and creative expression of others enhances and is generated by a high level of sociability. (Sociability here describes a certain kind of ontology: feeling involved in and having critical concern for the good of the other members of one's society.) This is the case because greater individuation, which increases alongside autonomy, emerges non-pathologically from an understanding of one's own and others' needs as determined by

---

[35] This is in line both with Marx's position and with an older liberal position, for example, that developed by Wilhelm von Humboldt in 1792–5. See Humboldt, *Ideen zu einem Versuch, die Grenzen der Wirksamkeit des Staates zu bestimmen* (Stuttgart: Reclam, 1967); R. Geuss, 'Liberalism and Its Discontents', *Political Theory*, 30. 3 (2002), and 'Happiness and Politics', *Arion*, 10. 1 (2002); for Marx references see section 5 below.

others' needs and by the social environment as a whole. This self-reflective knowledge generates a critical distance from everyday individual need satisfaction, which not only further reveals the prevalent generative mechanisms but also thereby strengthens the feeling of autonomy. Hence, *autonomy is a characteristic of full human functioning that either takes the form of a general ethical objective or is manifested in the form of control or power over immediate obstacles, decisions and outcomes, or at least the desire for it*. And, like the other agency needs, a minimum of autonomy is a necessary but not sufficient condition for full human functioning.

I have analysed the agency needs separately from one another, but in reality they develop interdependently. They advance together in a causally and cognitively discernible manner. Individuals will be and feel more autonomous if recognised intersubjectively as deserving of equal respect and if they are provided with the skills and opportunities to engage in either of the two kinds of meaningful work: active and/or creative expression and producing to meet other's needs. And, as a consequence of their autonomous actions, they receive increased (or at least properly intersubjective) recognition. This then gives them more self-esteem, which might spur them on to greater heights in either of their two kinds of meaningful work. And the cycle continues.

5 THE NATURES OF NEEDS: HISTORICAL, NORMATIVE, POLITICAL

In contrast to my account of need forms and need categories, most modern theorists of needs tend to focus on developing lists of *universal* human needs.[36] These lists normally involve analyses of the human condition and include many more elements than the three natural physical needs characteristic of earlier thought, and are significantly more subtle than the pared-down basic needs approaches of modern mainstream welfare economics. However, these modern needs theorists force their substantive advances into a form of understanding that is reminiscent of the earlier static conceptions and of modern economics. But they do so for opposite reasons: they swing too far the other way and develop purely normative accounts of needs.

---

[36] See, for example, Doyal and Gough, *Human Need*, chs 4, 9 and 10; Braybrooke, *Meeting Needs*, p. 36; M. C. Nussbaum, 'Aristotelian Social Democracy', in B. Douglas and G. Mara (eds.), *Liberalism and the Good* (New York and London: Routledge, 1990), reprinted in Brock (ed.), *Necessary Goods*, pp. 135–56, and *Women and Human Development: The Capabilities Approach* (Cambridge: Cambridge University Press, 2000), pp. 78–80. See below for more Nussbaum references.

They start from the uncontentious claim that the urge to act in a particular way must not be confused with the justification for doing so.[37] My drive
to do or consume something, like smoke cigarettes or drink large quantities
of alcohol, understood in terms of need, may be something that I do not
objectively need. And, conversely, I can have a need for something, like
exercise, and yet never have felt it as a drive. They then claim that the fact
that not all our 'need-drives' can be justified as needs is sufficient reason
why needs should be understood as universal goals.[38] This enables them to
make a sharp analytical distinction between needs and wants. Wants, they
maintain, are subjective and drive-based, whilst needs are objective, universal goals whose lack creates objective harm. The goals are understood as
ineluctable means or conditions for individuals to be able to make choices,
have preferences heeded, and create 'life plans', or the preconditions for
actualising rights and enabling freedom, and as such they are conceived as
the 'preconditions' for being a person.[39] They are understood in this way
because the prevailing liberal discourse understands individual freedom as
based on universal rights and as constituted by free preference formation
and choice. And these lists of universal needs are proposed as theoretical
blueprints for how to provide the conditions upon which individuals can
make effective use of their rights in order to secure this freedom of choice.
Consequently, it is assumed that these *theoretical* lists of preconditions or
needs resolve the problem of needs, and as such theorists who develop
these lists repeat the follies of natural law and natural rights: they propose
a *meta*-political theoretical solution for an inherently practical, political
problem.

This has unintended practical outcomes. If it is thought that the problem
of needs is resolvable at the level of universal normative theory, the theory
will either be so generalised as to have no practical significance or it will
impose its own values and definitions, particular to one context, on all contexts. For example, Doyal and Gough argue that autonomy, their second
'basic' need or 'precondition' for being a person, is constituted by understanding, mental health and opportunities for new and significant action

[37] Doyal and Gough, *Human Need*, p. 36; G. Thomson, *Needs* (London and New York: Routledge, 1987), pp. 13–14.
[38] Doyal and Gough, ibid., claim that these are good reasons 'why we should divorce the discourse of needs as universalisable goals from that of motivations or drives altogether'. They pay lip service to needs as drives and motivations but they think of these only in terms of biology and genetic structure, claiming that 'the emphasis on drives and motivations does alert us to the *biological background* to human needs: to the *constraints* on human needs given by our *genetic structure*'.
[39] Ibid., esp. ch. 4.

guaranteed via 'democratic participation in the political process'.[40] However, this would disallow the classification of some actual human beings as persons, since they have the misfortune of not living within a democratic political environment. This problematic outcome is a direct consequence of Doyal and Gough's understanding of autonomy as a universal condition – a moral premise – and the result is the universalisation of a particular manifestation of western thought that by definition excludes a whole swathe of actually existing, that is, functioning, persons. This form of understanding needs is based upon a Kantian ethics that understands autonomy as a moral premise for human existence and free will, which also underpins modern neo-Kantian liberalism with its assumption, *à la* Rawls, that certain primary goods can provide the conditions for all possible needs, preferences and 'life plans' over and above them.[41] But these problems are not confined to neo-Kantians; their neo-Aristotelian liberal cousins sing the same hymn, although they are more explicit about the 'good', or form of life, in question. For example, Nussbaum's capability approach with its 'thick vague conception of the good' amounts to a list of liberal (and North American) values.[42] And given that these are universal accounts of needs from within

---

[40] Ibid., pp. 60–8.

[41] Doyal and Gough's approach fits snugly into Rawls' theory of justice; ibid., ch. 7. For Rawls, primary goods are 'things which it is supposed a rational man wants whatever else he wants', and include 'income and wealth', the 'basic liberties', 'freedom of movement and choice of occupation', 'powers and prerogatives of offices and positions of responsibility', and 'the social bases of self-respect'. J. Rawls, *A Theory of Justice* (Oxford: Oxford University Press, 1973), p. 92. This 'index of primary goods' is further elaborated in Rawls, 'Social Unity and Primary Goods', in A. K. Sen and B. Williams (eds.), *Utilitarianism and Beyond* (Cambridge: Cambridge University Press, 1982), p. 162, and Rawls, *Political Liberalism* (New York: Columbia University Press, 1996), pp. 75–7, 178–90, although the index itself is left mostly unchanged. In *Political Liberalism* Rawls defines primary goods as 'citizens' needs', or the 'things citizens need as free and equal persons', and therefore argues that 'claims to these goods are counted as appropriate claims' (p. 180). In doing so, Rawls makes a spurious distinction between these objective needs of citizens – 'a special kind of need for a political conception of justice' – and other human needs, and argues that other needs, desires and aspirations 'play no role' (p. 189n). Thus he too is not concerned with felt needs and how they are generated. See chapter 4, section 4, for further discussion. For more on Kant and his relevance, see I. Kant, *Critique of Pure Reason*, trans. and ed. P. Guyer and A. W. Wood (Cambridge: Cambridge University Press, 1998); and Doyal and Gough, *Human Need*, pp. 52–3. Moreover, this modern form of democratic Kantian liberalism is an anachronism of the first order, since Kant was neither a democrat nor a liberal. R. Geuss, *History and Illusion in Politics* (Cambridge: Cambridge University Press, 2001).

[42] Nussbaum, 'Nature, Function and Capability: Aristotle on Political Distribution', *Oxford Studies in Ancient Philosophy*, suppl. vol., 1988; 'Aristotelian Social Democracy'; 'Aristotle on Human Nature and the Foundation of Ethics', in J. Altham and R. Harrison (eds.), *World, Mind, and Ethics: Essays in the Ethical Philosophy of Bernard Williams* (Cambridge: Cambridge University Press, 1990); 'Non-Relative Virtues: An Aristotelian Approach', in M. C. Nussbaum and A. K. Sen (eds.), *The Quality of Life* (Oxford: Clarendon Press, 1993); 'Public Philosophy and International Feminism', *Ethics*, 108. 4 (July 1998); *Sex and Social Justice* (Oxford: Clarendon Press, 1999); and *Women and Human Development*. The same criticism can be levelled at Braybrooke's otherwise subtle 'List of Matters

the hegemonic western discourse, these theorists can and do unproblematically export their solutions to those less fortunate far away. The result is a theoretical conception of needs that dictates practical politics in all contexts irrespective of local problems and felt needs and preferences over needs: a dictatorship of western theories and value systems, or a theoretical equivalent of contemporary free-trade imperialism with its roots in monotheistic colonialism.[43] This is reinforced by the fact that these theoretical solutions remove the point of politics: there is little point in evaluating needs in practice if theorists know our needs and can entrench them in the form of rights or entitlements. Thus in developing purely normative conceptions of human needs that fit the extant structure of rights and preferences, these theorists develop static accounts of human needs that fail to give the concept of needs any real significance in politics and political philosophy.

These unintended practical outcomes are related to a number of other problems. First, theorists who develop lists of needs as conditions assume that once these conditions exist all humans will possess equal security and freedom with regard to rights and preferences. That is, they assume that the same conditions apply to all preferences. This is a little hasty. As Arrow and Sen have noted, the (sometimes) large variations in the moral, intellectual and physical capacities of individuals means that any single set of conditions will enable different individuals in very different ways.[44] Moreover, some kinds of political protest, for example hunger strikes, involve rejecting the provision of conditions normally indispensable to heeding preferences *because* the preferences that the protesters most cherish are not being heeded. And this occurs in *democratic* states fortunate enough to meet all of Doyal and Gough's conditions. Doyal and Gough could argue that without health and autonomy the hunger strike would be impossible. Yet I can still have sufficient autonomy and health to hunger strike long before I reach their required levels of health and autonomy. In imagining that the same conditions could apply to all preferences, these theorists either confine 'preferences' to 'liberal preferences' or they imagine a world without the current (enriching) diversity of moral, political and material concerns.

---

of Need': Braybrooke, *Meeting Needs*. For the relationship between Sen's and Nussbaum's accounts of 'capability', see my 'A Theory of True Interests in the Work of Amartya Sen', *Government and Opposition*, 34. 4 (1999).

[43] See my 'Needs, States, and Markets: democratic sovereignty against imperialism', *Theoria*, 102 (December 2003).

[44] K. J. Arrow, 'Some Ordinalist Notes on Rawls' Theory of Justice', *Journal of Philosophy* (1973); see chapter 2, section 5 for Sen references and further discussion.

Second, these theorists conceive of needs purely as means, understood relative to lack and objective harm, that is, as those means or conditions whose lack creates objective harm,[45] and this excludes a wide spectrum of needs and most causal determinants of need. In conceptualising needs as means, most modern accounts of needs emphasise the logical form of everyday instrumental needs: *A* needs *X* in order to *Y*. This reduces needs to their everyday satisfiers, for the *X* in the formula is normally understood as the need in question, and thus does not allow for the fact that needs are satisfied in a number of ways by a number of satisfiers. Recall my example of the need for a car. The satisfier is the car but the need may not be; it may be mobility or social esteem or a combination of the two. Thus the everyday logical form actually confuses matters because it reinforces the reduction of all needs to instrumental means to meet other ends or goals; that is, it reinforces the assumption that needs are means rather than ends. This is obviously true of many needs in many everyday contexts, but it cannot cover *all* contexts and needs. Moreover, it tends to accept extant constellations of satisfiers and the goals for which these are means. In other words, it reifies the present, excluding the possibility of new needs and preferences in the future. A quick glance into history will make it clear that needs are formed over time, and that many contemporary needs used to be wants, for example, the need for a refrigerator. It follows from this that some particular human needs and their satisfiers may not yet be known, and thus that we cannot say anything of interest now about how to provide the conditions for the meeting of these needs or preferences. And in any case, some human needs are ends or goals in themselves, with certain attendant aspirations. Understanding needs exclusively as means excludes a whole spectrum of needs and thus artificially equates needs like my need for autonomy to everyday instrumental needs, such as my need for a battery to make my camera work.

In excluding need-drives from their analysis, these normative approaches cannot entertain the common fact that particular needs that were once normative goals become legitimised as needs, thereby becoming need-drives and forming part of the empirical 'facts' that are then described in more 'descriptive' work on needs as natural need-drives, or even 'biological' need-drives. That is, they fail to grasp the causal mechanisms through which needs are formed: that, for example, a corporation's or society's legitimation of the drive to compete as a need for competition is fundamental to the individual's interpretation of that drive in terms of need. Similarly, a society's

---

[45] Doyal and Gough, *Human Need*, p. 45.

legitimation of a certain goal as a need can over time cause that need to be felt as a need-drive. Those who think that needs are best understood purely as goals will omit the wide expanse of social and historical processes that have given rise to some of our seemingly most 'natural' and 'biological' of drives; that is, they will exclude an understanding of the formative institutions and practices of needs, material which is crucial to the evaluation of needs and related claims.

   Third, it simply is not the case that I lack whatever I need: many things that I already have are things that I need.[46] Or, in other words, I still need something that I no longer lack — I still need shelter even though I have a house and so do not lack shelter. Nor is it the case that I need everything whose lack creates objective harm. The objective harm created by lack is also experienced when strong wants are left unsatisfied; or in other words an unmet strong desire that is not a need can also cause objective harm. Consequently, the great irony is that this means of understanding need does *not* provide an adequate means of distinguishing need from want; this is reinforced by actual usage, where 'want' can be and is used in the sense of 'lack'.[47] There is no doubt that wants are distinct from needs. One way of seeing the distinction is to analyse the counter-claim, common amongst economists, that need is identical to want for it is a kind of want, a fully informed one. This argument accepts that some stated wants are not fully informed preferences, but argues that needs are always fully informed preferences. This is mistaken. What of the person who is fully aware of the dangers of smoking, and yet prefers to keep smoking? Or think of people who prefer to indulge in extreme sports, or people who prefer to put the needs of others ahead of their own — the UK medical doctor who transfers to Botswana out of concern for HIV/AIDS sufferers. Reducing needs to fully informed preferences wipes out the distinction called for in these common cases. Thus defining need in terms of lack is not only mistaken and unhelpful, it joins those with an opposing project.[48]

---

[46] D. Wiggins, 'Claims of Need', in Wiggins, *Needs, Values, Truth: Essays in the Philosphy of Value*, 3rd edn (Oxford: Clarendon Press, 1998), p. 6; A. R. White, *Modal Thinking* (Oxford: Basil Blackwell, 1975), p. 107.

[47] The OED's first entries under 'want' as noun and verb are: lacking, missing, lack of something desirable or necessary, to lack. 'For want of a naile, a shoe is lost, for want of a shoe the horse is lost, for want of a horse the rider is lost': G. Herbert, *Outlandish Providence* (1640), p. 499.

[48] As it does those with an opposing, though similarly flawed, needs project: the relativists. In arguing that needs are by definition subjective, felt drives that when left unmet create objective harm, the relativists equate needs with impulses or drives and thus undermine unintentionally the useful normative distinction between needs and wants. G. Rist, 'Basic questions about basic human needs', in K. Lederer (ed.), *Human Needs* (Cambridge, MA: Gunn and Hain, 1980); A. H. Maslow, *Motivation and Personality*, 2nd edn (New York: Harper and Row, 1970). For a more nuanced

Thus modern conceptions of needs rest upon an impoverished definitional triumvirate of means, lack and harm, which reduces needs to instrumental means in the attainment of other goods and de-politicises the
question of needs. Marx provides a means of moving beyond these problems in that he understands needs in normative, historical and instrumental
terms; that is, he conceives of needs as means *and* ends. However, as I will
argue, Marx retreats from the logical implications of his approach and ends
up developing an apolitical conception of needs.

Marx has two conceptions of needs. His first is restrictive and normative.
Implicit in it is the notion that some desires and goals are fundamental to
human functioning and others are superfluous (or even inimical) to human
functioning. Often this distinction corresponds to our ordinary normative
use of need in which people are said not to have needs for ice cream
and sports cars, but for food or exercise or meaningful work. This first
conception is found throughout Marx's writings, from the *Economic and
Philosophic Manuscripts* (1844) to the various versions of *Capital* and the
Notes on Adolph Wagner.[49]

Marx's second conception of needs is his expansive, developmental conception. This is a generalising and expansive conception of needs that covers
approximately the wide expanse of ground covered by 'wants' and 'needs';
that is, all the needs in the restrictive sense, and the desires and goals that
develop above and beyond them. This conception emphasises the historical, developmental side to needs and is most frequently and obviously
encountered in the *Economic and Philosophic Manuscripts* (1844), *Capital
Vol. I*, and other economic writings.[50]

relativist position, see K. Soper, *On Human Needs: Open and Closed Theories in a Marxist Perspective*
(Brighton: Harvester, 1981); and 'A Theory of Human Need', *New Left Review*, 197 (1993), pp. 113–28.

[49] K. Marx, *Economic and Philosophic Manuscripts (1844)*, in *Karl Marx Early Writings*, intro. L. Colletti
(London: Penguin, 1992; hereinafter *EPM*), pp. 359, 366; Marx, *The Poverty of Philosophy*, in *Frederick
Karl Marx Engels Collected Works Vol. 6* (London: Lawrence & Wishart, 1976; hereinafter *MECW*),
p. 160 — 'the necessary provisions for the sustenance of the worker', and p. 199 — 'the needs of the
population' (for food); K. Marx and F. Engels, *The Communist Manifesto*, intro. G. Stedman Jones
(London: Penguin, 2002); Marx, *Grundrisse*, trans. M. Nicolaus (London: Penguin, 1973), pp. 284,
852–3; Marx, *Capital*, 3 vols., intro. E. Mandel, trans. D. Fernback (London: Penguin, 1976–8), esp.
vol. 1; Marx, *Notes on Adolph Wagner*, in *Karl Marx Texts on Method*, ed. T. Carver (Oxford: Oxford
University Press, 1975). See D. Braybrooke, 'Two Conceptions of Needs in Marx's Writings', in
Moral Objectives; and for more on Marx's ethics see P. J. Kain, *Marx and Ethics* (Oxford: Clarendon
Press, 1988).

[50] Marx, *EPM*, p. 358; K. Marx, *Oeuvres* (Paris: Gallimard, 1965–82), vol. 1, p. 219 ('Wage Labour and
Capital'), p. 245 ('General Introduction to the Critique of Political Economy'), p. 277 ('Critique of
Political Economy'), where Marx talks about the 'objets de besoins humains', whether 'nécessaires,
utiles ou agréables'; vol. 1, p. 501 ('Wages, Prices and Surplus Value'); vol. 1, pp. 561–2, 569, 605,
612, 621, 650, 675, 697, 739 (all *Capital Vol. I*).

The basis for this second conception is Marx's understanding of the development of needs in terms of powers and senses. He describes and explains a continuous and circular process that brings to light the interdependence of needs, powers and senses as they develop historically. Marx argues that when we feel a need, be it 'crude' or 'human', we exercise a power to meet or satisfy the need. Through the satisfaction of this need, we develop the power as a consequence of its having been exercised. This provokes the development of a new sense, or the modification of an old one — the development of the power opens new connections and understandings (even kinds of cognition) that create a new sense. This new sense then gives rise to a new need, and attending to this need may require a new power. The process continues in this circular but (always) potentially developmental manner.[51] The potential is realised positively when it is developed in a 'human' or 'social' manner. Thus this second conception is related to the first, restrictive conception of needs: Marx argues that this process can only function properly under conditions of freedom; that is, needs develop fully and correctly when free from the restraints of external control, and when developed amongst other people who are developing their needs.[52]

Thus needs are expansive but they can develop on a positive trajectory, in a 'human' or 'social' manner, or on a negative, distorted trajectory, where the development of needs either takes an inappropriate route or stops. According to Marx, this occurs, at least under extant conditions, when

---

[51] '[O]nly music can awaken the musical sense in man and the most beautiful music has *no* sense for the unmusical ear... [it] can only be for me in so far as my essential power exists for me as a subjective attribute... In the same way, and for the same reasons, the *senses* of social man are *different* from those of non-social man. Only through the objectively unfolded wealth of human nature can the wealth of subjective *human* sensitivity — ..., sense able of human gratification — be either cultivated or created.' Marx, *EPM*, p. 353. (In all quotes emphasis is Marx's unless otherwise indicated.) Cf. J.-J. Rousseau, *Discourse on the Origin and Foundations of Inequality Among Men* or *Second Discourse*, in *The Discourses and Other Early Political Writings*, ed. V. Gourevitch (Cambridge: Cambridge University Press, 1997), p. 111.

[52] Part of the inspiration for this argument comes from P.-J. Proudhon's proposals for a future society in which economic exchange and relations are organised socially, or humanly; that is, free from the distortion of the right to private property, and associated property relations, and the imposition of external political control. Proudhon, *What is Property?*, trans. and ed. D. R. Kelley and B. G. Smith (Cambridge: Cambridge University Press, 1994), originally published in 1840 as *Qu'est-ce que la Propriété?*; Proudhon, *Système des Contradictions Économiques ou Philosophie de la Misère* (Paris and Geneva: Slatkine, 1982), originally published in 1846; and Proudhon, *Théorie de la Propriété* (Paris: Éditions l'Harmattan, 1997), originally published in 1866. There is no doubt that Marx read Proudhon's *What is Property?* soon after arriving in Paris in 1844, and before he began writing the *Economic and Philosophic Manuscripts*. See Marx, *EPM*, pp. 345–79; L. von Stein, *The History of the Social Movement in France, 1789–1850*, intro., ed. and trans. K. Bauer-Mengelberg (Totowa, NJ: Bedminster, 1964), pp. 348, 356, 400, 415, 422, 425–6; and Marx and Engels, *Selected Correspondence* (Moscow: Foreign Languages Publishing, 1956), p. 187. Two years later, in *The Poverty of Philosophy*, Marx develops a detailed criticism of Proudhon's solution, which I discuss below.

the sense of having and owning, and the need to have and own, is so overpowering that it replaces the other needs, or at least controls the other needs. For Marx, the workers are controlled in the sense that they are kept in conditions in which their needs remain 'crude'; that is, they can satisfy only their basic needs – sufficient food, adequate shelter – with the result that the development of their human powers is blocked by the constant immediate need to *have* things as a means of survival, or basic life. In the case of the relatively rich, Marx argues that despite the fact that their needs and powers are well developed (he says they have 'rich' needs), the sense of having and owning and the concomitant needs distort this development. The objective of the relatively rich becomes to accumulate and possess for the sake of having and possessing, not for the sake of human growth and development.[53]

Thus the second, expansive conception allows Marx to argue that, given the historical development of needs, humans have the capacity, the expertise and the means to develop and provide for everyone's needs. And the first, restrictive conception allows Marx to criticise the emphasis under capitalism on the wrong kinds of needs, which create the waste, alienation, class conflict and inappropriate need development that concern him.[54]

The central importance of these two conceptions is reinforced by the fact that Marx uses them together when he describes the rare type of practical activity in which participants do develop their real needs. A good example of this is his passage on the communist workers.[55] When people are involved in practical activity that has as its central objective the needs of society, an actual and instrumental need produces in Marx's expansive sense a new need that forms the most important part of his restrictive, normative conception: a 'need for society' which acts as the normative guide for the development of all the other particular needs. Obviously political and practical in nature, communal activity is for Marx one of the guiding principles, or goals, in the development of needs. Although the particular real needs cannot be

---

[53] See his point about estrangement, or alienation: 'Estrangement appears not only in the fact that the means of *my* life belong to *another* and that *my* desire is the inaccessible possession of *another*, but also in the fact that all things are *other* than themselves, that my activity is *other* than itself, and that finally – and this goes for the capitalist too – an *inhuman* power rules over everything.' For Marx, '[t]he *rich* man is simultaneously the man *in need* of a totality of vital human expression'. Marx, *EPM*, pp. 366, 356.

[54] Ibid., p. 366.

[55] 'When communist *workmen* gather together, their immediate aim is instruction, propaganda, etc. But at the same time they acquire a new need – the need for society – and what appears as a means has become an end. Smoking, eating and drinking, etc., are no longer means of creating links between people. Company, association, conversation, which in its turn has society as its goal, is enough for them.' Ibid. p. 365.

stipulated in theory — rather they emerge through practical action and suffering — Marx makes a clear normative distinction as regards the paths of preferred development of the powers, needs and senses, that is, of human capacities and potentialities. Needs should not develop, and ought not to be allowed to develop, along the path of egoistic 'having' created by the conditions of capitalist society, but rather along the shared concern of the wider needs of individuals and their society that accompanies communal activity and thought.[56]

Furthermore, Marx's first restrictive, normative conception does not contradict his idea about the constant development of needs; for he sees the latter as intrinsically connected to the development of human nature. Marx makes use of his two conceptions of need simultaneously to indicate how a purely instrumental need under the right conditions could be a real ineluctable need that is developing correctly. In the right conditions new needs are not stifled but are rather developed in accord with a *human* trajectory of the development of our human powers, needs and senses. But this does *not* (have to) mean that present felt indispensable needs will be disregarded, that is, will not continue to be met. For Marx can hold an argument about constant development and have a core idea concerning human nature. His restrictive conception does not delimit expansion. Later periods in the historical development of need can expand the category depending upon both the development of need satisfiers and human needs. The progress from 'animal' to human or real needs can occur without discrediting or removing the original animal need. For example, as an instance of food, an apple is a satisfier of animal need as desire need (mere want), and this animal desire need for food survives in the desire need for a balanced diet. Once I am more aware of what a balanced diet entails, the form of manifestation of my animal desire need is changed, but it still survives as part of my need. It could even be argued that it remains as the source of the

---

[56] Here Marx draws on Feuerbach's analyses of the necessity for communal cognition in a correct understanding of need and the social world, adding the idea that it can only be real human cognition if it emerges out of practical activity. L. Feuerbach, *Preliminary Theses on the Reform of Philosophy*, and *Principles of the Philosophy of the Future*, in *The Fiery Brook: Selected Writings of Ludwig Feuerbach*, trans. Z. Hanfi (Garden City, NY: Anchor Books, 1972); Marx, *EPM*, pp. 381, 389, 391. Following Max Stirner's critique in 1845, Marx explicitly repudiates Feuerbach's philosophy, and the notion of 'species-being' then becomes notable for its absence. M. Stirner, *The Ego and Its Own* (Cambridge: Cambridge University Press, 1995); Marx, '[Theses on Feuerbach]', *MECW 5*; Marx and Engels, 'The German Ideology', *MECW 5*. However, even in his later work Marx retains Feuerbach's main epistemological and ontological points on the communal nature of human knowing and being, and 'species-being' is simply replaced by the notion of the 'social individual' (as opposed to the 'private individual'). Marx, *Grundrisse*, pp. 161–2; 172–3; 487–8; 540–2, 706–12; 831–2. Cf. the orthodox interpretation: Marx abandons Feuerbach's approach and along with it any normative or voluntarist theme. G. Stedman Jones, 'Introduction' to Marx and Engels, *The Communist Manifesto*, p. 142.

desire: who ever really ravenously desired a balanced diet?[57] Similarly, the need for recognition still survives when the skills accumulated in the ego-istic quest for fame and social acclaim are adapted and developed for community-oriented means and goals; in the latter I need the skills to be ef-fective, but the reason I develop them is not solely for my own ends but also for some community-oriented good, or purpose. For Marx, the communist workers are not filled with different needs, but the form these same needs take is distinct. Certain capacities and potentialities — powers, needs and senses – that were always present in human beings have become actualised.

Marx's understanding of need, therefore, revolves around the claim that the development of powers, needs and senses will develop dependent on how they are allowed to develop; and that they can remain as mere potentials unless they are given the opportunity to be realised. This is a subtle kind of normative critique that owes its insights to two related factors. First, needs are understood in terms of means *and* ends, in terms of human functioning and the actual and possible historical development of needs, rather than purely in terms of means whose lack creates harm. Second, it follows from this that Marx does not separate the satisfiers of needs and the needs themselves, or more aptly, the human beings themselves, as is common in both earlier thought and modern approaches to needs. Moreover, given his expansive conception, he incorporates wants into this causal analysis and thus links them to needs and human functioning. Thus Marx has extended the Hegelian re-establishment of a normative nexus by deepening our understanding of how need and want satisfiers affect the development of human needs and thus human functioning. Once this is accepted it is only a short step to a political analysis of needs, which focuses on the choice of need trajectories, and the forms of collective coercion that will be required for these choices to obtain. However, this is a step Marx himself never takes; in fact, he does the opposite: he develops an apolitical conception of needs. Why?

If nothing else, politics is an activity defined by some notion of collective choice among differentially assessed paths or trajectories of need develop-ment, where the assessment is in terms of evaluated individual and public goods and interests. And any significant action in the light of the choice will ultimately involve coercion. There are various different paths down which the development of needs can progress and some of these can be

---

[57] See Marx's discussion (*Grundrisse*, p. 92) of the need involved in satisfying hunger by bolting down raw food, and that involved in satisfying the same thing, hunger, using a knife and fork on cooked food. He maintains that the form of the desire need has been transformed to such a degree that the need is different, but in the process the animal desire need for food survives.

evaluated as 'better' than other paths. And a political theory of needs is one that sees needs as variable in dimension depending on the state of politics, often with a concomitant claim that political action has some hope of influencing which paths the development of needs follows. Marx has an apolitical conception of needs because he argues that the problem of needs is fully resolvable, but only once the political evaluation of needs and political coercion cease to exist; in other words, his solution to the problem of needs is outside the realm of, or detached from, politics.[58] According to Marx, his goal or solution – the future society without classes, oppression, alienation or the 'bourgeois' state – will not require 'politics' as we understand it. This is because, for Marx, the current political order that involves the state, alienation and class division is a contingent consequence itself of the capitalist order, as well as a condition for its continued existence. In the long run 'politics' will therefore be abolished, or will have to be abolished, if we are to feel and meet our real needs, that is, under 'human' conditions free of external political control. This is axiomatic to Marx's position.

Although Marx's work generally was manifestly political in the sense that much of it was designed to motivate the contemporary political actors to act in a certain way in order to achieve a preferred path for the development of needs, his main claim (or belief) is that once this is achieved the evaluation and meeting of needs will no longer be a political issue.[59] This future society simply will be a society in which the need problem will be solved once and for all, for needs will be generated and satisfied under 'human' conditions. Thus although Marx's two conceptions open up an interesting and fruitful political arena, he closes this off with an idea that given the 'right' conditions not only will we know and satisfy our real needs but also they will be harmonious and communal by 'nature'.[60] This will not

---

[58] Normally by 'apolitical' we mean 'detached from politics', whilst 'unpolitical' means 'not political, not concerned or dealing with politics' (*OED*). I opt for 'apolitical' rather than 'unpolitical' to describe Marx's position because there is little doubt that Marx is both concerned and dealing with politics. And for obvious reasons I do not use 'political' (and so 'apolitical') in Marx's own technical sense, which means having to do with power in a capitalist state. For Marx, the problem is political, not the solution.

[59] The motivation to change the conditions amounted to a motivation for revolutionary change associated with a certain kind of faith in the outcome. Hence, this more obvious sense of Marx's political activity is less historically significant for a conceptualisation of the nature of needs.

[60] Thus Marx does not make use of a distinction between true and false needs. The fact that he claims that desire needs are egoistic under capitalism does not mean that they are false and others true, but that the conditions simply warp the process of need generation so that actual felt needs are ineluctable and yet egoistic. Given the right conditions, they will be generated in a different manner; the right conditions will give rise to real needs. Consequently 'real' here is not synonymous with

require forms of political evaluation, intervention or coercion.[61] In other words, Marx himself combines his two conceptions of need in an unhelpful, resolutely future-oriented manner: the first expansive conception provides the potential for the transformation of our needs and the restrictive sense can only be a real, 'human' guide once the conditions provide the correct ethical and structural environment.

This idea that needs could somehow be free from political and evaluative problems when under the right conditions is manifested generally in Marx's work after the failed revolution of 1848. He moves away from any political analysis of how to improve on the conditions of need development because he turns to a specifically 'economic' approach in attempting to solve what he sees as the source of the problem. Marx criticised Proudhon in *The Poverty of Philosophy* (1847) for his attempt to formulate a concept of use value based in labour, but by the middle of the 1850s Marx had developed his own concept of use value, which is presented later, in *Capital*, as a direct, static and naturalistic specification of human need.[62] Marx's concept of use value is the main ingredient in what would have been a full theoretical, apolitical 'solution' for the problem of needs. But for his radical anti-utopianism and incomplete project, we would have had a 'solution' for the future society that bypassed the state and the everyday evaluative problems related to the specification of individual needs: *meta*-political natural law turned on its

'true' as the polar opposite of illusory, imaginary or false needs. Rather 'real needs' describes our needs under Marx's notion of social organisation that is based on the principle of *human* need, forms of which can be identified within certain actual kinds of social interaction, as discussed above. Cf. P. Springborg, 'Karl Marx on Human Needs', in R. Fitzgerald (ed.), *Human Needs and Politics* (Oxford: Pergamon, 1977), pp. 162–3; 169, who argues that Marx does make use of a true/false distinction, as is common in later Marxist writers, such as Marcuse.

[61] He takes this to its extreme in the *Critique of the Gotha Programme* (1875) where he simply claims that '[i]n the highest phase of communism . . . society can inscribe on its banners; from each according to his ability, to each according to his needs'. *Karl Marx: Selected Writings*, ed. D. Mclellan (Oxford: Oxford University Press, 1977), p. 560. As Braybrooke notes in 'The Common Good', in *Moral Objectives*, p. 222, this sentiment of Marx's has its origins in the Bible: From one and all according to their ability, to one and all according to their need (Acts of the Apostles 4:34–5).

[62] Marx criticised Proudhon's solution, his 'corrective ideal' of equal wages, where a fixed notion of utility (use value) is determined by the basic labour time required to produce each product. Marx argued that Proudhon's solution rests on an imagined difference between use value and 'estimation'. For Marx, the perceived utility of a thing is dependent on the needs of the evaluator ('estimator'), which by their very nature are constantly changing, as well as the actual relation of the supplier (producer) and demander (consumer), which is a relation of conflict between the marketable value demanded by the supplier and the marketable value supplied by the demander. In other words, *under market conditions* the evaluation of utility is the consequence of an unequal conflict of power. Thus, *under market conditions* the search for an absolute use value is a futile one. Proudhon, *What is Property?*, pp. 177, 207, 211, 215; Marx, *The Poverty of Philosophy*, pp. 107, 117, 133–4. Yet later Marx developed an absolute use value based in what he termed 'labour power', or the capacity to work: the commodity the worker sells is his 'labour power' and the fact that labour power is normally paid below its value cannot alter its value. *Capital Vol. I*, chs VI, XXV.

head, metamorphosed into a kingdom of abundance, production for use rather than exchange.

Now, obviously, the control, evaluation and coercion that characterise the evaluation and satisfaction of needs do not have to take the form they do in the present, but Marx assumed not only that he had to find a theoretical solution to the problem but also that for that solution to have any force politics as he knew it would be completely changed. In contrast, I maintain that the specification of human needs in a particular context will always be a political problem, even if oppression, alienation and class structure were eradicated; that is, it will always involve evaluation and choice over different paths and the subsequent use of coercion to cause some groups to choose the evaluated paths. Hence, although Marx's two conceptions of need are an advance on modern conceptions in the sense that they establish an understanding of need in terms both of means and ends (and goals and drives), his particular combination of the two conceptions in the context of his solution is apolitical in the sense stipulated here.

In sum, then, whether in Kantian or Aristotelian vein, modern approaches to need develop purely normative positions that tend to undermine a causal, historical and evaluative and thus political understanding of needs. This is reinforced by an instrumental understanding of needs, in which needs are understood above all as means or conditions for individual choices and 'life plans'. This instrumental approach to need is given definitional logic by reference to lack and objective harm, and an analytical fetish over the relational formula A needs X in order to Y. My conception of needs is distinct from these modern conceptions in a number of ways. First, it does not confine needs to universalisable goals as conditions; rather my categorisation of needs includes needs as drives, goals and the necessary elements of human functioning. My distinction between particular and general needs is important in this regard. Particular needs, or needs in their particular form, are normally means and can be understood and explained using the formula A needs X in order to Y. General needs, or needs in their general form, are normally ends and cannot be understood or explained using this formula. Thus my different categories or forms of need correspond to different moments in everyday human existence, the beings and doings of humans. Particular social needs pertain to everyday means, while vital and agency needs pertain to the ends of life, the necessary component parts of full human functioning. Sometimes needs are the mundane, instrumental concerns and 'means' of everyday life and sometimes they are the ultimate requirements, goals and aspirations of human existence. And, as will be argued in chapter 2, these different forms are inter-related in causally significant ways. To reduce the category of needs to one or the other is to trivialise the reality of human needs and their causal significance and thus the concept of needs. Hence, second, needs are not defined in terms of means or conditions whose lack creates objective harm, but rather as necessary components of actual and possible full human functioning.[63] Human needs take the form of means or ends and drives or goals depending on context; together they constitute different equally significant moments in human existence and human individuality and freedom; and are therefore not solely means but means and ends. Third, needs therefore cannot be subordinated to static artificial concepts such as the concept of rights.

Fourth, wants are distinct from needs but not as proposed by modern theorists. Wants are always felt drives or desires that do not relate to human goals and functioning in the same way as needs do since they do not usually involve a normative connection to human functioning. In some cases they do, but this is because people often do want what they need, or in other words, needs are often experienced as wants, or in the form of wants. For example, my preference for a certain pair of shoes coincides, and arises from, my need to protect my feet and maintain mobility, and my preference for a car may coincide with and meet my need for mobility. And even when wants are not expressions of needs they can meet and causally affect needs. As a result, people sometimes present needs as wants, and conversely also (erroneously) interpret wants as needs. Thus, unless a want is a volitional expression of vital or agency need, wants are related to local (normally immediate) concerns and desires that do not have a necessary relation to human functioning, although they affect human functioning through their causal relations with needs.

In combining the normative and the instrumental elements of needs within an expansive, developmental understanding of needs, Marx delineates the causal relationship between needs and wants and why it is

---

[63] This definition is objective in the sense that the needs, as drives, goals or functions, or combinations thereof, can be ascertained and analysed objectively in terms of how they relate to functional necessity and objective general ethical objectives. But it is not objective in the sense entertained by, for example, Doyal and Gough. Their definition of needs as things that 'constitute goals which all humans have to achieve if they are to avoid serious harm' is objective 'in that its theoretical and empirical specification is independent of individual preference' (Doyal and Gough, *Human Need*, pp. 45, 49). The same cannot be said for my position. As will become evident in what follows, individual preferences are important in themselves and with regard to the evaluation and specification of needs in context. Needs are both objectively ascertainable and require subjective involvement. The measurement of the height and weight of a starving person can indicate need, as too can a population census of morbidity, but they also necessitate subjective analysis — the person in need may be pregnant, or fasting rather than starving, and she would need to be able to have the institutional means to relate that to the provider of the need satisfiers.

important to think of needs both as felt desires and objective goals that may or may not be felt or cause objective harm. His account of the inter-relationship between the satisfaction of needs and the development of human nature – his causal account of needs, powers and senses – clarifies how and why goals can become drives over time and vice versa. The existing objects of need change human nature itself and needs are determined to a significant degree by wants and the form of the extant need trajectory. Although Marx does not employ this notion, he develops in embryonic form an understanding of how an individual's needs are determined to a significant degree by the trajectory of needs (and wants) of her society. Thus the area of political interest lies between the guiding goals of vital and agency needs and the trajectory of actually felt needs and wants: the generation and legitimation of 'new' wants that make them determine human nature to the degree that they become 'new' needs. However, un-like Marx, I refrain from attempting to provide a theoretical solution to the problem of needs. My approach provides greater potential for a thoroughly political conception of needs because it argues that the problem of needs is and always will be a practical, evaluative question focused on develop-ing greater understanding of the generation, perception and evaluation of needs. For a need-based approach to be practically effective and, in some sense, causally explanatory, it should start with the felt needs, and actual institutions, practices and roles and criticise actual needs and their condi-tions in terms of whether they obstruct the attainment of vital and agency needs. A political conception involves analysis of this constant evaluation of needs and choice of need trajectories and an account of the requisite institutions for this kind of communal, practical exercise.

Thus, in chapter 2, I develop a more in-depth causal account of the formation and perception of needs. And in chapters 3 and 4 I use this causal understanding alongside my analysis of vital and agency needs in order to evaluate the extant institutions, practices and roles that have given rise to the actual trajectory of need development, and propose means of transforming them.

CHAPTER 2

The formation and interpretation of needs

In the previous chapter I developed an understanding of needs based on need forms and categories of human needs that identified the historical, normative, instrumental and thus political nature of needs. My account of vital and agency needs provides a general outline of indispensable human functional conditions and goals (or means, ends, values and ethical objectives) that can be gleaned from the phenomenological material of everyday need satisfaction. It does not make categorical distinctions between needs and wants; rather, it provides the possibility for a more dynamic understanding of their relationship. And it questions the adequacy of the relational formula A needs X in order to Y. As I have argued, this formula is problematic because it engenders an impoverished understanding of needs as means, but it also under-estimates the complexities of how needs are formed and interpreted. For example, the 'Y' (or end) in question may be a means mistakenly identified as an end, or a distortion of either means or ends. And these various possibilities concerning the interpretation of ends complicate the evaluation and choice of means to valued ends. Moreover, as I will argue, the nature and form of these ends, in particular the agency needs, can be transformed through time and across space depending upon how their particular manifestations are interpreted and legitimised in everyday experience.

This is of profound political significance. If my analysis of need is correct, not only are the long-neglected need determinants of significant political import, but also the claim that the use of the above logical form is normally enlightening and likely to lead to consensus is mistaken. I maintain that consensus over these kinds of issues is the exception rather than the rule, and that in any case political decision and action is not ultimately dependent upon whether the interrogation of A's more deeply held Y's enlightens A or engenders the possibility for consensus. In actual political practice there are a number of institutions and mechanisms that, prior to any evaluative use of the relational formula, determine which A's to include and which X's and Y's are legitimate means and ends. Thus it is surprisingly easy for A's needs to be left unheard, removed from the political agenda or interpreted as concerns that do not relate to needs. This is just as likely to be the case whether A is an individual or group. Hence, there exists an imperative for political theorists to undertake two related tasks: to unearth actual material and cognitive blocks to cumulative individual and communal learning in order to provide a greater parity of power in the interpretation of needs throughout society; and to think imaginatively about more causally efficacious kinds of participation that might improve rather than fragment this process of learning. This chapter is intended as a move in that direction. In particular it focuses on providing an understanding of the mechanisms through which different types of needs are formed in contemporary society via a thorough grasp of the dynamic between needs and wants and the causal and cognitive components of the generation, legitimation and perception of needs.

In the first section of the chapter, I develop a causal analysis of the contemporary processes of need generation and legitimation. By analysing how the needs that comprise the different need categories interact with one another, I highlight the causal and cognitive importance played by individual wants and articulated needs on the perception and articulation of agency needs. In other words, I show why it is important to understand everyday needs causally and politically, publicly rather than privately.[1] I analyse the production, satisfaction and articulation of need as determined by three different, phenomenologically distinct, societal processes: the production and consumption of commodities; the production of knowledge; and the non-discursive and discursive aspects of a society's informal structures of legitimation – beliefs, conventions and rules. In the second section I analyse how these different mechanisms interact with one another to affect the balance of normative power. In the third section I defend some general claims about the perception and cognitive status of needs, particularly with regard to interpreting need in oneself and others. Then, I focus on common legislative, normative and cognitive effects of vital and agency need perception under conditions of normative power imbalance. In the fourth section the discussion thus far is used to define oppression in terms of needs. The final two sections develop the main insights from the first chapter and the first four sections of this chapter, articulate the real and conceptual link between need and interest, and construct a contextually

---

[1] For a discussion of the specific issue of why and how political theory must eclipse conventional conceptions of 'private' and 'public', see sections 2 and 3 below.

applicable and intentionally political concept: the concept of true interest. I critically interpret what I maintain is the most sophisticated theory of true interests to date, Amartya Sen's capability approach, and distinguish the concept of 'true interest' from other concepts, such as self-love, rational interest and prudence.

I GENERATION AND LEGITIMATION

Category breakdown

The needs that constitute the different categories are not mutually exclusive. The same need often appears in two categories simultaneously or in different forms at different times in different categories. The needs in the different categories are, therefore, constantly interacting causally with one another. There are three different kinds of interaction and they highlight the causal importance of the two kinds of particular social need (category B) — public and private ineluctable needs.

(1) Vital needs (category A) are general needs, but in any given society at any given time they are manifested and experienced in particular forms that may (or may not) be specific to that culture or time or both. (a) These particular forms might be unproblematic direct expressions of one of the general vital needs, for example the need for shelter experienced by the homeless. (b) On the other hand, they may be more specific, either more culturally specific or more instrumentally specific (as a component part of a means to a more general end), or both. An example would be the need for a higher-paid job. (c) Different again, they may be pathologically distorted expressions of one of the general vital needs or a particular means to the distorted end; for instance, the perceived need to marry in order to 'seal' a loving relationship. (d) Finally, they could be a distorted means to a perfectly healthy expression of vital need, for example the felt need for a car to meet the need for mobility. The consequence is that one general vital need can have four possible forms, or particular manifestations. And, more importantly, all of these particular forms (or any particular one at any given time) appear, and are expressed and cognised, as particular social needs (category B needs) even where and when they are avowedly legitimated in terms of general vital needs.

(2) There is a subgroup of particular social needs that can simultaneously be experienced as particular social needs (category B needs) and be examples of agency needs (category C needs). As in (1) above, the possibilities for cross-category interaction are determined by the fact that

there are four kinds of particular agency needs to be found in category B. Or, in other words, in category B there are four forms in which general agency needs are expressed. (a) Direct expressions of agency needs, for example, the political claim for equal recognition of women in the workplace. (b) The indirect expression of an agency need, for example a claim for political autonomy by a political group (as an implicit or explicit means to the constitutive individuals' own increased autonomy). (c) Distorted expressions of agency need, for example an individual's need for recognition expressed in terms of the ownership of rare commodities, like highly priced sports cars. (d) Distorted means of attending to healthy expressions of agency needs, e.g., the violent expression in relationships of men's physical power over women (usually consequent on a low level of autonomy in both parties, but particularly in the man when extant practices expect him to be the main material provider). A non-distorted expression of this need would be the ability to contribute equally to the relationship and use reason rather than force.

(3) Category B is left intentionally rather all-encompassing for an important methodological reason. It tries to capture the empirical reality exemplified in the first of the following two points *and* to provide the means for a defence of the second, which is a claim. First, although theory might put vital needs and agency needs on a pedestal (most often in general form), the particular expressions of these needs display the same characteristics as less fundamental, more everyday, category B needs. Second, the form and perception of agency and vital needs are mediated by the other particular needs – by which I mean the individual in need experiences particular expressions of agency and vital needs within (and often even in terms of) the evaluative context of concretised wants and distorted expressions of vital and agency needs. Hence, because of the inherent particularity of the experience of vital and agency needs there is a third form of category breakdown that like the other three is mediated by category B but unlike them actually results in a breakdown between categories A and C: the interpretation of a particular agency need as an instance of a vital need and vice versa: for example, when my freedom of expression *per se* is interpreted as an essential part of my existence as a human, as is sometimes evident within the 'human rights' discourse.[2]

---

[2] The doctrine of 'human rights' is problematic if it provides people with a ready mechanism to defend actions (including speech acts) that otherwise a society would not allow on grounds related to the well-being and agency of its citizens. For an example of the problem, see the recent defence before a French court of Yahoo's dissemination and sale of Nazi propaganda and paraphernalia on the internet.

The above three points highlight the particular and general nature of needs, and show why strict analytical distinctions can cloud our causal understanding of need. In general, the generation of a particular desire for an object and its legitimation as a need is a complex process that may be influenced by an array of objects, events and mechanisms, but in the light of the above it would not be an over-statement to claim that the generation and satisfaction of wants hold significant causal importance. Needs emerge out of wants because the repeated satisfaction of a specific want, given the right conditions and the commonality of the want, transforms the felt want into a felt particular need; that is, transforms it from an individual luxury into a common requirement, into a *sine qua non* of normal existence. This does not of course mean that all wants necessarily become needs nor that all needs were once wants, but it may point to the fact that a certain kind of want satisfaction facilitates the legitimation of a particular desire in that it transforms it from a want to a need. Once the want and its satisfaction has been accepted as normal, in other words, not wildly extravagant or perverse, which normally occurs as a result of various mechanisms such as helpful technological advances and the emotional drive to emulate respected others, it often generates a need for the original object. This new need, *a new particular social need*, causally influences the experience of vital and agency needs in the three ways discussed above. The determinants of these causal mechanisms are explored more thoroughly in what follows.

The production and consumption of commodities: the want-need dynamic

In industrial societies the production, distribution and consumption of commodities are significant determinants of the generation of wants, the generation of needs and the legitimation of needs. *Prima facie*, the opposite seems true because the production and distribution of commodities is often taken to be the result of supply reacting to demand, production supplying satisfiers for people's wants and needs. However, because there is nothing 'natural' about wants and particular needs and because (in the case of need) an economic satisfier must necessarily satisfy a *particular* need, the causal sequence is often in the converse direction. New satisfiers (commodities), which amongst other things are inspired by new technological advances, scientific insights, and manipulation of everyday consumption needs, may themselves generate new wants and needs. This kind of causality in fact works within three different kinds of mechanisms. (1) Wants and needs are generated and satisfied by commodities that enhance and simplify everyday life in that they provide cheaper and more efficient means of meeting vital needs. For example, the kettle provides a means of simplifying the boiling of water. (2) Wants and needs are generated and satisfied by commodities that are directed specifically at satisfying *private ineluctable needs*. For example, the car is a commodity of this sort: it produces the need for a car. These commodities often satisfy other needs as unintended consequences of the formal generation, for example the vital need for mobility (or a distorted kind of agency need for recognition), and often ensure the continued interpretation of the former in terms of the latter. (3) Some commodities are produced purely for the satisfaction of particular luxury-wants, and are not intended to generate and satisfy needs in any sense. They are described as causally insignificant trinkets, but have unintended consequences that do generate, satisfy and distort new needs. For example, a new video game might generate a new kind of addiction that creates a need for specially trained child therapists. It is a characteristic of capitalism that each of these three different kinds of commodity production is *determined by the logic of profit to a degree equal to which the others are determined by it*. That is, despite their different relationship to vital and agency needs, they are all given the same value as commodities. And there is no means of distinguishing between kinds of commodities since commodities owe their existence to whether they are consumed or not; and the ability to choose amongst as wide as possible an array of commodities is, the argument goes, a good in itself (and even a form of 'autonomy'). Furthermore, in each case (1–3 above), once the new commodities have found a niche, they and their concomitant wants and needs generate new wants and needs. These developments generate unintended new needs, both in the form of new wants and in terms of the above-discussed want-need dynamic where over time wants become new needs.

The production of knowledge: the articulation of need

The production of knowledge occurs within the mechanisms discussed in the previous subsection and within the institutions and practices that constitute the production and dissemination of information and education concerning needs, especially vital and agency needs. The latter kinds of institutions and practices include those of government and those of non-governmental activity, as well as associated institutions like universities, schools, community organisations and churches. The activities of these kinds of institutions are particularly important for the generation of needs that emerge via the articulation of need-claims (though obviously they also generate needs in the three-fold manner discussed above (1–3)). The articulation of need is causally significant in the process of need generation for reasons that relate to political claims-making. The inherently non-individualistic nature of need explains why the simple articulation of a need (in other words, a need-claim) by one individual almost always generates a need in at least one other individual, especially when the claim is couched in manifestly political tones. These kinds of need-claims are normally a consequence of – at least they are *always* couched in terms of – a lack of possibilities for meeting vital needs or developing agency needs, or both. And only very infrequently are they relevant only to the individual, or even the group, making the original claim. Other individuals, who on hearing the need-claim perceive of themselves as being in a similar situation, frequently think about their situation in analogous terms and begin to feel the same need. This is especially true of need-claims that allegedly identify a disparity in treatment or possibilities for the development of powers and capabilities (otherwise known as the identification of oppression – see below, section 4). For example, the suffragettes' aim was to create a need in other women (and therefore all adults) to feel that they held the right to participation, out of something that was a luxury (privilege) for some alone, dependent on sex.[3] (This is also another example of the luxury-need dynamic, and, as discussed in the main introduction, generally the historical move from privileges to rights is a constant case in point.)

Legislation and general education are also significant determinants in the creation of possibilities and insights that generate and legitimate new needs. For example, a British commuter's need to take the train rather than use her car will be directly connected to whether or not the British government successfully legislates to impose charges for entering big cities like London by car as a means to commute to work (and whether it can provide a better and cheaper train service).[4] These kinds of institutions and practices are distinguishable from political claims-making because they are the formal

---

[3] I hold that they aimed to *create* a need in other women to feel that they had a right to participation, and not simply to point out to the authorities that they had the same right to participation as men, because it was (and is) just as important for this kind of political cause to illuminate to other women their own position and make them feel the need (and hopefully recruit them to their cause) as it is for them to fight the legal battle. This is generally true for these kinds of political movements for change because the extant legal framework is unable often even to entertain their claims. The stronger claim is that movements for change will have difficulty using the existing legal framework because it normally actively serves to silence the claims themselves and control the agenda so as to foreclose on any discussion of the issue. For more on power, silencing and control of the agenda, see S. Lukes' classic account in his *Power: A Radical View* (London: Macmillan, 1974), esp. ch. 4.

[4] This does not imply that the commuter could not feel the need simply for ecological reasons, or as a result of her concern for the needs of future generations, but rather that there is more chance that people will feel this need where it is supported by legislation. It is insufficient to rely on the moral virtue of the citizen.

structures that legitimise claims and wants so that they are subsequently interpreted as needs; or, at least, they provide the formal stamp on already legitimised needs. The more informal process of legitimation takes place through the naturalisation of needs achieved by their justification within extant structures of belief, convention and informal rules.

The production of beliefs, conventions, and rules: the recognition of need

An understanding of the generation of need will remain impoverished if the legitimation of need is understood only in terms of the formal codification of laws, rules and statutes concerning need; or, in other words, if the legitimation of need is taken to be constituted by that which occurs when a need becomes sufficiently objective or its object of satisfaction becomes widely enough accepted as a needed object for it to become legally recognised as a need by the state. There is a wide spectrum of less formal legitimation that takes place throughout society, that might best be described as the *recognition of need*. The recognition of need becomes noticeable when a particular need-claim becomes an accepted, legitimate part of general 'public' discourse. The legitimating beliefs, conventions, norms, attitudes, rituals and rules are either discursive or non-discursive, or some mixture of both. And because many of these legitimating structures, especially attitudes, norms and rituals, are non-discursive, they do not uniformly and unproblematically fit into the relational formula of A needs X in order to Y. Yet they are a central part of the legitimating background for the truth-claims used in defence of a particular need.[5] Hence, such legitimating structures *are* identifiable even when and where they are not discursive. The fact that a need (or need-claim) might find legitimation within a ritual or norm of which the individual concerned is not aware means that analysis of the claim must track back from the particular purposive needs to discern their particular relation to attitudes and beliefs. The motivation and genesis for the production of particular beliefs, conventions and norms are, however, less manifest than that which occurs in the mechanisms discussed in the previous two subsections. Fortunately, though, it is more important to analyse the functional roles that these belief structures play within the actual process of need generation or society concerned. For example, the belief that the degree of recognition one receives is dependent on the make of car one drives cannot be attacked for being erroneous or distorted in itself. But

---

[5] For an analysis of how different kinds of rules differentially affect this process of legitimation, see D. Braybrooke, *Meeting Needs* (Princeton: Princeton University Press, 1987), pp. 83–4.

it can be criticised if it provides significant functional support for practices that distort the perception of agency needs or the meeting of vital and agency needs in oneself or others.

The points in these sections about causally significant mechanisms in the generation of needs indicate the significance of the 'way the world is' for what persons need.[6] Moreover, needs are expressed (normally) in terms of some of the factual material there is at hand. However, I maintain that these points also show that the 'way the world is' does not determine what persons need. This is most evident in the case of claims-making, where need-claims are normally intended as means of changing the 'way the world is'. The need for a particular political transformation usually emerges in the form of a strongly felt desire for change and the need can become a need *qua* need without the actual provision of particular need satisfiers or means of attending to the needs, although there obviously must be some hope that existing forms of provision could be transformed or new ones could be created. In the case of the want-need dynamic there is never a direct or necessary dependence between a particular need and its antecedent want: during the time it takes for the particular want to become a particular need there is a constant process of historical and procedural legitimation that takes place, often under the guidance of agency needs. From the fact that most particular satisfiers of need were once objects of want it does not follow that ideas and criticism that emerge from consideration of categories A and C cannot influence the constant process of need legitimation, that is, make public and political the inherently evaluative transformation of an object of want to a satisfier of need.

2 NORMATIVE POWER AND THE INSTITUTION OF PRIVATE PROPERTY

An individual's or group's ability to affect the recognition of felt needs within the mechanisms of need articulation and the want-need dynamic will depend on their relative normative power. Normative power is both the power to affect norms in society and the power that derives from extant norms. Hence, force, knowledge, political authority and charismatic power could all be thought of as different kinds of normative power. However, here *normative power is understood as the power to affect the extant norms and beliefs that directly or indirectly affect how individuals perceive and are able to attend to their vital and agency needs.* The general thesis I defend is the

---

[6] D. Wiggins, 'Claims of Need', in *Needs, Values, Truth: Essays in the Philosophy of Value* (3rd edn) (Oxford: Clarendon Press, 1998), p. 6.

following: the greater an individual's normative power, the more enhanced is her ability to cognise and criticise a society's norms and beliefs, and thereby her own needs. However, this is the case only up to a threshold. Beyond the threshold, especially under conditions of large normative disparity, the normative power of some individuals becomes so great that they tend to believe that they have no need for others, to the extent that their need perception actually begins to deteriorate. That is, I can have too little and too much normative power, and for different reasons they both engender misperception of (and a related inability to meet) vital and agency needs.

There are two mutually dependent forms of distribution that strongly affect an individual's normative power: material distribution and the distribution of cognitive labour.[7] The state of both of these kinds of distribution heavily influences the productive processes discussed in the preceding sections and the state of these processes determines an individual's access to satisfiers for and control over her everyday needs. Material distribution is the less complicated of the two and amounts to the distribution of satisfiers for particular vital needs, and public and private ineluctable needs. The distribution of cognitive labour is the distribution and kind of cognitive access to procedures, institutions and practices that affect the society's mechanisms of commodity production, knowledge creation and beliefs (and their causal link to agency needs). Material distribution affects the distribution of cognitive labour but it does not determine it; and (more obviously) this also holds vice versa. In liberal capitalist societies material wealth and fully met vital needs do not guarantee a normal person the capabilities to cognise and criticise his and his society's norms and beliefs. But generally speaking, an increase in normative power is normally associated with an increase in parity of either one or other or both of the two kinds of distribution.

In terms of the discussion in the preceding sections, the production and consumption of commodities and the production of knowledge and beliefs do not only influence one another. The extent and kind of distribution prevalent at each level also affect the generation and legitimation of needs in general, and the capacity to cognise these mechanisms in particular. Under liberal capitalist regimes the scales of normative power are tipped in a direction that favours two kinds of normative imbalance: first, that exhibited in the uninhibited production of new commodities under the

---

[7] The latter phrase is taken from S. L. Hurley, 'Cognitivism in Political Philosophy', in *Well-Being and Morality: Essays in Honour of James Griffin* (Oxford: Oxford University Press, 2000), p. 192. Hurley makes a distinction between cognitive capacities at the individual level and the collective level and warns against oversimplifying relations between them. The next section explores these relations in terms of the perception of need.

logic of profit; and, second, the related imbalance in normative power between societal groups, especially between different consumer groups.

There are two main reasons for the first kind of normative imbalance. The first relates to the temporal and spatial order of generation and legitimation, and the second emerges from the contemporary assumption (or belief) that an increase in choice necessarily creates an increase in freedom. I do not go into the second issue here because it is taken up in section 3, but the first point concerns the following. As a consequence of the fact that need recognition is both temporally and spatially centred in institutions and practices that have secondary evaluative impact on the original locale of commodity production, they can only act as correctives to the main need-generative force. (Of course, legislation can be used to regulate or control production but this is necessarily *ex post* the generation of the need and its general public acceptance – recognition – as a need or otherwise.) Put differently, it is a logical consequence of the above understanding of the production of commodities, knowledge and belief that the generation of particular needs take place across all of society at a specific time (time *t*), while the subsequent recognition and legitimation of need is confined to ever more restricted environs and always at a later time (time $t + 1$). Hence there is not only a necessary time lag; the generation of need is also more pervasive than what could be called the critical evaluation of need.[8] And because the generation of need has as its main fount of inspiration the generation of new wants (generated via the production of commodities), it is under greatest normative influence from the unrestricted generation of commodities. In terms of my need categories, the power to generate new particular social needs (category B) and the power to ensure that the conventions and beliefs about needs are formed so as to ensure their eventual acceptance as needs is heavily biased in favour of commodity production. For, although the formal process of legitimation (codification and legislation) is separate (in principle) from the generation of need, the real business of legitimation (i.e. recognition of need) takes place under the normative sway of commodity production. In sum, the needs of individuals are generated as a direct outcome of commodity production, and therefore commodity production has greater normative power than is commonly accepted in modern political discourse.

The above scenario is not necessarily one that will create the pathological generation of individual agency needs but it does show that agency

---

[8] Normally, the evaluative mechanisms of public debate – where they exist – are separate from the generation of new needs.

needs and vital needs (categories A and C) are of secondary concern to a logic of production whose goal is the production of any and all kinds of particular social needs (category B) and wants. Furthermore, the production of commodities (first and foremost) is driven by the *practice* of producing and marketing commodities for profit. This practice is based in and legitimated by the same *institution* that legitimates the general belief that needs are private: the *institution* of private property. The institution of private property is too complicated and fraught with ideological division to be adequately covered in this study, not least because it would require an analysis of the different forms of private property (fixed (like land), capital and commodity); but these two issues of profit and privatisation of need indicate how fundamental private property is to our present manner of interpreting everyday needs.[9] Furthermore, the institution of private property has tangential importance in that it is one of the institutions that could be said to legitimate the contemporary belief that healthy competition generated by incentives, and advanced by the tendency to seek incentives, is destroyed when and where individuals are prevented from generating profit in commodity production.[10] The three-fold combination of this practice and institution, the beliefs and norms that naturalise them both, and the kinds of particular needs they generate constitutes the contemporary environment within which individuals interpret their vital and, more significantly, their agency needs.

A type of private property ownership also affects the second kind of prevalent normative power imbalance, the one that exists between groups. Think of the following example.[11] Jack feels the need for a car. Think of him

---

[9] A third issue is that it is arguably an empirical fact that thinking about change in terms of entitlement and rights only reinforces the belief that one's property is an essential part of oneself and one's means of being recognised, expressive and autonomous. (I discuss this below, in section 3.) Some examples of different ideological positions on property are: A. Ryan, *Property and Political Theory* (Oxford: Blackwell, 1984); C. Reinold Noyes, *The Institution of Property* (New York: Longmans, 1936); J. Waldron, *The Right to Private Property* (Oxford: Clarendon Press, 1988); and J. Tully, *A Discourse on Property: John Locke and his adversaries* (Cambridge: Cambridge University Press, 1980).

[10] G. A. Cohen, 'Incentives, Inequality and Community', in G. Petersen (ed.), *The Tanner Lectures on Human Values*, vol. XIII (Salt Lake City: University of Utah Press, 1992).

[11] My example is mundane. It is chosen for its ordinariness for two reasons. First, issues surrounding the concept of need arise in most 'everyday' considerations, especially those linked to public policy. Second, adopting the concept of need to think about issues that are 'everyday' but not immediately related to public policy, especially those conventionally labelled 'private' concerns, is a good way of uncovering their inherently 'public' character and adjusting policy accordingly. This is achieved by transforming that convention that presumptively 'confined' them to the 'private', which is only possible if 'external' justification (reason-giving) is sought in place of 'internal' justification. For more on the last point see B. Williams, *Moral Luck* (Cambridge: Cambridge University Press, 1981), ch. 8; and section 3 below. For more on the contentious history of the distinction between 'public' and 'private', see R. Geuss, *Public Goods, Private Goods* (Princeton: Princeton University Press, 2001);

as a representative member of a population group whose felt needs would normally be considered (heeded) by social policy. Jack needs a car because amongst other things he needs to get to work in the morning, take his child to school on the way and buy food on the way home. To achieve all that on the inadequate (and recently privatised) 'public' transport system would take four hours out of his day. Taken as it stands and besides his own felt and expressed need for a car, analysis could utilise various collections of 'basic' needs, like the fact that humans need fulfilling work, humans need time to relax and exercise, humans need to sleep and humans need companionship, to justify Jack's need for a car. It will provide him with an efficient means of saving enough time to accomplish all these stated needs and meet his more general vital need for mobility. But why does his collection of needs concertina together to produce the need for a car and not a need for some other means of transport? What effect does his professed need have on his perception of, and ability to attend to, his other vital and agency needs? And how does his satisfaction of his particular needs and his perception of his (and others') agency needs affect the way the other members of his society meet and perceive their needs? Together, full answers to these questions unearth Jack's normative power and the effect this has on his and others' perception of, and ability to attend to, their vital and agency needs.

An answer to the first question would incorporate analyses of the society's prevailing norms and their determinants. For example, the belief that private ownership of certain kinds of goods is an indicator of personal status and wealth – the more I have the more I am worth and respected; the contemporary production practices and regulations; consumption patterns; state provision and legislation; and other influencing factors such as the prevailing restrictions on and practices within advertising. Answers to the second and third questions will involve analyses of Jack's perception of his agency needs and how this relates to the general perception of, and ability to attend to, vital and agency needs. The analysis might pick out the legislation that determined the privatisation of the transport system, and its subsequent inadequacies as a service, as being a significant determinant in Jack's coming round to the idea that he needs a car. Once he had a car, once it was his, he might feel more 'autonomous' (free) and he might enjoy being recognised for being an owner of a particular kind of car. He and other members of his group (e.g. other car owners) may scorn the need for recognition in general and, say, recognition as a citizen in particular. If they

and J. Dunn, 'Public and Private: Normative map and political and social battleground', presented at conference on 'Asian and Western Conceptions of Public and Private', Cambridge University, 13–15 September 1999.

are able to do so with confidence and without regret, they possess a great degree of normative power. Jack's group has this degree of normative power because it has the material and cognitive opportunity to set the normative agenda within the existing norms. These opportunities are created by the group's greater brute purchasing power and their greater cognitive control over the legitimation of particular manifestations of agency needs, which are consequences of the extant material and cognitive labour distributions. However, this kind of power can be detrimental to how Jack's group perceives their needs, especially their agency needs, because in undermining the importance of agency needs they necessarily misperceive the basis of needs: the intersubjective communality of needs. There are various different kinds of consequences that emerge as a result of this and other effects and they relate both to how Jack treats those with less normative power, how Jack's normative power indirectly affects those with less normative power, and how this then affects his and their perception of their vital and agency needs. But, before expounding on these consequences, first I need to say something about the perception and interpretation of need.

3　PERCEPTION AND INTERPRETATION

When I speak of the 'perception' of need I do not simply mean the act of 'seeing' need in oneself or another. I mean the manner in which the experience of felt need (and desire) is *interpreted* by the individual; how and why a particular need is interpreted as the outcome of X rather than Y, or as a particular kind of A (vital) or C (agency) need (A+X rather than C+Y, etc.). As was established earlier, the feeling of need is always mediated by cultural and historical interpretation because all needs (even the most seemingly 'basic' ones like the need for food) are manifested in particular forms. As a result, all feelings of need are verified by the existence and feelings of, and interaction with, other individuals; a particular need only becomes a need if it is actually felt by others, or at least cognised by others as being causally connected to another commonly felt need. The needs of others are never simply or uniquely 'the needs of others'. They are understood and interpreted as needs and have a tendency to create a feeling of empathy and a desire to emulate because they are particular manifestations of a common, frail ontology of feeling and function. One can see another's need and hear about another's need, but the perception of need requires either the existence of the same feeling of need or the cognition of the need as a necessary means or goal for human functioning. And the latter form, cognition without the physical experience of the need, always involves thinking about the need 'as if' one were experiencing it. However, this does not require or involve the kind of neutrality or impartiality common in many liberal arguments, for example the notion of a 'common standpoint' of impartiality as found in Rawls' account of justice as fairness. This is the case because in speaking of the perception of need in others I am talking about empathy rather than impartiality, and empathy does not require impartiality or neutrality; in fact empathy would not be necessary and important if it did require impartiality or neutrality. We are able to empathise with others' needs, especially when and where we have felt a similar kind of need, but we cannot simply simulate a felt need in the same way that we play a role in acting a part in a play.[12]

Although the interpretation of need in oneself obviously involves different processes to the interpretation of needs in others, the difference is one of degree rather than kind. This is especially evident in the case of agency needs, which are infrequently felt as physical drives. Needs of this kind emerge from a perceived lack, but (as in the interpretation of need in others) their perception requires a degree of distance from everyday physical experience and position. This distancing process does not, however, entail less effective interpretation of need because the interpretation and perception of non-experienced need resort to existing concepts and beliefs about need. Hence, the perception of need in both oneself and others is dependent on the extant concepts and beliefs about actual needs and need in general.

Needless to say, then, 'perception' here is not based on a positivistic epistemology that reduces perception to observation of an external reality based on a dichotomised mind/world ontology. But just as cognition cannot be reduced to the recording of sense data, so the world cannot be reduced to our concepts, beliefs and forms of cognition. There are actual institutions and practices that (in part) determine mechanisms at the level of individual cognition and vice versa; and, as is argued below, these institutions, practices

---

[12] Thus, I maintain that Rawls has misunderstood the nature of needs and interests if he really imagines that, given certain restrictions on information, we can adopt, even *hypothetically*, a position that enables us to act as if we were rationally autonomous representatives of citizens in society reasoning for principles of justice. J. Rawls, *Political Liberalism* (New York: Columbia University Press, 1996), pp. 27, 304–5. If I am right about the nature, generation and perception of needs the notion of neutrality and impartiality with regard to our particular needs, interests, desires and aspirations is pure pie in the sky. (And this is reinforced by my analysis of roles and practical reason in chapter 3, sections 3 and 4.) These facts about needs, roles and practical reason create a number of problems with the idea of representation as it is understood and practised in liberal democracies, but apart from a few comments in chapter 4, I do not discuss these issues here. I intend to cover this central concern of modern politics in my future work, provisionally entitled *States and Markets of Needs*.

and mechanisms are real in that they exist beyond our perception of them, and would continue to exist were we to stop perceiving and interpreting them.

Substitute gratification as cause and effect in agency need perception

How do the likes of Jack's need affect the perception by others of their own vital and agency needs and their ability to attend to them? Although there are manifold unintended consequences of a particular need of Jack's combined with the extant ideologies and institutions of production and consumption, I am particularly interested in two. First, individuals who are unable to 'compete' at the designated level of consumption are reduced to variables within state welfare calculations and thus no longer constitute 'effective demand' in the market.[13] Second, these individuals can become addicted to the allegedly innocuous trinkets whose existence as wants and needs are legitimated originally by Jack's consumption, that is, his demand, and the logic of production. I deal with the first consequence, welfare provision and its effects, in the next subsection. The second phenomenon is especially prevalent in conditions of stark material inequality when and where the development of some individuals' agency needs have stagnated, but it also occurs under 'healthier' conditions. It is an empirical fact that below a certain threshold of normative power, some individuals substitute particular means to meeting their vital and agency needs for particular wants. They do so in order to be seen to consume as others do. This kind of process has been understood generally as 'substitute gratification'.[14]

Substitute gratification occurs when a person alleviates the negative feelings that emerge from exploitation or frustrated satisfaction either by adopting another satisfier or by a feeling of recognition, expression or autonomy different in kind from the original object of want or need (non-recognition, exploitation, oppression, etc.). In the former case, the satisfier can take the

---

[13] The fact that these people actually fall out of the market because they do not constitute any 'effective demand' ensures that the demands and needs they do have that cannot be met by the state will normally remain unheeded, and definitely unmet. A classic recent case in point is the situation in much of Africa concerning HIV/AIDS retroviral treatment. Until the South African government legally defeated the challenge of the major drug companies' claims about breach of their patent rights, it simply was not in the economic interests of the companies to lower the price of these drugs to meet the demand for drugs in Africa. It was more profitable to keep prices as high as the 'first world' demand could handle and claim that there was no 'effective demand' from Africa. They may continue to do so if they cannot compete with the cheaper generic versions, or once humanitarian international concern has a new cause.

[14] For more on 'substitute gratification' and 'adaptive preferences' see (particularly) J. Elster, *Sour Grapes: Studies in the subversion of rationality* (Cambridge: Cambridge University Press, 1983).

form of another commodity, and thereby usually satisfy the same want or need differently, or satisfy a cousin desire. In the latter case, the alleviating feeling of recognition, expression or autonomy works via a process of re-routing the feeling of exploitation into another (often related) complex of oppression or exploitation, which can be more easily recognised and alleviated. This kind of substitute gratification has become common in theory and practice through the celebration of some more easily *identifiable* difference, like being of a different race, colour, and/or sex. That is, the race, colour or sex is celebrated for itself, often in culturally essential terms, irrespective of whether this celebration in fact hinders the satisfaction of the agency and vital needs of those being exploited as a consequence of their race, colour or sex. And this celebration often acts to alleviate the feeling of being exploited to the degree that the individual stops short of reaching to the depths of the main causes of exploitation. These *might* be the fact that the individual concerned is of a different class, comes from a certain area, or fills certain kinds of roles.[15] The common notion that exploitation is resolvable via an essentialisation of difference emerges from the same practices and ideology that help legitimate the less well-off consumer's substitution of her agency needs for a new commodity. In other words, Jack's needs are also significant determinants of this commodification of identity.

Substitute gratification is one of the main mechanisms that provide the conditions for addiction, especially in the former commodity (satisfier) substitution case. For example, many unemployed people who are consequently unable to develop their agency needs for recognition, active and creative expression and autonomy become addicted to watching television as a kind of substitute 'activity'. This claim about the connection between the stagnation of agency need development and addiction is supported by the fact that individuals normally control their addictions not after special addiction therapy but when they are given the opportunity to develop their agency needs, especially in the form of meaningful work.[16] The commonplace

---

[15] This does not downplay the fact that in a specific place in a specific time, the experiences of 'being black' or 'being a woman', say, might be associated with being oppressed by the way *others* treat me and how this affects the allegedly equal institutional treatment. However, a simple acceptance of the possibility that the various kinds of exploitation present may have similar causes is an important breakthrough that could undermine the 'market' of difference and lend some solidarity between movements for distinct collective 'rights'. See chapter 4, section 4 for an analysis of strategic group needs.

[16] It has been argued that an exception to this claim (and observation) might be severe physiological addiction, like that associated with heroin consumption. There is, however, an obvious counter to this claim: the conditions for the onset of this kind of addiction are (in most cases) even more obviously connected to the stagnation of agency need development. On a different note, there is another kind of mechanism that has received significant philosophical attention in the explanation

that controlling addiction equates to 'kicking a habit' is, therefore, misplaced. The significance of substitute gratification in the provision of the conditions for addiction is important because the mechanism of substitute gratification has a unique bi-directional causality: it is generated by disparities in normative power and the associated agency need stagnation *and* it has a significant causal influence on the misperception of agency and vital needs (and the concomitant inability to affect the normative power balance). Thus, although substitute gratification conceivably crops up across the full spectrum of needs, it and its concomitant effects are particularly common under conditions where material distribution creates a large gap between those who struggle to meet vital needs and those that are so free from necessity that they tend to trivialise agency needs.[17]

Normative power imbalance, the possibility effect, and the endowment effect

Here the emphasis shifts to two mechanisms of motivation and perception that affect the cognition, satisfaction and development of needs. I call the first the 'possibility effect' after John Dewey's analysis of how we only really yearn and strive for that which might conceivably be actually attained, that which is realistically possible of attainment.[18] The possibility effect is crucial for understanding how different groups of people in society seem to strive differently both in terms of how they strive and what they strive for; that is, how their aspirational agency needs are causally influenced by possibility or its lack. This effect and the 'endowment effect' are generated by blocks to need development that are created by legislation and biased procedures, and within perception and motivation mechanisms working to reduce 'cognitive dissonance'.

---

of addiction: *akrasia*, or weakness of will. I am less sure than some that the notion of weakness of will takes us very far, unless of course weakness of will were understood in the context of my need-based discussion as: acting intentionally counter to one's 'own best judgement' brought on by a pathological dependence on one or more extant satisfier of (or activity as a means towards the meeting of) a particular vital or agency need. Hence, if the notion of *akrasia* is to be helpful, it should not be understood as a kind of metaphysical weakness of will, a lack of virtue, or simple logical blunder; and *not only* as a weakness at the moment of choice and judgement. For a subtle account of *akrasia* see D. Davidson, 'How is Weakness of the Will Possible?', in *Essays on Actions and Events* (Oxford: Clarendon Press, 1980), ch. 2, p. 21. For more on addiction from a variety of theoretical perspectives see J. Elster and O.-J. Skog (eds.), *Getting Hooked: Rationality and addiction* (Cambridge: Cambridge University Press, 1999).

17 For an example of how this affects macroeconomic legislation, which then creates skewed conditions for the satisfaction of needs, see P. Bond, *Elite Transition: From Apartheid to Neoliberalism in South Africa* (London: Pluto, 2000).

18 J. Dewey, *Human Nature and Conduct* (London: Allen and Unwin, 1922); and 'Theory of Valuation', *Int. Encycl. Unified Sci.*, 2. 4 (Chicago: University of Chicago Press, 1939).

Jack's need for a car will have certain public political ramifications, especially with regard to the provision of services and welfare, which affect other individuals' possibilities in ways that engender restricted or pathological perception of agency needs. Welfare provision is a modern and mostly 'western' phenomenon. Basically, it is the contemporary form that *public* need provision has taken for the meeting of vital needs *and* (infrequently) those particular needs perceived as indispensable for enabling individuals to attend to their agency needs, which earlier I combined under the general label of public ineluctable needs. This is an important point in itself because, as has been noted, many theorists tend to envisage a necessary link between questions (and the politics) of need and the activities of the welfare state.[19] There is obviously a contingent link, but that is as far as it goes: the welfare state is simply one empirical example of one kind of political *redistribution* of goods and benefits. There have been (and are) others: feudal patronage, charity and other forms of supererogatory benevolence. To return to the main concern here, recall two earlier points. (1) Public ineluctable needs are dynamic; that is, like needs and wants generally, they change over time within any particular society. What particular provisions are deemed ineluctable for an individual to survive and function minimally will change depending on which *particular* needs are perceived as involved in normal functioning, or in other words are interpreted as manifestations of vital needs. These are dependent on which tasks individuals are expected to perform, which roles they fill, and which capacities and achievements they should display. (2) There is always a lag between the general use of a particular new need, say a television, and the public provision for it even beyond its general perception as a need, a necessity; that is, even long after it has moved from being a luxury want to becoming a need it may still not be a public ineluctable need. There is a further process of legitimation beyond general public recognition that transforms a need into a public ineluctable need. This process of legitimation could be thought of as the final concretisation of an actual felt need as need; or, in other words, the point at which a particular need satisfier is fused with the original felt need.

Hence, like the other needs in category B, public ineluctable needs are generated by the surrounding practices and institutions of consumption and production, the material conditions of the society concerned, the context-specific values attached to individual human well-being, and the existing

---

[19] See, for example, R. Goodin, 'Vulnerabilities and Responsibilities: An Ethical Defense of the Welfare State', in G. Brock (ed.), *Necessary Goods: Our Responsibilities to Meet Others' Needs* (Oxford: Rowman and Littlefield, 1998).

imbalances in normative power. The beliefs, values and normative power influences that generate Jack's need for a car at one pole are the same as those that generate public ineluctable needs at the other. Evidence for this fact appears in two effects, the one directly explicable in terms of the state and its fiscal health and policies, and the other (more cognitively) in terms of how welfare provision determines possibility. First is the obvious point that given a fixed level of taxation the amount government can spend on welfare will be directly related to how much it spends on other public works and services, and this is affected by normative power differentials. For example, Jack might form part of an interest group (with an efficient and well-connected lobby) whose single objective is the construction of a new motorway that would halve the time private owners of cars of a certain area take to travel to work. If this interest group does manage to lobby government successfully – they get their motorway – it is very likely that the resources and time (at least in the form of contracts and negotiations) invested in that project would be prioritised above other issues and projects, such as the claim made by Jill and others with similar needs for investment in an improved train service (not to mention the other kinds of necessity-constraints on the building of the motorway, for example those of an environmental kind). The causal significance of the normative imbalance in this case is relatively transparent since the imbalance directly effects the prioritisation of need-claims that determine legislation.[20] The second effect relates to the above point that the kinds of things that are valued as basic and fundamental in the society are concretised in the form of welfare provision. The form and emphasis of welfare provision are important indicators and stimulants for possibilities and initiative in the individual development of agency needs. For instance, the fact that unemployment benefit in most Western European societies is in the form of money and basic training for menial tasks fits the demands of the market rather than the demands of agency

---

[20] But like the other kinds of effects discussed here, individual causal origin and responsibility is difficult to pin down. Jack will not significantly affect legislation and policy unless there are other consumers in a similar position and unless this group as a whole holds a relatively high degree of normative power in the society concerned. In these kinds of cases, individual responsibility is dispersed between the individuals that compose the group and often between the different groups (where there is more than one). It is, therefore, less likely to be controlled beneath modern society's everyday structure of public (moralised) criticism of individual action. Nor will it fall under the remit of the majority of ethical work on rights, responsibilities, obligations and virtue, especially that developed within the framework of 'virtue-ethics'. And this situation is not remedied by a move away from rights to obligations, for the question is still understood in overly legalistic and individualistic terms. For an example of this move, see O. O'Neill, 'Rights, Obligations, and Needs', in Brock (ed.), *Necessary Goods*, pp. 95–112. For an insightful critique of virtue-based ethics in general, see R. Geuss, 'Virtue and the Good Life', *Arion*, 8. 1 (2000).

need development and can restrict the unemployed from cognising their agency needs. Not only is it a fact that possibilities are restricted to either receiving handouts or undertaking menial, repetitive tasks, the individuals within this cycle literally learn not to strive for further possibilities beyond these menial tasks.

I will now turn to various kinds of possibility effects that are *not* determined by legislation. Under liberal capitalism, the normatively powerful recognise one another for what they have. That is, they do enjoy a certain kind of recognition. But often they feel no need to recognise or be recognised by the normatively less powerful. The latter become merely a means to the attainment of the former's 'private' needs and wants and their instrumental needs in achieving these objectives.[21] (The notion that members of two groups with very different normative power could nevertheless recognise one another as citizens with equal rights is therefore not only unlikely but also inconsequential.) The effect on the perception and development of the agency needs of the less normatively powerful, those for example that are the butt of Jack's disrespect, varies depending on the power differential. At the most brutal level, in some of the harsher places on earth, the imbalance often generates violence against the physical persons and vital needs of the less powerful.[22] With regard to agency needs in less harsh places, the worst case scenario is the effect it has on those with much less normative power. First there are the more institutionally mediated ways in which agency need development is blocked, and how this affects perception. An example is the aforementioned Stephen Lawrence case in Britain. As has become quite clear this case is not simply an instance of one-off racist violence and prejudice. It in fact highlights institutional racial prejudice and injustice that, it could be argued, is a direct consequence of a highly class-stratified society. The more numerous and less

---

[21] As is common, these things cut both ways: Jack's own agency need for intersubjective recognition, therefore, will either remain unmet or be an instance of distorted recognition.

[22] The dangerous empirical reality of a lack of a co-ordinated public transport system in both Brazil and South Africa is a wave of violence against those without private cars (and there is some danger to those with cars too). In South Africa the gun-toting *taxi* (minibus) companies, which arose as a consequence of apartheid-era policy that failed to satisfy the transport needs of black South Africans, not only kill passengers every day in their constant turf wars but use their mafia-enforced monopolies to escape accountability for their involvement in the majority of road accidents and for their complete disrespect for consumer demands. In Brazil, especially in the Northeast, pedestrians and cyclists are knocked down on a daily basis due to a combination of total disrespect for pedestrians on the part of owners of private cars and the fact that insufficient private bus companies service the poorer *bairros* – they prefer to stick to more central (especially tourist) routes for obvious reasons of increased profit. There is no other way to describe these situations than in terms of violence perpetrated against these persons resulting from a particular kind of institutional arrangement. I thank Chico dos Santos Santana for this insight into the Brazilian case.

qualified individuals in the British police tend to display racist attitudes, or in other words a form of non-recognition, towards blacks, brought on itself by an under-recognition of this class of police force recruit. This is a contingent outcome of Britain's highly class-stratified society, for it is a common reaction to under-recognition and disrespect to find someone else to disrespect, and for various historical reasons related to colonialism the easiest target has been non-white Britons. And, obviously, the low numbers of blacks and other ethnic minorities in the police force exacerbate this problem. That is, Britain's police force is institutionally racist both in the sense that it has racist procedures, which in themselves distort treatment and restrict recruitment, and because its constitutive individuals display racist attitudes; and blacks and other ethnic minorities are, therefore, subjected to various forms of unfair treatment that are not only the direct effect of non-recognition, but also a more indirect effect of under-recognition of the perpetrators. With regard to the possibility effect being discussed here, black people's perception of the possibility of being justly treated by the police force has been severely foreshortened by the kind of treatment highlighted in this case. And this has affected the way that oppressed groups have perceived one of their agency needs, intersubjective recognition; they see it in a negative light.

Then there are the more subtle forms of distortion of agency need perception. It is helpful here to think of agency need perception in the form of a skewed normal curve of successful need satisfaction that descends back to zero rapidly beyond a certain threshold of met needs. The least distorted agency need perception is normally just prior to the threshold and the worst is found at the two extremes. Individuals at both extremes display distorted agency need perception, and unmet agency needs, but for manifestly different reasons and under opposing conditions of normative power. The individuals at the first extreme are forced by necessity to spend all their energy and time on meeting vital needs rather than cognising and developing their agency needs, and usually they have little normative power. In contrast, the individuals at the other extreme (like Jack) have no trouble satisfying their everyday needs and meeting their vital needs and have the resources, time and energy to interpret agency needs, and yet they tend to interpret agency needs and their causality in a biased and asocial manner. They misperceive agency needs because they are so free from necessity that they trivialise and distort the importance of agency needs in overcoming necessity and other obstacles. Unfortunately, besides the fact that they can satisfy all their everyday needs, they tend also to have a great deal of normative power, and are often quick to use it to propagate their warped interpretations of agency needs.

In between these two extremes there are various levels of distortion. On the one hand, those who envisage that they have a chance of acquiring a car often perceive their agency need for recognition in similar terms to Jack, although they will trivialise the commonality of the need to a lesser degree. On the other hand, those with no hope of acquiring a car normally trivialise the need for recognition just as much as Jack but for different reasons; for reasons related to the fact that they tend often to prioritise the need for a car under conditions of little normative and purchasing power. Their resentment of Jack's position often manifests itself as scorn for the underlying need and usually produces complete social isolation rather than (the theoretically imagined) solidarity for change. This last kind of possibility effect is the subtlest of all. It is an example of how individuals foreshorten their own horizons of possibility as a result of a tendency in humans to reduce individual cognitive dissonance.[23] Cognitive dissonance of this latter form arises when the poor person is able to experience the commodities and feel the wants and needs of the less poor while simultaneously having his possibilities objectively curtailed by poverty. The universal reach of the media and advertising and, at least in Europe, the relative well-being and mobility provided by welfare state provision for public ineluctable needs makes certain lifestyles seem closer and more attainable than they really are. Yet there are constant everyday reminders of the impossibility of attaining these alleged possibilities. This contradiction between alleged possibility (or fantasy) and actual possibility (or reality) would create a constant state of cognitive discord if some mechanism did not restore harmony or consonance. The mechanism is what I call the possibility effect.

Another kind of common cognitive mechanism that tends to restrict possibilities and agency need development has become known as the 'endowment effect' and involves people placing a 'higher value on rights or goods that they currently hold than they place on the same goods when in the hands of others'.[24] It consists, that is, in the over-valuation of what I

---

[23] L. Festinger, *A Theory of Cognitive Dissonance* (Stanford: Stanford University Press 1957). For some social and political ramifications see Elster, *Sour Grapes*; and his *Alchemies of the Mind: Rationality and the Emotions* (Cambridge: Cambridge University Press 1999), pp. 20, 42.

[24] C. R. Sunstein, 'Democracy and Shifting Preferences', in D. Copp, J. Roemer and J. Hampton (eds.), *The Idea of Democracy* (Cambridge: Cambridge University Press, 1993), p. 201. Cf. Elster's discussions in *Alchemies of the Mind* (pp. 21–2) of opposite kinds of phenomena, such as 'forbidden fruit' (or 'reactance') and 'the grass is always greener on the other side', as modes of dissonance *creation*.

own or have, especially when they are given to me as my own property in the form of rights, and the under-valuation of what others own or have; in other words, a converse of the last form of possibility effect discussed above. This kind of effect captures the main reason why avowed needs and wants (preferences) cannot be taken 'as they are'. This is the case not only because of the kind of issues I have been discussing above concerning interpretation, but also because the endowment effect also affects the theoretically and practically alleged government neutrality and equilibrium. Government neutrality is not a possibility because the reason that people have a need or preference for a commodity, or entitlement of any sort, is in part a function of whether the government has allocated it to them in the first place. The simple allocation of a right or good normally makes the person value that entitlement more than if it was allocated to someone else.[25] Hence, if the meeting of particular ineluctable needs is carried out in terms of individual entitlements it has a tendency to create the kind of cognitive response described by the endowment effect and in so doing reflects, reinforces and legitimates the need for (and presumptive associated rights to) exclusive private ownership. In contemporary 'advanced western' societies and discourses welfare is legitimated and provided under this ideology of entitlements, as are rights in general.[26] This is of central concern and significance.

4   OPPRESSION AND NEED

I have analysed the causal blocks to satisfying needs as well as the cognitive mechanisms that develop within individuals as a consequence of normative power imbalances. The latter cognitive mechanisms distort the constant and necessary process of the interpretation and development of agency needs, and they are generated by imbalances in possibilities for meeting vital needs and the development of agency needs.[27] In the light of this discussion I

---

[25] Sunstein, 'Democracy and Shifting Preferences', p. 199. For examples, references and analysis of the source and use the term 'endowment effect' see especially pp. 199–201 and fns 8–17.

[26] For how acknowledgement of government and state-institutional *non-neutrality* affects our conception of the state, see below, end of chapter 3 and chapter 4.

[27] The various kinds of mechanisms I have been discussing are often understood as examples of 'preference adaptation', although endowment effects are both different and more pernicious than the other varieties since they support the very legitimating discourses and structures themselves. I have not discussed these mechanisms in terms of 'preference adaptation' for obvious reasons: needs are not preferences and the kind of adaptation and pathology under consideration is not simply of preferences but also of needs, beliefs and discourses. In any case, preference adaptation is a new term for a long-considered phenomenon. See for example M. Wollstonecraft, *A Vindication of the Rights of Woman*, intro. M. Warnock (London: Everyman, 1992) – she makes constant reference to how

can now conclude that individuals can be oppressed in three different but inter-related ways: in how they are treated directly and indirectly by the normatively powerful; in the greater possibility there is for them to undergo the kinds of distortions of perception analysed above; and in their lack of participative control over the legitimation of need, that is, over the recognition and legislation of particular needs. In other words, they can be oppressed in a direct causal way, cognitively, and institutionally. Therefore, I define oppression as those causal, cognitive or institutional conditions of generalised need generation that block, distort or trivialise the development of any individual's attempts to meet her vital needs or develop her agency needs.[28] The situation is bleak for Jill (and others with similar needs), whose demand for an improved train service is prioritised below Jack's group's motorway. Nearly all their agency needs are being blocked, especially recognition and autonomy, and even their vital need for mobility remains unmet.

To sum up, we interpret our needs in terms of the particular wants, feelings, needs and satisfiers perceived in ourselves, in others and in the market, and as determined by our position on the normative power continuum. It is, therefore, of significant political importance how the constitutive members of any society are needing and wanting; the historically and institutionally determined natures of individuals leave no room for a de-moralisation and de-politicisation of needs *or* wants. The non-individual ontology of needs *and* wants ensures that, more often than not, needs and wants have public consequences of a kind that affects the way we react politically to our felt needs at a particular point in time. Furthermore, individuals verify their needs in a process of recognising others and being recognised by them: a process necessary both for cognition and autonomy. That is, in modern society we are dependent on others for the gratification of our particular social needs, which include particular vital needs, *and* for the cognition and development of our agency needs. The self does not develop and become more autonomous independent of others; it is actually dependent on others both materially and cognitively for the enhancement of its autonomy. Given all of this, how could we begin to improve upon how we evaluate our needs and control the trajectory of need development? This question is

women's beliefs, desires and needs have been shaped by a status quo that demeans them as human beings. See also J. S. Mill, *The Subjection of Women*, same volume.

[28] Cf. I. M. Young, *Justice and the Politics of Difference* (Princeton: Princeton University Press, 1990). Her general definition of oppression – 'the institutional constraint on self-development' (p. 37) – incorporates only one of my three kinds. Yet her five kinds of capacity inhibition (oppression) stretch beyond her own general definition and (arguably) obtain when one or more of 'my' three agency needs are left unattended.

addressed in philosophical terms in what follows; then, in the next chapter, the philosophical findings are problematised and their political implications investigated.

5 TRUE INTERESTS

I have established thus far that although needs are causally related to wants they are not equivalent to wants, fully informed or otherwise. Similarly, it is mistaken to claim that interests are equivalent to wants or kinds of wants, say fully informed preferences – that is, that something is in my interest if I prefer it under conditions of full knowledge. For, what of the smoker who is fully aware of the dangers of smoking, and yet prefers to keep smoking, or the medical doctor who transfers to Botswana out of his preference to put the needs of others ahead of his own? Reducing interests to fully informed preferences wipes out the distinction called for in these common cases, where even under conditions of full information the individuals' 'interests *[do] not reduce* to what answers to their preferences'.[29] A better way of conceiving interests is in terms of needs. Something is in an individual's interest if it meets one of needs or is constitutive of the resources or means to meeting these needs. And I argue here that it is in fact possible to go one step further by remaining aware of the above insights concerning pathologies of perception and by using the concepts of vital need and agency need in a contextual evaluative approach. This section develops a practically employable concept of true interest, distinguishing it from other concepts such as rational interest, prudence and self-love.

Unlike vital and agency needs, I claim that the concept of 'true interest' is best employed if restricted to a particular issue at a particular time and understood substantively in terms of vital and agency needs. If something is in my 'true interest' it designates a particular 'post-reflective-evaluation' vital or agency need of mine in the here and now, or a satisfier thereof that can be justified causally as a means of meeting my vital needs and developing my agency needs. It is my 'true interest' X at time t. At time $t + 1$ (despite my vital and agency needs not having changed) my 'true interest' might be Y. This explains the complete omission from my approach of the concept of 'agency interest' – an individual's interest must always be related to a particular context and situation, though that does not mean it has to be restricted to it. This is the case because one's true interest is constantly under reflective reformulation under the guidance of the general vital and

[29] Braybrooke, 'Needs and Interests', in *Moral Objectives, Rules, and the Forms of Social Change* (Toronto and London: Toronto University Press, 1998), p. 9.

agency needs. This also explains why I do not speak of 'true needs'. As was touched on in the first chapter when discussing Marx's non-adoption of a distinction between 'true needs' and 'false needs', the notion of true need would not only fall into the trap of reifying extant particular needs, it also more easily provides theoretical legitimation for paternalist politics, *dirigisme*, or the dictatorship of needs. That is, a distinction between 'true needs' and 'false needs' might condone (and in relatively recent history has condoned) the notion that individuals can be wrong about their needs, while other individuals or institutions with more knowledge (for instance the government) can know their 'true needs'. It is not very far from this theoretical slip to a practical nightmare in which the state dictates the needs of the populace under the guise of having antecedently to organise production to meet their 'true needs'.[30] The following account of true interest shows how political theory might capture the fundamental importance of a fully substantive understanding of need while ensuring that the dictatorship of need remains well out of court.

Theories of true interests

A theory of true interests is not simply a list of what the theorist takes to be in people's true interests, because besides the moral disquiet this quite rightly creates, it would not deserve the label 'theory' and it would emerge from a static conception of human nature. As a theory it is concerned with how and why the idea of true interests is adopted in discussion of how to organise society, and pivots on the notion that working from people's interests rather than their wants, preferences and desires is a better starting point for substantive political discussion of the *good life*, or *good lives*. The concept of interest was introduced into philosophy to mediate between reason and desire (the passions); that is, between people's wants and certain rational ideals. Historically, much emphasis has been placed on the role of reflection and self-evaluation, in an attempt to bridge the gap between the Humean line of thought, exemplified by Hume's own dictum that 'reason is, and ought only to be the slave of the passions',[31] and the Kantian faith

---

[30] The theoretical slip is evident in some authors I have already discussed, like Doyal and Gough, and Nussbaum. For an astute and important analysis of the practical manifestation of this problem within the (then) Soviet Union, see F. Fehér et al., *The Dictatorship Over Needs* (Oxford: Basil Blackwell, 1983).

[31] D. Hume, *A Treatise of Human Nature*, 2nd edn, ed. L. A. Selby-Bigge (Oxford: Clarendon Press, 1978 – 1st edn 1888, orig. edn 1739–40), Bk II, Part III, Section III, p. 415. For more on the development and use of the idea of 'interests', see A. O. Hirschman, *The Passions and the Interests: Political Arguments for Capitalism before Its Triumph* (Princeton: Princeton University Press, 1997 [1977]).

in reason – that showing that something is rational will give me a reason to do it and having a reason will make me want to do it.

A theory of true interests is distinctive because: (1) it covers interests in the context of individuals and groups (along the lines of my earlier discussion of the needs of individuals and groups); (2) it connects wants to rational reflection; (3) it requires both an internal perspective – the agent's own account – and an external perspective – other people's (external evaluators') points of view; (4) the substantive issues that constitute this perspectivally diverse reflection (ideally) revolve around how particular felt needs relate to vital needs and agency needs; and (5) what should emerge is an understanding of what is in the true interests of the individual rather than simply their (initial) avowed interests. The importance of (3) is that it does not give epistemic priority to wants in the sense of revealed preferences. Although there is an acknowledged difficulty in interpersonal attributions within all approaches, there is a tendency to assume that the attribution of preferences (wants) is, somehow, less problematic. However, Davidson has shown why the belief that the attribution of preferences (wants) to individuals is free from the epistemological difficulties of interpretation is unfounded.[32] The ranking, comparison, and even the apparently simple coming to know people's wants does not occur independently of the assignment of a set of beliefs to the individual. These processes involve the following assumptions: (1) that the individual is rational; and (2) that the interpreter can understand (comprehend) the individual's beliefs – that there is a basic similarity between the belief systems involved. Problems of interpretation, therefore, will occur in every evaluation of wants, beliefs and interests; there is much less of a gulf between attributing preferences and attributing interests than is commonly assumed.

By using both an external and an internal perspective, a theory of true interests does not take the internal perspective – the individual's perceived interests – unconditionally. It uses this experiential knowledge,[33] which might be a statement of merely apparent interests, and the extra information the observer(s) might have, to ascertain the true interests of the individual

---

[32] D. Davidson, 'Judging Interpersonal Interests', in J. Elster and A. Hylland (eds.), *Foundations of Social Choice Theory* (Cambridge: Cambridge University Press, 1986); and *Inquiries into Truth and Interpretation* (Oxford: Clarendon Press, 1984).

[33] I call it experiential knowledge because it is knowledge that is acquired as a result of having lived a particular life, under particular circumstances and experiences. It is the sort of knowledge that an external evaluator might never be able to acquire or fully understand in its particularity. The issue of whether extended ethnographic work can bring one into another culture's (and person's) sphere of knowledge is a distinct and more thorny one that does not concern this discussion. It is unfeasible to think that for each policy decision the external observer will have the time, resources, or will to involve an ethnographer.

in question. That is, a theory of true interests accepts Davidson's view as regards the two assumptions and stipulates that the participants (the observer and the observed) should come from similar cultural contexts so as to increase the chances of a basic similarity between the belief systems involved. It also assumes, realistically, that despite their similar belief system, the observer might have extra knowledge about medical science, say, or even about the belief system itself, about how it legitimates certain needs while silencing others or how it foreshortens the possibility horizons of some groups and not others. This knowledge should form part of the process of reaching an understanding of an individual's true interests because once the observed is aware of (and accepts) this knowledge he might re-value some of his interests, preferences and assumptions via the re-evaluation of some of his needs. Hence, although all stated interests are considered, a person's true interests are those that are generally agreed upon as being constitutive of the *good life* in that cultural context determined by constant reference to vital and agency needs.[34] This does not violate the epistemic demand of liberalism – that the individual is the best final judge of what is in her true interests – because the reflective process of interpretation and understanding is in the early stages. At the end of any particular evaluation, the individual remains the last court of appeal.

A refined analysis of 'true interests': Amartya Sen's capability approach

Sen has been developing his capability approach ever since his 1979 Tanner lecture, 'The Equality of What?',[35] where he wishes to shift attention 'from goods to what goods do to human beings'.[36] The central features of the approach are: certain valued functionings ('doings' and 'beings'), the capability to achieve these functionings, and the freedom to pursue goals that are relevant to the person in question (which together make up a person's

---

[34] The context can be, of course, the whole globe. To claim that the group of elements that constitute the process of valuing the *good life* must be restricted to those that are found only within a single cultural context is to shift the parameters unrealistically. Every society, 'traditional' or otherwise, is constantly in contact with and influenced by other societies; this dynamic is what informs ideas, creates diversity and influences change. As Sen argues, internal criticism has a standing and force that criticism from outside cannot match, and there are reasons to pay special attention to critique coming from within the society, community or culture in question, but to imagine that some ideas do not, or should not, come from without even in what emerges in internal criticism is artificial. A. K. Sen, 'Positional Objectivity', *Philosophy and Public Affairs*, 22 (1993); M. C. Nussbaum and A. K. Sen, 'Internal Criticism and Indian Rationalist Traditions', in M. Krausz (ed.), *Relativism: Interpretation and Confrontation* (Notre Dame: University of Notre Dame Press, 1989).

[35] A. K. Sen, 'The Equality of What?', in S. M. McMurrin (ed.), *Liberty, Equality, and Law* (Cambridge: Cambridge University Press, 1987), pp. 137–62.

[36] Ibid., p. 161.

capability set); rational reflection to escape illusion; and an open-endedness that can still inform political decision-making. It will be argued that, unlike some other contemporary theorists who have developed broad and positive political theories, for example Gerry Cohen, Sen has a flexible conception of true interests. He does not simply describe a static list of functionings but emphasises the role freedom plays in the achievement of well-being and the *good life*.

Sen's illuminating work has grown out of his uneasiness with welfarism in general and utilitarianism in particular, in which value is seen only in individual utility, defined in terms of some mental characteristic, such as pleasure, happiness, or desire.[37] Sen maintains that these approaches are guilty of both 'physical-condition neglect' and 'valuation neglect'.[38] The latter results because no room is given for the possible evaluation of states and conditions. By taking wants as given and the informational basis for an assessment of the 'well-ness' of someone's life, they create 'premature fixity'.[39] The former arises because by only considering mental states no account is taken of the freedom the person had in reaching these states, and her objective condition is not considered separate from any reference to how she feels about it. This is a central issue for Sen. The very poor person whose conditions of existence would give him a very low objective well-being might score quite well on a utilitarian scale that only tests his own analysis of his situation in terms of his happiness or pleasure (the welfarist approach). He may do so because: (1) he has a naturally sunny outlook on life; or (2) he has become accustomed to penury and hardship – he has formed adaptive preferences; or (3) he has both. This exemplifies the circumstantial contingency of desires and supports Sen's point that internal criteria alone are bad indicators of what most people would think of as good criteria for an analysis of well-being.

Sen also takes issue with some of the reactions against the utilitarian approach, for example Rawls' set of 'primary goods', and Dworkin's notion of 'equality of resources', which provide the means to a life of free choice as regards the *good life*.[40] The belief is that the individual should be free

[37] A. K. Sen, *Inequality Reexamined* (Oxford: Clarendon Press, 1992), p. 6.
[38] A. K. Sen, *Commodities and Capabilities* (Amsterdam and Oxford: North-Holland, 1985), pp. 20–1.
[39] Ibid., p. 30.
[40] Primary goods are 'things which it is supposed a rational man wants whatever else he wants', and include 'income and wealth', the 'basic liberties', 'freedom of movement and choice of occupation', 'powers and prerogatives of offices and positions of responsibility', and 'the social bases of self-respect'. J. Rawls, *A Theory of Justice* (Oxford: Oxford University Press, 1973), p. 92; further elaborated in Rawls, 'Social Unity and Primary Goods', in A. K. Sen and B. Williams (eds.), *Utilitarianism and Beyond* (Cambridge: Cambridge University Press, 1982), p. 162; and Rawls, 'Priority of Right

to choose whichever *good life* she wishes, and the state should ensure that this choice can be made. Not only do both Rawls and Dworkin fall into the trap of assuming that the development and expression of all needs and preferences have the same set of preconditions, they also assume that means can be valued outside any valuation of the ends. Sen argues that this is impossible and unrealistic;[41] he *begins* with valued 'doings and beings', the valued ends themselves.[42]

Capability and functionings

Sen's approach seeds the middle ground between the subjectivist (internalist) utility angle and the more 'objective' (externalist) resource-based position. The basic notion in Sen's 'capability approach' is a person's functionings, 'which represent parts of the state of a person – in particular the various things that he or she manages to do or be in leading a life'. The capability of a person 'reflects the alternative combinations of functionings the person can achieve, and from which he or she can choose one collection'.[43] The capability to function comprises the various combinations of functionings – the set of vectors of functionings – that reflect the person's *freedom* to lead one type of life or another; that is, it reflects the person's ability (which includes her living conditions) to choose from possible lives. The actual functionings of a person therefore make up part of the capability set but are not equal to it.

The capability set is the 'primary informational base'. This is the case because there are four conceptual categories in the capability set which are all valuable for the quality of life but are not functionings *per se*.[44] They are: well-being achievement, well-being freedom, agency achievement, and agency freedom.[45] Unlike some approaches that see the person as being able to have an adequate well-being achievement without having had much freedom of choice, Sen maintains that there is more to an assessment of well-being, and especially the broader *quality of life*, than the achievement of

---

and Ideas of the Good', *Philosophy and Public Affairs*, 17 (1988), pp. 256–7. R. Dworkin, 'What is Equality? Part 2: Equality of Resources', *Philosophy and Public Affairs*, 10 (1981).

[41] Sen has a series of examples that forcefully indicate how the same means (primary goods, resources) enable people to varying degrees (and are put to very different use by people) depending on physical conditions such as metabolic rate, pregnancy, debilitating disease, etc.

[42] Sen, *Inequality Reexamined*, pp. 79ff. (my emphasis).

[43] A. K. Sen, 'Capability and Well-Being', in M. C. Nussbaum and A. K. Sen (eds.), *The Quality of Life* (Oxford: Clarendon Press, 1993), p. 31.

[44] Ibid., p. 38.

[45] A. K. Sen, 'Well-Being, Agency, and Freedom: The Dewey Lectures 1984', *The Journal of Philosophy*, 82. 4 (1985), pp. 202ff.; Sen, *On Ethics and Economics* (Oxford: Basil Blackwell, 1987), pp. 60ff.

well-being. He places much importance on the *ability* to achieve well-being and the freedom to choose between different lives that lead to well-being. As I have argued more fully elsewhere, Sen's replies to Cohen's criticisms indicate the important role freedom plays within the capability approach.[46] Sen argues convincingly that Cohen's midfare, which is somewhere between goods and utilities, leaves out a fundamental aspect of what Sen claims is in the true interest of the individual: her freedom (what I call, 'autonomy', or 'control over one's life'). Sen holds that freedom and freedom of choice are important not simply because an increase in choice *might* provide better alternatives, but because acting freely and being able to choose, having well-being freedom, might itself be 'directly conducive to well-being'.[47] Sen's argument is that 'doing *x*' is distinct from 'choosing to do *x* and doing it', and the latter is, and ought to be, more highly valued.[48] Freedom is not being seen in the 'negative' way in which it is often represented, as principles of rights and non-interference, but rather the 'issue is the positive *ability* to choose',[49] which is constitutive of the *good life*: 'the "good life" is partly a life of genuine choice, and not one in which the person is forced into a particular life – however rich it might be in other respects'.[50]

Self-evaluation and objectivity

I have been trying to show that the structure of Sen's theory of true interests lies in his elaboration of functionings and capability, but that it is to be found neither solely in one nor the other: it comprises certain valued functionings, the capability to achieve these, and the freedom to pursue personal goals. These are the types of things that Sen values and argues people have reason to value. But what if people do not in fact value these things? Sen replies with an argument for the dynamic of change in moving from illusory

---

[46] G. A. Cohen, 'Equality of What? On Welfare, Resources and Capabilities', in Nussbaum and Sen (eds.), *The Quality of Life*, pp. 9–29; Sen, 'Capability and Well-Being'. The crux of Cohen's criticism is that he thinks that Sen is too 'athletic' with his conception of freedom and capability; but this, I argue, is because Cohen is more concerned with a static notion of well-being that assigns no positive value to freedom as regards the ability to choose and act. Cohen ends his article (p. 28) with: 'No serious inequality obtains when everyone has everything she needs, even if she did not have to lift a finger to get it.' (This may be true, but as my analysis of need indicates, 'inequality' might not be everything and agency is indispensable.) For a full account of my critique, see my 'A Theory of True Interests in the Work of Amartya Sen', *Government and Opposition*, 34. 4 (1999).

[47] Sen, 'Capability and Well-Being', p. 39.   [48] Sen, *Inequality Reexamined*, p. 52.

[49] He says a very similar thing in another work: 'Capabilities . . . are notions of freedom, in the positive sense: what real opportunities you have regarding the life you may lead.' Sen, *The Standard of Living*, 1985 Tanner Lectures, ed. G. Hawthorn (Cambridge: Cambridge University Press, 1987), p. 36.

[50] Sen, *Commodities and Capabilities*, pp. 69–70.

interests to true interests, which involves an account of self-evaluation, positional-objectivity, and objective illusion.

According to Sen, self-evaluation is a reflective exercise undertaken by each agent that tells us each person's assessment of her own quality of life *vis-à-vis* that of others.[51] It does not occur in a vacuum, but takes place within the framework of contemporary standards and beliefs, as does 'standard-evaluation' which evaluates issues like well-being and the standard of living objectively as outcomes.[52] If contemporary standards are widely shared these two forms of evaluation can converge, but both need to be held under the microscope of critical scrutiny that aims to answer '*why* these opinions are held and these values cherished'.[53] Hence, on the one hand, self-evaluation is not a purely subjective exercise and can be critically evaluated using evidence and analysis from external positions, and, on the other, 'standard-evaluation' requires agent-centred reference. In other words, apparent interests are *used* and tested in the light of additional information and different positions. This is not paternalistic because though interpretation might depart from direct reference to utility, a move that many utilitarians would deem the definition of paternalism, the outcome of self-evaluation is not rejected. Sen's point is that in the process of evaluation, reference is made to the subject herself, but the reference must only be made after, not before, the process of self-evaluation has occurred. The difficulty, however, is that self-evaluation is under-determined compared to standard-evaluation and the result can be a remoulding of agent-centred standards to that of the larger community, which may have the opposite effect to that desired − the ability to distinguish between true and illusory interests.

Sen maintains that he overcomes this difficulty via his account of objectivity. He argues that objectivity should not be seen *only* in the form of invariance with respect to individual observers and their positions, a 'view from nowhere', but also as a view 'from a delineated somewhere'.[54] He uses the following analogy: the statement 'the sun and moon are the same size' is an objective one if others who stand in the same position on the earth verify it, and there is no other information available (of the sort, say, that we have now for measuring their sizes). His point is that it is possible to check the claim by noting what other people observe in the same position. Yet there

---

[51] Sen, *The Standard of Living*, p. 31. This is not to be confused with utility because it is 'quintessentially an *evaluative* exercise'. Ibid., p. 32 (Sen's emphasis).

[52] Ibid., p. 30.   [53] Ibid., p. 32 (Sen's emphasis).

[54] Sen, 'Positional Objectivity', p. 127. Sen is making reference to Nagel, *The View From Nowhere* (Oxford: Oxford University Press, 1986).

is also another sense of objectivity: 'trans-positional objectivity'. Sen argues that beliefs are, and should be, tested 'trans-positionally', beyond positional-objectivity, and verified if there is still convergence thereafter. Hence, with this binary sense of objectivity a statement can be objective and false. For example, a community that has no knowledge of optics could be shown to be mistaken about their belief that the sun and the moon are the same size; this will not make their belief a subjective one, but it will show that their objective belief is mistaken. It will lose its positional-objectivity over time and no longer be a legitimate belief. This final step is left unstated by Sen but it is clearly assumed.

But will this analogy work in the sphere of beliefs, interests, wants and choices? Sen thinks it does, as is evidenced by his analysis of 'objective illusion'.[55] For a belief to be shown to be objective and illusory it has to be shown to have had general agreement, or coherence, within a certain observational and deliberative context, from a certain position, *and* it must be diagnosed as erroneous with the use of extra information and critical scrutiny. As Sen puts it: '[I]llusion relates to beliefs that are formed on the basis of a limited class of positional observations. And these beliefs – false as they may be – could nevertheless have been derived objectively in the absence of access to other positional scrutiny'.[56] He gives two convincing examples of 'objective illusion': the difference, in Indian states with different levels of health awareness, between the self-perception of morbidity and the observed life expectancy; and the gender bias in self-assessment of morbidity related to observed mortality. These examples demonstrate that beliefs are often erroneous, though objective, because of a general lack of exposure to information – a lack of 'trans-positional' scrutiny.

In both examples, the moon and mortality, however, there is a relatively secure truth touchstone; the laws of optics and the ability to measure the life expectancy of people are not hugely disputed in the world today. In contrast, competing belief systems can be distant poles apart over some issues. It seems that for Sen the truth of something emerges after sufficient trans-positional scrutiny and some form of agreement is what is ultimately

---

[55] The backdrop of this discussion concerns Sen's position as regards the nature of 'beliefs' within the natural sciences and the nature of 'beliefs' within the human or social sciences. He holds that there is little to distinguish a belief in the natural and the human sciences. Once accepted as trans-positionally objective, they are taken as objectively *true*, but this does not mean that they always have to remain so. This is evidenced in the oft-quoted Kuhnian paradigm shifts in natural science. See also C. Taylor, 'Explanation and Practical Reason', in Nussbaum and Sen (eds.), *The Quality of Life*, pp. 208–31; and H. Putnam, 'Objectivity and the Science-Ethics Distinction', in ibid., pp. 143–57.

[56] Sen, 'Positional Objectivity', p. 133.

valued. *If* this is the assumption, is it not excluding the reality of political interaction?

Incompleteness, evaluative spaces and social choice

The point of the 'positional objectivity' thesis, which allows for the possibility of 'objective illusion', only holds force within a conception of human nature that delineates a set of capabilities which include valued functionings: *being* adequately nourished, adequately housed, adequately clothed, etc., allowing the individual, for instance, to *do* certain things like take part in the entertainment of the community and appear in public without shame.[57] It is a theory of true interests because it tries to encompass all of these and yet leaves the substantive process open; it emphasises incompleteness, thereby refraining from providing a theoretical blueprint.

This is what Sen calls 'assertive incompleteness' and he defends it at two levels: (1) at the level of the theory; and (2) at the level of practical political decision-making. He criticises the unrealistic metaphysical assumptions of both the Rawlsian and Habermasian versions of neo-Kantianism: the belief that a theory can incorporate the answers to the means to a just society *in abstracto* from actual political reality (exemplified in Rawls' hypothetical 'original position');[58] and the claim that if theory fails there is always the transcendental rationality of practical discourse portrayed in the Habermasian universal 'ideal speech situation' that assumes agreement. Sen argues that the relevant issues cannot be fully solved at the level of theory and that it is to ask too much of human rationality to begin with the assumption concerning agreement.[59]

Rather, Sen focuses on the idea of consensus over an evaluative space. He argues:

There are substantive differences between different ethical theories at different levels, from the meta-ethical (involving such issues as objectivity) to the motivational, and it is not obvious that for substantive political and social philosophy it is sensible to insist that all these general issues be resolved *before* an agreement is reached on the choice of an evaluative space.[60]

---

[57] Sen, *Inequality Reexamined*, pp. 115–16.
[58] This, and what follows, comes from personal communication with Amartya Sen.
[59] Yet he does not want to discard the foundationalist position. He wants to overcome it by depicting its incompleteness. Moreover, he defends Rawls' priority of liberty (the first principle). Sen, 'Freedoms and Needs: An argument for the primacy of political rights', *The New Republic*, January 10 & 17 (1994).
[60] Sen, 'Positional Objectivity', p. 49. See also pp. 32–3.

Yet, in the light of his analysis of capabilities and functionings, agreement on the evaluative space, I maintain, is a strong true interest claim. He is valuing certain ends that form part of the 'evaluative space': the valued functionings, capabilities to function, and the different freedoms. Moreover, Sen's evaluative space *excludes* or rejects the things a theory of true interests rejects: sole emphasis on the psychological, on mental states, exemplified by the utility-based approaches that rely on professed wants, or on only *desire fulfilment*; and proposals such as *primary goods* (Rawls) or *resources* (Dworkin), or commodities for their sake alone.[61] Instead, Sen takes the state of being happy as one among many objects of value, desire as evidence – though frequently distorted and imperfect – of what the person values,[62] and primary goods and resources as instrumentally valuable and valuable only in so far as they promote valued capabilities.[63] The evaluative space, therefore, clarifies certain interests that are valued in the theory. Decision on what these are – *valuation* – is intrinsically important, therefore unavoidable, because although some functionings, such as being adequately nourished, are so elementary that they will be strongly valued by all, there are others that are more complex and possibly less obvious that still require valuation.

Now, when substantive issues cannot be decided through evaluative deliberation, Sen emphasises the role of social choice, although not in terms of traditional social choice theorising that has revealed difficulties with combining individual preference orderings into aggregative social welfare judgements (Arrow's impossibility theorem) and then retreated into a purely procedural view of social decisions (*à la* James Buchanan). Rather, in a very similar fashion to his analysis of ethics more generally, Sen argues for the need to incorporate consequences into procedural concerns and defends the role of practical reason in public discourse: '*many of the more exacting problems of the contemporary world... actually call for value formation through public discussion*'.[64] Social choice, therefore, must be seen in the light of the fact that public discussion has, and should have, an educative role. Theories of social choice have tended to assume that people's preferences are given, but it is a fact of life in democratic politics that on a lot of

---

[61] Sen notes: 'The possessing of commodities... has derivative and varying relevance' in assessment of things such as the living standard, well-being, and the quality of life. Sen, *The Standard of Living*, p. 25.

[62] It is more plausible to think about desire and value in the following way, 'I desire *x* because I value *x*', rather than, 'I desire *x*, therefore I value *x*'. Sen, *Commodities and Capabilities*, p. 32.

[63] Sen, 'Positional Objectivity', p. 48.

[64] Sen, 'Rationality and Social Choice', *American Economic Review*, 85 (1995), p. 18 (my emphasis).

issues people do not have clear preferences. It is through practical discourse that true interests are not simply collated but refined, changed and decided upon.

Criticisms of Sen's account

There are two possible criticisms of Sen's account in the light of my analysis of needs. The first questions why Sen does not use the language of needs and interests. The second claims that his conception of practical reason is too simplified to deal with two inter-related issues: the institutional sources of objective illusions that create imbalances in normative power; and role-relative evaluative criteria. Here I focus on the second criticism because I have discussed the first issue elsewhere,[65] and because in doing so I identify issues to be covered more fully in chapter 3. I only introduce the issues here.

If practical reason is to be understood, as Sen would seem to condone, as involving the critical comparison, evaluation and ranking of alleged human goods and ends,[66] he needs to analyse the types of coercion, power and needs that must be taken into account. There is none of this in Sen's account, and this might be a consequence of the fact that he seems to *assume* we can sort out what we mean by substantive notions such as 'a life of quality' via discussion and practical reason. As I hope is clear from my account of the nature and formation of need, and normative power and its effects, this is not as unproblematically evident as might seem the case. I maintain that Sen's inaccurate assumption emerges as a result of a questionable faith in practical reason. Imagine the difficulties inherent in transposing his theoretical evaluative condition of *intersubjectivity* based on the goal of 'trans-positionality' into a practical mechanism for ascertaining true interest or changing conditions in order to improve the meeting of vital needs and the development of agency needs. Avowals of vital and agency needs will depend on both short-term practical means and goals and longer-term aspirational goals, and these (and the consequent analysis of true interests) will be relative to felt feelings of lack and possibility that themselves are relative to the roles an individual normally fills. That is, Sen has unrealistically excluded problems of normative imbalance, role

---

[65] In my 'Theory of True Interests'.
[66] O. O'Neill, *Constructions of Reason: Explorations of Kant's Practical Philosophy* (Cambridge: Cambridge University Press, 1989); and O. O'Neill, *Towards Justice and Virtue: A constructive account of practical reasoning* (Cambridge: Cambridge University Press, 1996).

disparity and role-relative perception in his account of practical reason in the 'evaluative space'. What is required is a means of analysing the formative structures that arguably constitute Sen's 'evaluative space', which pays particular attention to the distribution of roles and their legitimating institutions and practices. This assessment of roles will provide an account of the actual conditions for practical reasoning, and the degree of distortion in people's perception of their capabilities. The kind and distribution of roles is the central concern because they are, so to speak, the positions from which people evaluate needs generally and perceive vital and agency needs in particular. If certain kinds of roles confine individuals to certain environs, experiences and needs, or if there is an unequal distribution of roles between the individuals who comprise society, or if some groups of people's needs are poorly attended to and developed, the evaluative space within which capability-inspired practical reasoning occurs will not meet any of Sen's ethical objectives. I address these concerns at greater length in chapter 3, particularly sections 3 and 4.

6 THE CONCEPT OF TRUE INTEREST

The concept of true interest is understood here as distinct from the notions of rational interest, prudence and self-love. An individual's true interest is epistemologically and ontologically based in her needs. And her needs are determined by either one or a mix of the following: agency needs, that is, practical and theoretical ethical aspirations (only one of which is autonomy, or freedom); vital needs, or ineluctable conditions for human functioning; the particular manifestations of these two general groups; and what I have called either luxury-wants or desire needs. In line with my account of needs, the notion of true interest does not suggest a single subject-blind and all-pervasive aspect (or viewpoint) prevalent in discussions of rational interest and rights; it allows for difference in choice depending on other issues like personal goals and self-interest. 'True interest' is not the same as prudence because a theory of true interests does not accept the assumption that practical wisdom is necessarily always driven by self-interest (psychological egoism) or the argument that self-interest is necessarily always the best guide (ethical egoism). Given the above concerns about our natures as needing individuals and the generation and legitimation of need, and given the dearth of empirical and normative support for the two kinds of egoism, it is quite conceivable that I might have a true interest determined by agency needs or strongly felt vital need that it would *not* be very prudential for me to pursue. For example, given the state of public transport, it might be prudential for Jill to buy a car instead of cycling around the motorways between the trucks, but it is not necessarily her true interest, especially if it were part of a political campaign of hers to diminish the use of cars and affect public transport policy. Self-love in both of its formulations, *amour de soi-même* (love of oneself) and *amour-propre* (love of self, which engenders the desire for esteem and self-esteem), is either too basic and hypothetical – i.e. simply concerned with a self-preserving pre-social animal with no imaginative faculties – or too self-obsessed and individualised. Self-love is not necessarily the same as either psychological or ethical egoism, but both forms of self-love fail to take into account the cognitive and constitutive nature of human needs in the manner (arguably) achieved by the concept of true interest in a theory of true interests.[67]

Finally, it is important to stress that the concept of true interest developed here is not a compound of 'true' and 'interest' but a separate and distinct concept in its own right. If something is found to be in my 'true interest' it designates a particular 'post-reflective-evaluation' need of mine in the here and now that can be justified via its causal link to preferable means of meeting my vital needs and developing my agency needs. The evaluation is constituted by external and internal evaluation and the last word is the individual's; however, there are structural means of improving the interpretation and perception of needs so that this process of evaluation becomes less dominated by others and their powers and biases. Consequently, the notion of 'truth' being adopted is not to be understood in any sense as a metaphysical or final truth, but rather as one centred in a particular context and time, and one that could change with an improvement in the meeting of vital needs and development of agency needs. 'Truth' in a theory of true interests is not some atemporal end-state but rather what is attained with an increase in knowledge or change in position or condition that necessitates input from others and critical scrutiny based on vital and agency needs. And, following Nietzsche, nor is 'truth' in this sense dependent on, or an example of, a universal 'God's eye view' of the world, a single position of *ultimate* judgement;[68] the 'truth' in true interests is particular to context,

---

[67] For more on self-love, especially *amour-propre*, see J.-J. Rousseau, *The Discourses* in *The Discourses and other early political writings*, and *The Social Contract* in *The Social Contract and other late political writings*, both ed. and trans. V. Gourevitch (Cambridge: Cambridge University Press, 1997); and the French moralists, especially La Rochefoucauld. For a modern analysis, see Elster, *Alchemies of the Mind*, esp. pp. 85–96, 130, 417.

[68] This has its source in Nietzsche's accounts of objectivity and truth, which are expressed most clearly in: F. Nietzsche, *On the Genealogy of Morality*, ed. K. Ansell-Pearson, trans. C. Diethe (Cambridge: Cambridge University Press, 1994); and F. Nietzsche, *The Birth of Tragedy and Other Writings*, ed. R. Geuss and R. Speirs, trans. R. Speirs (Cambridge: Cambridge University Press, 1999).

time and individual or group. Hence, a theory of true interests explicitly *rejects* the possibility of a 'view from nowhere'. This shows that a set of true interests necessarily will include certain 'objective illusions', from which the individual or group concerned might, or might not, escape in the future. It is important, therefore, to refrain from completeness and foreclosure that could stifle the possibility of new forms of human functioning, but rather to see theory as working like a filter, undermining illusory interests and supporting true interests. If this is the case, why use the concept '*true interest*' and not something less final? The answer is short. The notions of agency or vital need do not provide the feeling of lack and urgency that might engender attention to the meeting of needs. For urgent and pressing practical concerns to retain their level of urgency, the notion of 'truth' is not only unavoidable, it is felicitous.

CHAPTER 3

The political evaluation of needs

The account of need formation in the previous chapter raised significant problems for a rational and discursive approach to the understanding and evaluation of needs in particular and politics in general. And it was argued that the theory of true interests as it stands is too naïve and could even be said to fall into the same traps as the more discursive analyses against which it is posited. In this chapter I conclude the argument and overcome this problem by attending to my two criticisms of Sen noted at the end of the last chapter in manifestly political or institutional tones. But first I dispose of a conceptual candidate for understanding these issues that relies on a similar kind of faith in practical reason and discursive deliberation to that found in Sen and the need theorists discussed in chapter 1: the concept of 'civil society'. In the first section of this chapter I uncover what underpins the use of the concept, and why these assumptions make the concept inadequate for critical political theory, especially a needs-based critical account of the kind developed here.

In the remaining three sections of the chapter I develop an alternative conceptual framework for the political evaluation of needs and interests rooted in an account of practices, institutions and roles. I emphasise the causal significance of institutions, the epistemological significance of roles and the function of a coercive authority. I show how such an approach provides the core means of escaping the utopian and naïve true interest theory reliance on direct intersubjective interaction between individuals and policy-makers. It can be used on two levels. First, it can be employed as a means of evaluating the extant breadth and differential access to available information about needs. In other words, it can be used to *understand* the evaluative terrain. Second, it can be used as an objective means of transforming the conditions under which the individuals of a society perceive and interpret their true interests and satisfy their needs. This alternative approach is better as a means of both evaluating need-claims and engendering the meeting of needs than the rights-based 'civil society' approach, meta-theoretical accounts of rights, or the tradition of utilitarianism. The defence of this claim involves an evaluation of institutions and roles within the logic of what I call 'institutional consequentialism', which involves a more elaborate and frequent census designed to engender the articulation of needs. The chapter ends with a few comments on practical reason, especially the prevalent moral conception of practical reason and its inadequacies in the light of this account of needs, practices, institutions and roles.

I   FREEDOM AND RIGHTS: A CRITIQUE OF THE CONCEPT OF 'CIVIL SOCIETY'

The concept of 'civil society' has become the fundamental conceptual apparatus within most 'critical' thinkers' attempts to overcome exactly that phenomenon that has the potential to block agency need development: the disparities of normative power vested in different groups of the citizenry and some associated institutions and practices. The most common assumption or argument underpinning the many conceptions of 'civil society' is that the concept and creation of 'civil society' generates deeper forms of democracy and citizen power. However, as I will argue, contemporary conceptions of 'civil society' are based on idealistic notions of states, markets, freedom, rights and citizen power, and therefore hinder rather than facilitate the attainment of deeper forms of democracy.[1]

I focus most of my attention on one theoretical account: Cohen and Arato's voluminous study, *Civil Society and Political Theory*.[2] Why this particular theoretical analysis? One reason is that it was well received: one commentator heralded it as 'undoubtedly one of the most significant treatises in the realm of political theory to have been published in the last two decades'.[3] I question that assessment, but I maintain that Cohen and Arato's

---

[1] Theories of globalisation are particularly prone to a reliance on the concept of 'civil society'. In these theories, globalisation is perceived as representing a threat to democracy, and thus it raises concerns with how to advance citizens' rights and deepen democracy. 'Civil society' is used as a means of developing an understanding of how to do this. Therefore, the problems I identify in what follows are particularly true of the notion of cosmopolitan democratic citizenship within a global 'civil society'. For the project of cosmopolitan democracy and its use of 'civil society', see D. Held et al., *Global Transformations* (Cambridge: Polity Press, 1999). In governmental and non-governmental (NGO) analysis and policy the concepts of 'civil society' and 'globalisation' (or related terms) often appear together. For typical examples, see the recent speech, 'NGO's in a Global Future', by the Rt Hon. Clare Short, MP, at Birmingham University on 13 January 1999, and the references in J. Hearn, 'Foreign Aid, Democratisation and Civil Society in Africa: A Study of South Africa, Ghana and Uganda', *Institute of Development Studies Discussion Paper*, 368 (March 1999).

[2] J. L. Cohen and A. Arato, *Civil Society and Political Theory* (Cambridge, MA: MIT Press, 1992).

[3] R. Wolin, 'Review of Jean L. Cohen and Andrew Arato, *Civil Society and Political Theory*. Cambridge: MIT Press, 1992', *Theory and Society*, 22. 4 (1993), p. 575.

study is important for three reasons. First, it is the most developed recent attempt to defend 'civil society' as a means of 'deepening' democracy.[4] Second, it is the most widely cited and influential theoretical tract across the whole range of 'civil society' discussions. Third, it is illustrative of the theoretical weaknesses, unrealistic assumptions and empirical flaws within current usage of the concept.

The discourse of 'civil society' is characterised by a large number of vague and confused conceptions of 'civil society'.[5] However, underlying this conceptual disorder there exists a common problem: theorists right across the political spectrum assume or argue that 'civil society' is an autonomous arena, or in extreme cases even causally independent from the state.[6] I argue

[4] Cohen and Arato, *Civil Society*, p. 3.

[5] I have identified at least eight different conceptions of 'civil society'. They can be grouped within three different traditions or approaches to 'civil society'. (a) *Liberal* conceptions, including J. Rawls, *Political Liberalism* (New York: Columbia University Press, 1996), pp. 14, 220; P. B. Lehning, 'Toward a Multicultural Civil Society: The Role of Social Capital and Democratic Citizenship', *Government and Opposition*, 33. 1 (1998); E. Gellner, *Conditions of Liberty: Civil Society and Its Rivals* (London: Penguin, 1996); S. Giner, 'Civil Society and Its Future', in J. A. Hall (ed.), *Civil Society: Theory, History, Comparison* (Cambridge: Polity Press, 1995). (b) *Civic virtue* conceptions, including A. B. Seligman, 'Animadversions upon Civil Society and Civic Virtue in the Last Decade of the Twentieth Century', in Hall (ed.), *Civil Society*; Seligman, *The Idea of Civil Society* (Princeton: Princeton University Press, 1992); E. Shils, 'The Virtue of Civil Society', *Government and Opposition*, 26. 1 (1991). (c) *Post-marxist anti-statist* conceptions, including Cohen and Arato, *Civil Society*; J. Keane, *Democracy and Civil Society* (London: Verso, 1988); K. Tester, *Civil Society* (London and New York: Routledge, 1992). However, even within these groupings there is little agreement as to the exact specification of 'civil society'. Tester epitomises the problem with the use of the concept 'civil society': he gives at least four definitions of the term. For more on these different conceptions, see my '"Civil Society": Critique and Alternative', in S. Halperin and G. Laxer (eds), *Global Civil Society and Its Limits* (London: Palgrave, 2003).

[6] This is true of all the above-cited analyses, in particular the liberal and post-marxist anti-statist conceptions. For example, Rawls and Lehning argue that 'civil society' is a space of voluntary association between government and the private sector that is free from the coercive structure of the state. And they make typical liberal assumptions and distinctions between the 'private' (or 'nonpublic') and the 'public'. Rawls, *Political Liberalism*, pp. 14, 220; Lehning, 'Multicultural Civil Society', p. 223. But this is not true of earlier conceptions of 'civil society' both in the liberal and civic virtue traditions. For example, in Montesquieu and Locke's otherwise distinct conceptions, 'civil society' is synonymous with 'political society', while Hegel uses it to refer to more specific economic and political institutions and practices that have direct causal links to the state (about which more below). For Locke, a 'civil society' is a legitimate political order that remedies the inconveniences of the state of nature; that is, it is 'the state liked' as determined by pre- or meta-political natural law. In Montesquieu's more 'political' conception of society, the rule of law and the *'corps intermédiaire'* stand and fall together; that is, the autonomy of 'civil society' is not achieved in contra-position to the state. J. Locke, *Two Treatises of Government*, ed. P. Laslett (Cambridge: Cambridge University Press, 1988); J. Dunn, 'The Contemporary Political Significance of John Locke's Conception of Civil Society', *Iyyun, The Jerusalem Philosophical Quarterly*, 45 (1996); C. Montesquieu, *The Spirit of the Laws*, trans. and ed. A. M. Cohler, B. C. Miller and H. S. Stone (Cambridge: Cambridge University Press, 1989); C. Taylor, 'Invoking Civil Society' and 'Liberal Politics and the Public Sphere', in *Philosophical Arguments* (Cambridge, MA: Harvard University Press, 1995); I. Hont, 'Liberty, Equality, Prudence', *The Times Higher Education Supplement*, 9 October 1992.

that this is mistaken and that it is the result of a misconceived understanding of freedom in which individuals are conceived as being 'free' only if completely uncoerced; and are therefore unfree if coerced in any sense. This problem in particular is clearly evident in the work of Cohen and Arato, whose conception of freedom is heavily dependent on a Habermasian theoretical template of the requirements for 'free' dialogue, and of what it means to interact 'freely'. This discursive approach to politics fosters a misunderstanding of rights that generates conformity rather than the (intended) celebration of difference and a consequent lack of institutional focus that undermines a critical theory to 'deepen' democracy. Thus I focus on Cohen and Arato's conception in order to pinpoint the source of this serious problem within the 'civil society' discourse, and to avoid an extended taxonomy of shortcomings.

The autonomy of 'civil society'? Cohen and Arato and Habermas

Cohen and Arato's conception of 'civil society' is in the tradition of Tocqueville, Gramsci, Parsons and Habermas, and their main aim 'is to further develop and systematically justify the idea of civil society'.[7] They see themselves as defending the theoretical aims of Hegel's synthesis bar his 'statist bias'.[8] As a theoretical springboard, Hegel is as good as any, for he has come closest to depicting an unambiguous concept of 'civil society', called *bürgerliche Gesellschaft*. But Hegel's conception is completely distinct from that developed by Cohen and Arato, and it is not 'statist' in the way they understand the term. For Hegel 'civil society' *includes* the economic sphere – the 'system of needs' and relations of exchange and production – and the institutions of the administration of justice, welfare policing, and the corporations.[9] It is a broad notion within which there are certain institutions whose role it is to begin the process of overcoming the fragmentation created by individualist need satisfaction, exchange and production. These institutions connect 'civil society' to the state; they are intended to mediate between the individuals and their state in such a way that the individuals are able to feel part of a larger whole and begin to see the 'other' not simply as a competitor within the market. These institutions are at once part of 'civil society' and the state and thus are neither autonomous nor causally independent of the state. If this conception can be called 'statist' it is only in the sense that without the state, the individuals that make up society would remain fragmented.

---

[7] Cohen and Arato, *Civil Society*, pp. 409–10, 17.   [8] Ibid., p. xiv.

[9] G. W. F. Hegel, *Elements of the Philosophy of Right*, ed. A. W. Wood, trans. H. B. Nisbet (Cambridge: Cambridge University Press, 1991), §§ 189–208; §§ 209–29; §§ 230–48; §§ 249–57, respectively.

Cohen and Arato are also concerned about individual fragmentation and power but they provide a different solution or at least use different means in their attempt to overcome the problem. They argue that the solution emerges out of feelings of 'solidarity', 'self-limitation' and 'societal community' that surface in an arena separate from the institutions that constitute the state and those that comprise the economy. They call this arena 'civil society' and argue that it is characterised by a form of interaction, discourse and institutional configuration in which individuals are free from the control and power relations of both the state and the economy. They argue that this arena is autonomous and its participants exercise universal individual rights to defend this autonomy. They lay most emphasis on the alleged fact that interaction in 'civil society' is characterised by the kind of discursive interaction that can only obtain in conditions of non-coercion; in other words, in a discursive environment that is, or at least can be, sealed off from the coercive forces and power differentials present in the state and economy.[10] Hence, 'civil society' is defined in terms of its spatial situation and in the light of its characteristic *linguistic* activity, coercion-free discourse. It comes as no surprise, therefore, that Cohen and Arato adopt Habermas' Discourse Ethics (hereinafter DE) as a normative analysis for what occurs within civil society. They defend DE as a 'political ethics' and as a 'theory of democratic legitimacy and basic rights' that provides a 'standard with which we can test the legitimacy of socio-political norms'.[11] Following Habermas, they argue that the participants can *evaluate* empirical norms, traditions and consciousnesses in terms of the meta-norms provided by DE: they can be evaluated in comparison to the norms that would emerge within the 'ideal-speech' situation. For Habermas, communicative interaction in the ideal-speech situation is characterised by rational discourse undistorted by differences in power or position or status. Thus, for Habermas and Cohen and Arato, the main evaluative criterion is the degree and kind of discursive freedom the empirical institutions allow and engender.

This discursive evaluative framework is supplemented by an analysis of the role of social solidarity. According to Cohen and Arato, it is within 'civil society' that social solidarity is created and out of which arises an allegedly more refined conception of Habermas' stress on the 'general interest'.[12] They maintain that the associations that constitute 'civil society' presuppose solidarity. This is the case because they involve direct participation, which eliminates power and monetary relations: 'civil society' is characterised by solidarity because the individuals that comprise it 'respond to

---

[10] Cohen and Arato, *Civil Society*, pp. 480ff.   [11] Ibid., pp. 21, 350–1, 357.
[12] Ibid., pp. 370ff.; J. Habermas, *Theory of Communicative Action, Vol. 1: Reason and the Rationalization of Society*, trans. T. McCarthy (Boston, MA: Beacon Press, 1984).

and identify with one another on the basis of mutuality and reciprocity...
without calculating individual advantages, and above all *without compulsion*'.[13] The first half of this statement *may* be descriptively accurate, but
the same could not be said for the two claims in the second part. For, even
if there was a degree of discursive freedom, it does not follow from this, or
from the fact that the arena abounds in mutuality, that self-interest, coercion and compulsion somehow evaporate in the solidary ether. And even
if the claim were intended as a purely normative wish, it would still need
more reference to reality to carry any political significance.

Cohen and Arato use illuminating empirical examples to substantiate
these theoretical claims. As in their previous works, their main focus is
on the form of what they call 'self-limiting' social movements that arose
under the banner of Solidarity in the former communist East European
countries, especially Poland.[14] They compare this to 'civil disobedience' in
western nation-states and social movements in the democratisation of Latin
America.[15] They maintain that these activities have two things in common:
they defend a set of universal rights; and they are self-limiting. That is, they
are not interested in state power but rather the defence of a set of rights
that delineate an area within which individuals and collectives are 'free' in
the discursive sense outlined in the work of Habermas.

The case of Solidarity provides a seemingly excellent example of anti-state
'civil' (uncoerced) activity. Consequently, it is tempting to extrapolate from
this particular movement to make universal claims about the general form
of 'civil society' activity. However, there is significant empirical evidence to
show that this is a highly problematic theoretical move. As in the case of
Latin American democratisation, Solidarity were fighting an authoritarian
and blatantly coercive state (rather, Party) and, as a consequence, began
to envisage freedom as equivalent to activity within a 'sphere' of 'civil
society' free from coercion. Yet they were not so much fighting from within
'civil society' but *for* an imagined (usually western) 'civil society'; and their
apparent (and avowed) opponent, the state, became their ally once they
destroyed their actual opponent, the Party. Solidarity's self-awareness within
their context allows them to see that it is not the state *per se* against which
they are fighting, but rather the Party and its (ab)use of its coercive power.[16]

---

[13] Cohen and Arato, *Civil Society*, p. 472 (my emphasis).

[14] A. Arato and J. Cohen, 'Social Movements, Civil Society, and the Problems of Sovereignty', *Praxis International*, 4. 3 (1984); and Arato, 'Civil Society Against the State: Poland 1980–1', *Telos*, 47 (1981); and Arato, 'Empire vs. Civil Society: Poland 1981–2', *Telos*, 50 (1981–2).

[15] Cohen and Arato, *Civil Society*, pp. 61–3, 492ff.

[16] M. Neocleous, *Administering Civil Society: Towards a Theory of State Power* (London: Macmillan, 1996), p. 167n.

In importing the concept of 'civil society' to explain these movements and changes, Cohen and Arato force a mismatch between empirical reality and normative theory.

Cohen and Arato repeatedly force causal reality to fit normative theory. Their argument is particularly problematic at two points, which highlight how their mistaken assumptions about freedom underpin the flaws in their account as a whole. First, Cohen and Arato identify the partial insulation, autonomy and 'free' discourse of certain institutions and practices within 'civil society', and argue that it follows that the 'sphere' as a whole is free and autonomous. This is illusory: it does not follow from the fact that parts of the alleged 'sphere' called 'civil society' are characterised by partial autonomy that the 'sphere' as a whole is autonomous or independent. Moreover, their argument for the alleged autonomy of 'civil society' (based on its unique communicative co-ordination) is contradicted by their own argument for its causal significance or influence over the rest of society. The claim that 'civil society' can causally influence the creation of law implies (at least the possibility for) the opposite causality:[17] that the state and economy affect the needs and values of 'civil society'. Although *in principle* there could be only one-way causality from 'civil society' to the rest of society and the state, it is empirically highly unlikely. Second, Cohen and Arato reduce various kinds of freedoms into one form and area of interaction. They conceive of 'free' acts in terms of their linguistic components alone and exclude an array of causally significant components. They thereby misconstrue coercion, consent and rights. I explain these points with the help of an analysis of Gramsci.

Freedom, coercion, consent and rights

Cohen and Arato's analysis fits well with the common anachronistic interpretation of Gramsci's account of 'civil society', which they invoke and follow.[18] However, the common understanding that Gramsci was the archetypal theorist of 'civil society' as an arena between the economy and the state (of a kind similar to Cohen and Arato) belies a more ambiguous and confused textual and empirical reality. At different points in his work Gramsci (1) contrasts the state with 'civil society';[19] (2) argues that the state encompasses 'civil society';[20] and (3) maintains that the state is

---

[17] Cohen and Arato, *Civil Society*, pp. 480–7.   [18] Ibid., pp. 142–59.
[19] A. Gramsci, *Selections from the Prison Notebooks*, ed. and trans. Q. Hoare and G. Nowell Smith (London: Lawrence & Wishart, 1971), p. 238.
[20] Ibid., pp. 262–3.

identical with 'civil society'.[21] Why this ambiguity? Gramsci is determined to explain why the 'bourgeoisie' hold near complete hegemonic power in western societies, and he makes various attempts. He first argues that the preponderance of 'civil society' over the state in the west as the mode of 'bourgeois power' indicates that it is the cultural ascendancy of the ruling class that creates stability in the capitalist order. As Anderson notes, this is not sufficient because it fails to see that the 'principal ideological lynchpin' is the general form of the representative state in bourgeois democracy.[22] Later, Gramsci argues that hegemony is distributed between 'civil society' and the state. Here he makes the mistake of placing coercion at the level of the state *and* 'civil society' because he argues that hegemony is constituted by coercion and consent.[23] But, as Weber has argued convincingly, coercion, or 'the monopoly of legitimate physical violence', lies fairly and squarely within the (modern) state; a defining feature of the modern state is that it alone controls the ultimate coercive force.[24] Gramsci's final attempt occurs when he includes both political society and 'civil society' within the state.[25] This leaves us with a totalising picture, later picked up by Althusser with his analysis of 'ideological state apparatuses', which fails to give any real *causal* significance to capitalism rather than, or alongside, the state.[26]

These problems and slippages emerge because despite Gramsci's insights into the nature of hegemony, he tends to under-emphasise the relationships and differences between consent and coercion. This simplifying tendency is the result of a voluntarist hangover that informs his work;[27] that is, he holds that there are arenas, or at least he holds out the hope that arenas could be created, in which individuals can or could act (and consent) completely free from coercion. He has a normative conception of freedom that is all or nothing – that is, any coercion amounts to complete unfreedom – and this affects his analysis of 'civil society'. Cohen and Arato fail to take full cognisance of the ambiguities in Gramsci's account of 'civil society' and

---

[21] Ibid., pp. 159–60.

[22] Ibid., p. 170; P. Anderson, 'Antinomies of Antonio Gramsci', *New Left Review*, 100 (1976–7), p. 26.

[23] Gramsci, *Prison Notebooks*, p. 246.

[24] M. Weber, 'The Profession and Vocation of Politics', in *Weber: Political Writings*, ed. P. Lassman and R. Spiers (Cambridge: Cambridge University Press, 1994), pp. 310–11; Weber, *Economy and Society*, ed. G. Roth and C. Wittich (Berkeley: University of California Press, 1978), pp. 54–5. This is not to say that there aren't other 'illegitimate' and more subtle forms of coercion, within the family, the economy, etc., but just that the threat and use of legitimate violence is the right of only the state, and is called coercion.

[25] Gramsci, *Prison Notebooks*, pp. 160, 261.

[26] Anderson, 'Antinomies of Antonio Gramsci', pp. 34ff.

[27] I do not hold, though, that Gramsci was unambiguously voluntarist. For more on this issue see A. Gramsci, *Pre-Prison Writings*, ed. R. Bellamy, trans. V. Cox (Cambridge: Cambridge University Press, 1994), pp. xiv–xvi, 43–57.

thus do not attempt to understand why this is the case. Consequently, they conceive of freedom in the same way.

The problematic ramifications of this approach to freedom are exemplified in Cohen and Arato's treatment of civil disobedience and rights. They argue that civil disobedience is the paradigm case of 'free' democratic and rights-based activity. Its locus is 'civil society' and it is by definition extra-institutional and above the law; but its 'self-limiting' nature distinguishes it from criminality and outright revolution.[28] They maintain that this limitation is self-imposed, or self-created, since it is constrained by rights that are self-created. According to Cohen and Arato these rights are antecedent to positive law, but are not supported by natural law dogma. Rather, Cohen and Arato link 'the idea of rights to the metaconditions of discourse...'; '[R]ights can be interpreted as normative requirements for participation in practical discourses about society.' For Cohen and Arato, these meta-conditions are grounded in a Kantian and Rawlsian conception of autonomy that rests on: (1) 'self-determination and individual choice'; and (2) 'the ability to construct, revise, and pursue one's own life plan'.[29] Hence, although Cohen and Arato claim to connect the *formation* of rights to a discursive arena, their own analysis of the rights under which the movements actually develop indicates that the rights are metaphysically prior to the movements in question. Cohen and Arato wish to connect rights to the historical development of an autonomous 'sphere' called 'civil society' that encompasses these self-creative movements, but in fact they base them in a set of 'communication rights' which themselves are grounded in *a priori* transcendental assumptions about human rationality.[30] Thus Cohen and Arato base this self-creating sphere's activity on a set of rights that are clearly not self-created.

Cohen and Arato claim that their account of rights can be supported by the fact that those involved in civil disobedience are united around the creation and defence of the rights that delineate 'civil society'.[31] But anyone with even a brief experience of civil disobedience would question this interpretation of the evidence. Diverse groups often unite over a single issue, even constitute a single movement – say for the equal recognition of women in the workplace – while otherwise supporting a wide variety of goods not all of which are either compatible with or in defence of rights generally or can be reconciled with the conditions under which the rights emerged. For example, the Marxist anti-WTO activist who joins

[28] Cohen and Arato, *Civil Society*, pp. 564ff., 592ff.
[29] Ibid., pp. 397–8. Recall the need theorists and their ideas concerning conditions for 'life plans'.
[30] Ibid., pp. 399–402.   [31] Ibid., p. 472.

the movement for equal recognition of women in the workplace might specifically and vehemently not support the discourse of rights, one part of which allegedly provides her with the freedom to protest. Meanwhile, some feminists involved in the same movement might disagree with the Marxist position more generally and yet also strongly oppose the conceptualisation of their claims in terms of rights – a significant conceptual support of the gendered discourse against which they stand. Probably the single most assured thing that could be said of single-issue movements is that they attract widely diverse groups, who in other contexts are discordant. Cohen and Arato are under the grip of an idea that collective action indicates a great deal more than it actually does. It is too much of a leap to infer from normal collective action that: (1) there exists an underlying solidary consciousness (either in terms of rights or otherwise); and (2) those involved in collective action are all defending the same set of political and moral values. This is not to say that those involved in civil disobedience do not create change, but that, as the activities of Italy's *centri sociali* and Brazil's *Movimento Sem Terra* highlight, civil disobedience is most effective when it is neither 'civil' nor constrained by an antecedently imposed structure of procedural means for the articulation and recognition of demands.

The most alarming aspect of the theoretical and empirical flaws within Cohen and Arato's account is that it is more likely to create conformity than criticism, difference and disobedience. The theoretical idea that there exists a place within which citizens freely defend their values and differences has the effect of providing the illusion amongst citizens that they are in fact doing as much even when and where they are not. The *idea* that I and like-minded others defend our difference in a causally significant arena, when in actual fact we do not, might gratify our need to 'self-create' while actually keeping us from criticising those institutions and practices that forced us into a position in which we felt the need to emphasise our difference. It is not inconsequential that the granting of rights, even special rights, in line with citizen demands is often concomitant with a failure even to begin the transformation of relevant pathological extant institutions and practices; or at least often adds little to our comprehension of the relation between extant institutional matrices and the institutions that 'grant' us our rights.

This problem about conformity is reinforced by the fact that an emphasis on 'civil society' is normally coupled with arguments for identity politics.[32] There are two things wrong with this sort of approach. First, contrary to

---

[32] Cohen and Arato and Taylor are obvious examples. For examples of the conception of a unified self that underpins identity (and difference) politics see C. Taylor, *Sources of the Self: The Making of the Modern Identity* (Cambridge, MA: Harvard University Press, 1989); and A. MacIntyre, *After*

the intentions of the theorists, the result of the emphasis is paradoxically an essentialisation of these categories within a 'market' of other equally essential and valuable identities; that is, they defeat their own emancipatory cause because they reinforce an existing tendency to create a 'market' of mono-significant identities that are competitive *vis-à-vis* one other. Second, because this discourse is often connected to a discussion of 'democratisation' from within 'civil society', the forms of different kinds of exploitation are made to conform to the requirements of the rights-guided and supposedly voluntary nature of 'civil society'. Although the various groups may have or represent widely divergent and even contradictory needs, they are examples of self-limiting acts of civil disobedience only if they remain within the rational and procedural confines of deliberative discourse.[33] The alleged 'difference' is, therefore, an antecedently legitimised one within a formulaic structure. An initial emphasis on difference actually ends in conformity.

It is more realistic and potentially transformative to acknowledge that freedom (and various different freedoms) do not occur completely free of coercion. Rather, freedom should be thought of as positioned somewhere along the continuum between the polarised analytical distinctions of the Hobbesian notion of freedom at the one pole and Kantian autonomy at the other; that is, as somewhere between the understanding of freedom that argues that an individual is only free if *free from* interference and the notion that to be free is to be *free to* act in a certain morally autonomous manner.[34] I maintain that it is at least possible to construe freedom in non-metaphysical terms as a multi-dimensional concept; and to think of freedom in terms of degrees of freedom that will depend on concrete issues like the form of the society's institutions (including those of the coercive authority), the level of agency need development, and the nature of possible alternatives. Alternatives are important. I may have two or more choices but none of them may be meaningful or they may all have the same general

---

Virtue: A Study in Moral Theory (London: Duckworth, 1981). M. Bull, 'Slavery and the Multiple Self', *New Left Review*, 231 (Sept./Oct. 1998), has shown how this emphasis on a unified self that is especially prevalent in contemporary moral philosophy is an example of master morality, as opposed to the Hegelian dual consciousness of slave morality. Following Bull, I maintain that the idea of a unified self is a misconceived and elitist conception that reeks of aristocratic stolid confidence. Consequently, the philosophical support it provides for identity politics is not only explainable, it is also sharply illusory since most claims concerning exploitation emerge from a demand to be treated equally, to overcome rather than support special aristocratic privileges.

33 It is a mistake to assume, as most deliberative democrats do, that the procedural parameters that define deliberation do not in fact exclude the substantive issues that are expressed within excluded forms of discourse. (They maintain that these same issues could be expressed deliberatively.) To restrict discourse to rational deliberation pre-interprets which substantive issues can be included; inarticulate or hysterical forms are left outside the forum. I thank Lisa Brown for this point.

34 R. Harrison, *Democracy* (London and New York: Routledge, 1993).

outcome. To argue that I am free simply because I am free to choose is to avoid the issue completely. For example, I may have the alleged choice between staying on income support or coming off it to take up a job, but if the job is in a labour market different from the one that my skills prepare me for, or if the pay does not meet my needs and leaves me uninspired, this is a meaningless choice. To argue that I am 'free to choose' in this case is to trivialise the notion of freedom by thinking of choice and its lack as an issue about choice *per se* rather than what might be called 'meaningful choice'. Furthermore, in order for me to be able to choose, I require not only meaningful possibilities from which to choose but also the knowledge, agency and security to make the choices. And, as Nietzsche and Foucault have shown in different contexts, these constitutive elements of the capacity (and freedom) to choose involve self-discipline and certain kinds of imposed discipline. The imposed discipline is commonly known as coercion. As will be argued further at the end of this chapter, coercion (or at least a coercive body) is both a pre-requisite and an ongoing functional necessity for the freedom to choose: there is both a logical and an empirical connection between freedom and coercion, and freedom is never in fact 'complete'. Thus the conception of political freedom I am describing here is not a negative concept (or at least not only) but always presupposes (and then involves) some element of coercion.[35] An individual can be more or less free, and theory can distinguish between forms of coercion and how they relate to, impinge upon, or enhance individual freedom.

Now, if freedom and coercion are understood in this way, that is, *not as polar opposites*, it can be shown that the act of consent must also involve coercion, but *that any actual motivation to consent* may have little to do with coercion (or its alleged lack). The motivation to consent is dependent normally upon other institutional factors and evaluative power differentials. Conversely, the fact that we are able to dissent does not necessarily mean that where we do so we are free from coercion, whatever that could mean, or that power disparities are at a minimum.

Consent is created both in the state *and* within the institutions that make up the rest of society; that is, economic, educational, judicial, and leisure

---

[35] My conception of freedom and coercion, and how they are inter-related, is therefore quite distinct from two prevalent types of modern 'liberal' conceptions. On the one hand there are accounts inspired by Hobbes and J. S. Mill, for example those found in the work of theorists such as Hayek and Isaiah Berlin, and on the other there are approaches inspired by Kant, most clearly evident in the theories of Rawls and Habermas. But it is no coincidence that they both result in the same mistrust and misunderstanding of any form of coercion. See F. A. Hayek (ed.), *The Constitution of Liberty* (London: Routledge, 1960); A. Gamble, *Hayek: The Iron Cage of Liberty* (Cambridge: Polity Press, 1996); I. Berlin, *Four Essays on Liberty* (Oxford: Oxford University Press, 1969). Coercion is discussed fully in section 4 below and in chapter 4, section 2.

institutions, some of which are included by different authors under the concept 'civil society'. Moreover, the rights that Cohen and Arato claim are created and defended in 'civil society' are by definition always first granted by the state; that is, they would not exist, could not be granted, without the state and its coercive authority. The realities of how consent and rights are 'created' is clouded if the act of avowed consent and communicative discourse is identified with freedom, and universal rights are understood as the outcome of this communicatively free process. In arguing that 'civil society' is the arena of coercion-free interaction while failing to maintain a strict conceptual distinction between coercion and consent, Cohen and Arato ride roughshod over the institutional inter-relationships between coercion, consent and freedom. This lack of institutional focus and critique allows them to think of rights as logically and historically distinct from privileges, immunities, or estate-type liberties.[36] This is empirically false. As I argued in the main introduction, most of the rights that are now the *objective* property of political subjects that are *universally* equal (before the law) were once rights in the form of special privileges or liberties for property ownership and political participation. In line with mainstream liberal discourse, this mistake acts to legitimise and forge consent for the 'liberal' state: the accountability for the form and scope of rights and their consequences is removed from actual states, state forms, governments and political philosophies and situated in an ephemeral sphere of 'free' communicative interaction. Thus Cohen and Arato's main achievement is to create an illusory 'sphere' of freedom and rights that supports the hegemonic ideology of the liberal state.

Although the *aim* of much of the 'civil society' discourse is to conceptualise and enhance the power of citizens, or in other words, to engender the fair and efficient recognition, evaluation and satisfaction of needs, the concept of 'civil society' is self-defeating. It emerges out of two pivotal blocks to our critical understanding of contemporary political experience and action, that is, of the realities of freedom, coercion and necessity: (1) a conception of freedom reminiscent of the more libertarian quarters of liberal thought, where freedom and unfreedom are positioned at opposite sides of a categorical divide; and (2) a certain liberal ideology of formal equality and freedom that has become codified in terms of 'rights', a broad category that also includes powers and liberties that inhibit the attainment of a realistic *degree* of freedom. Consequently, 'civil society' actually reinforces institutions and practices that act counter to these goals. Thus it would not help simply to propose a more apt conceptualisation of freedom and rights that fine-tunes

---

[36] Cohen and Arato, *Civil Society*, p. 413.

the concept of 'civil society'. Like other theoretical concepts, the concept of 'civil society' is a kind of political act, inasmuch as it can (be made to) *actively* hide its own origins: 'civil society' is not only an outgrowth of a misconceived notion of freedom, it also obfuscates the source of its own inadequacy. Thus it is better to discard the concept completely.

2   PRACTICES, INSTITUTIONS, AND THE EVALUATION OF INSTITUTIONS

In what follows I develop an alternative framework for achieving the same goals without the idealised presuppositions about freedom and rights, and without the illusory garb of the concept of 'civil society'. It is a means of understanding more fully the existing practices, institutions and roles within and between which needs are generated, interpreted and satisfied. And as a consequence of this understanding it is intended as a practical intervention in two related senses. First, it is proposed as a means of engendering institutional changes that enhance the individuals' power over the generation and satisfaction of their needs. And, second, it aims to direct theoretical attention to these causally significant mechanisms. If modern political theory embraced political sociology and political economy and rejected the dominance of moral philosophy it might begin to grasp the significant causal mechanisms that exist between certain forms of oppression and particular institutions and practices. The alternative framework proposed here is an attempt to re-kindle that theoretical attraction, to provoke political economic analysis of the normatively significant practices, institutions and roles in the formation of needs. In other words, the aim is to create the conceptual framework for an approach to politics that relegates moral philosophy to its true position within rather than above or prior to the history of political and economic institutions: that prioritises politics, ethics and institutional history above abstract reason and individual morality. Thus, although this involves a practical evaluative interaction with actual need-claims, the point is not simply to criticise the needs themselves, or, worse, the agents themselves, but rather to understand (and then evaluate) causally and normatively the extant trajectory of need. The concepts of practice, institution and role serve two functions within this approach as a whole. They facilitate the understanding of how needs are generated and legitimated in contemporary society, and they engender imaginative forays into how the formative environment might be controlled and changed in order to create greater parity in the recognition and satisfaction of needs. The latter is particularly important since it focuses on the constant context-bound political question of needs: how to change the trajectory of need development in a manner that improves the evaluation of true interests.

Practices

The concept of 'practice' is a relatively ample concept, but a practice can be distinguished, on the one hand, from a social regularity and, on the other hand, from an institution. A social regularity is a pattern that a society merely exhibits, for example its murder rate, while a practice is something the individuals of a society actually *do*. Social regularities do not necessarily have to display any human intentionality, agency or concern with human goods. Practices definitely do: they are arrays of human activity that display aspects of these three elements and they do so in a more norm-governed fashion than mere social regularities. Thus, by 'practice' I mean something more complicated than the everyday understanding of the term as it is used for example to describe what I am doing when I practise the piano. Rather, what I mean by practice is the performing of an action that is part of a 'temporally unfolding' collection of linked 'doings and sayings',[37] which involve at least some degree of or relationship to human intentionality, agency and goods. Some examples are eating an evening meal together with friends and relatives, industrial practices like flexible specialisation, and rights-discourse or 'rights talk'.[38]

Practices are norm-governed human activities: they involve practical understanding and the following of rules. The disputed point in much 'practice theory' is the degree to which those involved in a practice (and its norms or rules) are conscious or self-conscious of what they are doing and of the norms that govern their action. More specifically, there is disagreement over the explicitness of rules,[39] and, concomitantly, over the exact nature and significance of intentionality, human agency, and a practice's internal good. I cannot directly address these issues here, but I maintain that the relative emphasis placed on these three is illuminating of a theorist's political stance. Typically conservative positions, for instance those taken by MacIntyre and Oakeshott, emphasise habit and tradition ahead of intentionality, and stress the significance and relevance of a practice's internal good. For example, MacIntyre thinks of practices in terms of internal standards of excellence

---

[37] T. R. Schatzki, *Social Practices: A Wittgensteinian Approach to Human Activity and The Social* (Cambridge: Cambridge University Press, 1996), pp. 89–90.

[38] For more on 'rights talk' as a social practice, see R. A. Primus, *The American Language of Rights* (Cambridge: Cambridge University Press, 1999), esp. pp. 28–32.

[39] See the various contributions in T. R. Schatzki, C. K. Knorr and E. von Savigny (eds), *The Practice Turn in Contemporary Theory* (London and New York: Routledge, 2001).

that constitute the pasts and presents of the practices. He uses the concept of practice to denote 'any coherent and complex form of socially established co-operative human activity through which *goods internal to that form of activity* are realised in the course of trying to achieve those standards of excellence which are appropriate to, and partially definitive of, that form of activity, with the result that human powers to achieve excellence, and human conceptions of the ends and goods involved, are systematically extended'.[40] My conception of practice is manifestly distinct from this kind of understanding in two fundamental ways. First, I maintain that because practices are forms of activity that involve practical understanding and explicit (or at least evident) goods they are characterised by a significant degree of intentionality and human agency. Second, I maintain that practices can be evaluated, i.e. there can be good or bad practices, but that the internal perspective, or the internal good, is only one of the possible perspectives or goods. Moreover, in evaluating the practice one cannot draw any normative consequences about the practice as a whole merely from the fact that it is good for somebody, or some particular group. National Socialism may have been good for some high-ranking Nazis (while it was able to maintain itself). In evaluating practices it is, therefore, important to make three different distinctions: (1) between internal and external goods; (2) between different internal goods, dependent on whose internal perspective one chooses; and (3) between what the participants think is good about the practice and what *is* good about it.[41] Some practices can, therefore, be shown to be indefensible no matter how well they are performed or how allegedly indispensable their internal good is for some people, while others should be condoned even if they are not (even could not be) performed and defended with finesse, beauty, exactitude and courage. I claim that a practice is evaluated best in terms of the following external goods: how it meets vital needs, develops agency needs, and facilitates the evaluation of true interests, and whether it aids the legitimisation of institutions that do or do not facilitate the achievement of these three goods. However, before

---

[40] MacIntyre, *After Virtue*, pp. 187–8 (my emphasis). See also MacIntyre, *Whose Justice? Which Rationality?* (London: Duckworth, 1988). He is most interested in practices such as chess, football and architecture. For M. Oakeshott's account see *Human Conduct* (Oxford: Clarendon Press, 1975); and *Rationalism in Politics and Other Essays* (Indianapolis: Liberty Press, 1991), especially 'The Tower of Babel'.

[41] MacIntyre does the opposite: he fails to discriminate between practices in abstraction from their actual performance, and he defines goods purely within the 'framework of practices, crafts and traditions'. E. Frazer and N. Lacey, 'MacIntyre, Feminism and the Concept of Practice', in J. Harton and S. Mendus (eds), *After MacIntyre: Critical Perspectives on the Work of Alasdair MacIntyre* (Cambridge: Polity Press, 1994), pp. 268, 274. See also D. Miller, 'Virtues, Practices and Justice', in ibid., pp. 250–1.

I can analyse the causal relationship between practices and institutions, I must give an account of institutions as distinct from practices.

Institutions

There has been a recent resurgent interest in the study of institutions, sometimes called 'new institutionalism', but most of it is characterised by a confusion.[42] Institutions have either been thought of very generally as 'stable, valued, recurring pattern[s] of behaviour',[43] or (restrictively) conceptualised in terms of concrete organisations.[44] The former is too vague and analytically unhelpful due to its all-encompassing character. And the latter creates an erroneous association. In organisations, action is directly and authoritatively prescribed through enforced rules and roles and in the light of specific outcomes.[45] Institutions, as I understand them, are not necessarily purposively driven in this sense and they have what could be called a 'reciprocal' and 'cyclical' relationship to social norms.[46] They reinforce extant social norms and concretise changes to social norms, affected by individual action; they are, therefore, both enabling and restricting. Here, 'institution' is understood as the stabilised outcome of the interplay between past practices, intentional action that is purposive towards specific institutional ends, unintended consequences of (intentionally) unrelated action, and societal discourses more generally.[47] Some examples of institutions are: groupings of rights, such as private property rights; rights-based institutions, like liberal constitutions; money; social security provision; political parties; the police force; markets, and market-based institutions such as the business firm; religion and particular religious institutions, for

---

[42] Goodin's introductory essay in R. Goodin (ed.), *The Theory of Institutional Design* (Cambridge: Cambridge University Press, 1998), pp. 1–20.

[43] S. P. Huntingdon, *Political Order in Changing Societies* (New Haven: Yale University Press, 1968), p. 12.

[44] Cf. C. Offe, 'Institutions in East European Transitions', in Goodin (ed.), *Institutional Design*, p. 203.

[45] Offe puts it as follows: 'The latter [organisations] . . . can and do actually subordinate (in accordance with Weber's notion of "purposive rationality") "duties" to (expected) "outcomes".' Ibid., p. 203.

[46] Ibid., p. 199.

[47] First, I am assuming for now that some kinds of entrenched discourses, especially the discourse of rights, can be legitimately categorised as kinds of institutions. At the very least, they can be said to be kinds of practices that give rise to particular institutions, for example rights-based institutions. Rights talk (and rights-discourse) is a practice that both reinforces and depends upon certain rights-based institutions. Second, besides the 'hegemonic' function I emphasise in the above definition, there is also the purposive element: that institutions (to survive) have to complete the missions set for them within the remit of extant resources. Offe, 'Institutions', p. 200. Goodin is simplifying somewhat when he says: 'After all, institutions are in essence just ossified past practices.' Goodin (ed.), *Institutional Design*, p. 10.

example the church; institutions of education, such as the school; and marriage. The reason some thinkers assimilate 'institution' and 'organisation' is precisely because some forms of institution appear in practice as concrete organisations, for instance a given school is simultaneously an organisation and an example of an institution of education. Different institutions display various degrees of rigidity, stability and possibility for change, but what is important is that they are understood as expressed above. In other words, institutions are the relatively contingent concrete outcome of past and present individual intentional action and belief, but the complex of extant institutions provides the overarching normative framework within which and between which actual individuals act – believe, need, decide, choose and want.

Institutions are distinguishable from practices in that they are more determinate along three axes. Their rules are more explicit, their structure is more formal, and their constitutive human activity is more obviously intentional. An institution's 'reciprocal' and 'cyclical' relationship to social norms provides more possibility for change than is the case with practices. Hence, it does not follow from the determinacy of institutions that institutions are necessarily more stable than practices. This is evidenced in the fact that the practice of eating an evening meal together with friends and relatives might be *more* stable than virtually any institution one can think of, for example the police force, which is only 200 years old, or the Windsor dynasty, which is only 300 years old. Although practices constitute the temporal and behavioural filling (the 'everydayness') between the more concrete institutions – they are the loci of everyday legitimation of extant forms of need interpretation – it is the more explicit, formal and intentional nature and consequences of institutions that make them significant elements in an evaluation of true interests. I will defend the claim that because institutions are more determinate than practices, they are more politically controllable (and therefore significant) than practices.

The evaluation of institutions

In theory, institutions can be evaluated in terms of their causal role within five different mechanisms that determine the meeting and developing of needs and the evaluation of true interests. First, they can be assessed in terms of their direct effects on meeting the particular vital needs and developing the agency needs of a society's individuals. This is especially relevant for those institutions that react to (or are designed to react to) need-claims, either indiscriminately or in a manner that is intended not to retard meeting or developing the needs of the claimant or those of other people. Classic examples of this category are institutions such as markets and market-related institutions, and various state institutions or educational arrangements which function either to meet or to develop needs. Second, institutions can be evaluated in the light of whether they tend directly to distort the evaluation of true interests by creating or reinforcing substitute gratification, the possibility effect, or the endowment effect. These effects must be evaluated in all the contexts stipulated in the previous chapter: the want-need dynamic; the articulation of need; and the recognition of need. As has already been discussed, a good example of this mechanism in contemporary industrial societies is found within institutions of production, for instance those of the automobile industry. Third, institutions can be evaluated in the light of their causal role in the legitimation of norms that tend to govern practices: if these norms legitimise practices that act counter to the perception and meeting of vital and agency needs, the relevant institutions can at least be labelled suspect. Recall from above that although institutions and practices have causally determinate relationships with social norms, institutions are less norm-governed and more explicitly determined by human intentionality and agency than practices. Hence, if the practices in question act counter to the perception and meeting of vital or agency needs and they are underpinned or (at least partially) legitimised by identifiable institutions, the institutions are suspect. For example, the institution of rights is suspect since it legitimises, amongst other things, the practice of inviolable legal safeguards for the inheritance of property and the patenting of medical drugs in the face of ineluctable need. There is much evidence to show that without these two practices many more vital and agency needs could be met than are met at present, not least of all the basic health needs of large swathes of the earth's human population. Fourth, institutions can be evaluated in terms of how they affect the balance of normative power in the everyday analysis of true interests. This can be undertaken in the direct manner identified above in the first and second means of evaluation or the more indirect manner of the third mechanism. This is the case because institutions, or configurations thereof, or the combined arrangement of institutions and practices, are significant determinants of the distribution of normative power within a society. For example, unless they are otherwise regulated, large business corporations accumulate massive normative power through the control and ownership of media institutions. Fifth, institutions can be evaluated with regard to the nature and distribution of roles they tend to 'naturalise'. (See section 3 below.)

All five mechanisms of evaluation are relevant in a full evaluative exercise. Furthermore, there will be at least three perspectives on the institution in question: the internal descriptions of the institution (of which there may be many); the idealised (normally official) internal perspective; and the external perspective. And they may be very different from one another even where and when the goals and consequences of the institution are blatantly opposed to the recognition and satisfaction of needs – for example, think of the varied interpretations of the institution of apartheid in South Africa. Needless to note, in this approach the first and the third of these perspectives are more significant than the second.

Institutional consequentialism

Consequentialism, as it has come to be understood, is the term for the view that all *actions* are right or wrong in virtue of the value of their consequences.[48] My need-based approach to political evaluation is consequentialist only if this emphasis on individual action is replaced by a wholesale focus on the effects and consequences of actions and institutions. Institutional consequentialism, as I call this kind of evaluation, assesses institutional outcomes (and some related practices and actions) in terms of their effects upon the objective human goods stipulated above – in terms of whether the institutions meet vital needs and develop agency needs, or at least affect either or both, or facilitate the evaluation of true interests by individuals. As a result, the evaluation proposed here is quite distinct from the two prevalent kinds of meta-ethical and practical processes of evaluation: utilitarianism and rights-based approaches.

Although utilitarianism is a kind of consequentialism, institutional consequentialism is distinct from utilitarianism in two fundamental and related ways. First, it does not emphasise one single evaluative criterion, be it pleasure, happiness, or desire, since it rests on the valuation of human functioning as determined by how well vital needs are met and the relative development of three equally important agency needs. Second, it does not aim to maximise the valued objectives. It is concerned with a kind of political (rather than moral) evaluation that takes the maximisation of agency needs and the evaluation of true interests to be the concern of individuals; it functions to evaluate (the provision of) the conditions for these and the rectification of imbalances in normative power in the everyday evaluation of true interests. The most important subset of conditions includes the meeting of vital needs.

---

[48] J. P. Griffin, 'Consequentialism', in T. Honderich (ed.), *The Oxford Companion to Philosophy* (Oxford: Oxford University Press, 1995), p. 154.

At the other extreme, institutional conseqentialism is sharply distinguished from rights-based approaches to evaluation in the various ways that have been adumbrated throughout. (1) Rights constitute a significant institutional structure that this approach argues must itself be evaluated. To make rights the basis of an evaluative structure is, therefore, to beg the question.[49] (2) Actual existing rights can and do distort the meeting of vital needs. (3) The historical and actual philosophical underpinnings of the notion of rights, which determine that rights are the property of human persons understood as jural agents, tend to blur the line between givens and claims. They blur this line (counterproductively) because they classify actually existing rights *and* ethical aspirations under one single 'naturalising' concept of right. This is especially true of developments in the last fifty years, where rights in the form of human rights are claimed irrespective of whether anything or anybody has responsibility or power to enforce them. Rights, as they are now understood, thereby simultaneously distort two things. First, they make a necessity out of an aspiration: they transform a political goal into a part of human nature, thereby unintentionally reducing the *political* significance of the goal. Second, they trivialise the real priority of necessity by giving vital needs and agency needs the same essential properties: both are reduced to the same inalienable properties of humans. Rights are, therefore, self-defeating: both of these erroneous moves are the consequence of a notion of agency that takes individual power to be at base an individual capacity, which is the individual's private, inalienable property.

The determinacy of institutions

The above-discussed five means of evaluating institutions may look relatively neat in theory, but are things as tidy in practice? Is there ever enough institutional determinacy for practical evaluation to be able to identify particular institutions as significant determining causes within these five mechanisms? Does the relative determinacy of institutions as against practices translate unproblematically into a politically significant determinacy?

Unfortunately, the answer to these questions as they stand is not straightforwardly positive. Some institutions are more determinate than others:

---

[49] The fact that our modern institution of rights arose (originally) as a consequence of a voluntarist defence of individual subjective right, in which right is seen as the property of the individual and therefore property is taken as the paradigmatic right, problematises their contemporary positive interpretation. This is the case because the contemporary language we employ to evaluate them often begs the evaluative question: it uses ideas and concepts to interpret (and even criticise) the present status quo, ideas and concepts that can be shown to have a significant causal role in legitimising the same status quo.

some have explicit rules, an identifiably formal structure, and a causally obvious intentional structure. For example, some state institutions with specific functions are of this kind. Other institutions are too causally protean in themselves to be determinate as such, for example some market-related institutions. In the case of identifiably determinate institutions, the above five means of evaluation can be applied directly. In the case of those institutions that display less causal determinacy, these five evaluative processes are complicated. However, they are still possible because the determinacy of an institution can be identified using means other than these five ahistorical and strictly causal means of evaluation. The first depends on the use of historical analysis and narrative to identify the institution's formative or originating practices and the reasons for its continued existence. It is an empirical historical fact that the character of any one extant institution can be traced to earlier practices (or at least earlier discourses, if you think the former cannot include the latter) alongside the influence of other institutions. Once the institution, its determinacy and its scope are identified all five evaluative mechanisms can be applied. Or, where this is still practically impossible, the natures of the determining practices can be evaluated in their historical context in at least the last three of the five ways stipulated above. This would involve an historical and conceptual account of the emergence of the practice (or collection of practices) concerned and its transformation into an institution. If either the original practice, the process of transformation, or the resultant institution were characterised by a tendency to multiply unmet needs, distort the perception of needs, or create biases in normative power or role naturalisation the institution can at least be earmarked as deserving of further analysis. It is unwise to rely only on historical evidence for that would be tantamount to performing the genetic fallacy – damning institution X in the light of the nature and conditions of its origins alone. For example, it would be like arguing that train transport is suspect because it was invented during the era of slavery.

This first means of identifying and labelling an institution can be reinforced by a second approach. This relates to an analysis of the actual functioning of an institution in terms of the roles it tends to naturalise. Institutions in any particular context tend to be characterised by, or give rise to, certain concrete and causally transparent organisations and associations. These organisations will tend to 'naturalise' certain empirical roles. If the naturalised roles prohibit some individuals from meeting and developing their needs and evaluating their true interests, the organisations are themselves counterproductive to these procedural goals. The combination of these two means of identifying the worth of a relatively causally indeterminate institution is sufficient to label that institution suspect and identify it as requiring further investigation along the lines of the original five means of evaluation.

3 ROLES: RECLAIMING THE CENSUS

My account of how the evaluation of institutions may require an analysis of the empirical roles occupied by the individuals in any given society is one reason why theory must take roles seriously. A more important and obvious reason is that the nature and distribution of roles *directly* influence the evaluation of true interests. This is the case for two reasons. First, it is from the individual that policy receives information concerning the evaluation of true interests, and individuals occupy different roles in society. An agent's evaluation of her true interests involves evaluation of particular needs and resources in terms of the requirement to meet and develop her vital and agency needs, but the *perspective* on these concerns will be determined by the individual's access to and position within the complex of societal roles. In other words, the substantive concerns that are constitutive of any evaluation are determined not only by institutions and practices but also by the nature and distribution of the society's roles. The second reason is that normative power is determined in some part by the roles individuals fill. And, as will be argued, the process of true interest evaluation requires constant intervention by the coercive authority with regard to the distribution of normative power. There is, therefore, a practical imperative to understand the extant matrices of roles in order to control and maintain the most proficient form of this kind of intervention.

By 'role' I mean something at the same time specific and general. In specific terms I see roles as the societally pre-given slots (or 'sites', to use a Foucauldian notion) into and within which individuals move, develop and are organised within the existing institutions and practices. The general sense in which I will use the term 'role' is the normative one which I introduced in chapter 1, section 4: a role is a position (or 'function') in society within which certain valuable social tasks are performed – for example, the roles of carer, householder, worker, citizen and their associated 'tasks'. They are valuable because they are 'meaningful' in either or both of the two senses discussed in chapter 1, section 4: they involve active and creative expression; work that requires active and creative expression; or work in which the occupant of the role is functionally significant, in the sense of having an indispensable role in a combined effort to produce goods and services which meet other people's valued needs.

The specific sense of roles as extant empirical slots or sites has been associated with inherently conservative modes of thought – for example, the woman's role within the household – but it can be rescued from this kind of formulation by thinking of roles in both senses at once. Roles are the sites that extant individuals occupy, and whose actual value can be assessed in terms of how they relate quantitatively and qualitatively to the more general (valued) positions that all individuals should be given the opportunity to fill. The actual roles are merely contingent sites, but ideally the provision of the possibility for filling the valued roles would provide each individual with a more all-encompassing view of society from which to evaluate needs and interests. That is, the greater the diversity of roles I fill, the greater the diversity of my experience of different needs and the greater my knowledge is of needs generally and their legitimating institutions and practices. Conversely, then, the less the diversity or richness of the roles I fill the more reduced my knowledge is of needs and legitimating institutions. Hence, any claims I make as to my true interests may omit a whole spectrum of my vital and (especially) agency needs. This occurs if my matrix of roles objectively restricts my perception of my agency needs to the extent that I do not invest time and effort into developing these needs or making claims related to their development.[50]

Allow me to clarify the relationship between roles and need perception and true interest evaluation. As discussed in chapter 2, it is an empirical fact that the experience of need is an important (though not necessary) means of acquiring knowledge and evaluative understanding of the need concerned. For example, if I have never been given the opportunity to work or my work has never been meaningful, I might have no significant 'knowledge' of the need for active and creative expression or my need for recognition and its link to this kind of expression. I may, therefore, under-value or even disregard these agency needs (or particular means to their development) when and if I am asked, say by local government, to state my needs and preferences. Needless to say, as was also argued in chapter 2, my interpretation of these needs might be distorted by a variety of different kinds of cognitive effect, some of which I may not be aware of. The same could hold for other variants of incomplete role-filling, for example the woman who is a carer and a citizen, but has never worked in the labour market; or the high-flying businessman who feels no need for recognition

---

[50] Obviously, there are certain things that governments and policy-makers have to do, like repress crime, that do not necessarily have to take into account the 'internal', in this case 'criminal', perspective – although this 'internal' perspective can be extremely helpful for the creation of policy aimed at *preventing* crime.

as a citizen or carer because of all the (distorted?) recognition he gets at work. The epistemological effects of incomplete role matrices are found not only when and where individuals display a complete non-awareness of these needs. Complete non-awareness is, in any case, quite unusual. These effects can even obtain when an individual feels acute frustration and self-awareness about her lack of normative power and the imbalance in normative power generally, but remains objectively restricted by the kinds of roles she occupies; roles, that is, that restrict her possibilities and choice relative to that of other individuals. This is the case for two related reasons. First, I may simply accept my fate of comparatively less normative power aided by various mechanisms that naturalise my condition. For example, as a member of the Dalit caste in the state of Bihar, India, I might be all too aware of how little power I have and even argue vehemently about how unfair it is, but so long as I keep believing that my position (or 'role') is God-given or determined by nature there seems little hope of my being able to escape it (under my own steam or that of any other agency). Second, since I can actually be, and feel as if I am being, recognised, act autonomously and express myself within a *restricted* set of roles, I might actually want to stay in the roles I occupy. This might continue to be the case even when I am aware of my comparatively small amount of normative power.

Given these existential conditions, what might be done to make the process of true interest analysis more practical and transformative? The goal is a mechanism through which individuals can be involved in a more or less constant way in identifying their needs and roles so that policy can use this information to constantly transform the configurations of institutions and roles in line with the requirements of meeting vital needs and developing agency needs. One possible method is through the use of a more elaborate and frequent census: one, that is, that does not focus on spurious and even dubious concerns such as identity and how long one has been out of work,[51] but that ascertains specific information on a number of important objective and subjective facts. The objective facts could include the following. (1) The roles one occupies and the kinds of freedom they allow. (2) The objective state of one's vital and agency need development, for example, the quality and quantity of one's food, exercise, participation in politics, and whether and under what conditions one is employed. (3) The means to the development and satisfaction of one's vital and agency needs, for example, one's income, dependants, capital, and significant personal

---

[51] These two issues were the main concern of the 2001 Census of Britain. The second was obviously for reasons related to fighting social security fraud and cross-referencing with other sources of information on unemployment and work-seekers. In Britain the census is only once every ten years.

property (such as a car or other means of mobility) and so on. (4) One's area of residence and type of accommodation. The subjective facts could include some or all of the following. (1) One's role preferences; that is, one's desired role matrices. (2) One's avowed particular vital and agency needs and preferences over the means of meeting them. (3) One's concerns and preferences over actual and possible need trajectories, as discussed in chapter 4, and one's concerns and opinions on past policy and its consequences.

This information could be used to draw a broad sketch of which kind of role matrices are generally associated with which kinds of objective conditions and which kinds of avowals and preferences over needs and need trajectories. The objective conditions give a broad outline of the kinds of institutions and practices that exist in certain areas and their relative significance on roles and the avowal of needs and preferences. This kind of information can only really be ascertained through an elaborate and frequent census, but it can be supplemented with more macro-level empirical analysis of the existing significant institutions and practices. Taken together, this information could be used to evaluate the way certain institutions generate and meet needs and naturalise roles along the lines of my five means of institutional evaluation: that is, in terms of their direct causal effects on meeting and perceiving vital and agency needs, on the evaluation of true interests, on the balance of normative power, and on role naturalisation (see section 2 above). Thereafter, all these empirical facts can be combined under conditions of evaluative participation, as discussed in chapter 4, and used in decisions over what institutional changes might transform both the manner in which needs are satisfied and the extant matrices of roles. As will be discussed further in chapter 4, this information would have to be made public in order that it become part of the knowledge individuals use in their participation in the evaluation of needs, institutions and need trajectories. But ultimately these decisions and changes would need to be legislatively enforced.

This kind of more elaborate and frequent census would provide policy with an important causal account of how role matrix Y of one or more subgroups affects the interpretation of everyday needs. The articulated needs, preferences and beliefs of a representative sample of individuals who fill role matrix Y as compared to those of individuals who fill matrix Z can be *evaluated* both in comparative and role-relative terms. Their needs and demands can be understood and then evaluated in the light of the roles they do in fact fill, the roles they could valuably fill and the condition of their vital and agency needs. Articulated concerns and demands can be analysed in the light of objective measurements of met vital need and subjective and objective analysis of agency need development. This is a true interest evaluation with the added objective criteria provided by analyses of the *source of the avowed interests*, where the source of the avowed interests is ascertained from the objective conditions of role occupancy and met need that are stipulated in the census.

I have highlighted incomplete role matrices within different extremes of material wealth and normative power because it is important to emphasise that this kind of census must not prioritise a set of avowed interests over another simply because they are those of an individual with a wider set of roles. I can fill a large selection of different roles, in the specific sense of societal sites, and yet they can all be instances of one or two kinds of valuable social roles in the general sense; for example, I may have a number of different roles but all of them might be instances of my role as a citizen, or a citizen and a worker. In this case, despite the breadth of my roles, my opinions and interests might either be skewed by a lack of connection to the needs of individuals who fill the other valuable social roles, or at least be somewhat non-representative of these individuals. Conversely, I might only fill a few specific roles and yet have experience of all the (general) valuable social roles. Consequently, the issue of role-relativity does not revolve around the number of roles alone, but also the nature of the roles concerned; and the nature of a role can be objectively evaluated itself in terms of how it relates empirically to the valued social roles and the meeting and developing of vital and agency needs. Therefore, a census for the evaluation of true interests must incorporate information that would be required for both a quantitative and a qualitative evaluation of role occupancy.

4 PRACTICAL REASON AND PRACTICAL IMPERATIVES

The emphasis on roles and a more elaborate and frequent census furnishes a means of overcoming Sen's relatively naïve intersubjectivity condition for the evaluation of true interests. Moreover, it does so in a way that actually undermines or at least complicates one of Sen's main assumptions: the notion of trans-positional objectivity. It rejects the claim that transpositionality actually achieves objectivity. What I mean depends upon a kind of scepticism about the extent and practicability of the notion of practical reason that is advanced at the level of theory. My claim is that until individual X is actually given the opportunity to 'escape' his extant role matrix, his set of post-evaluation true interests will be relative to that set of roles. And since 'escape' here does not entail an escape from roles entirely, but rather a move into more and different roles that provide more and different sites from which to feel needs and view interests, post-evaluation true interests will always be relative to a set of roles, however many roles one occupies. To argue that I can perform the counterfactual over concerns about my own set of needs and interests and thereby escape from my objective condition, and can thereby come to hold or feel the same set of interests as another person with a different set of roles, that is, objective conditions, is to forget the all-important defining characteristic of true interests. This is that my true interests are particular to an individual or group context in the here and now. This is ultimately dependent on the nature of need perception and the relationship between needs and true interests, as discussed in chapter 2. Hence, true interests may be reached trans-positionally and intersubjectively, but they may still not be universal to my society, let alone my world. This does not mean that they are never empirically universal: it is an empirical matter of fact that most people will claim that nuclear disarmament is in their own and everyone else's true interest. But it does mean that the idea of a veil of ignorance or ideal speech situation, behind or within which I might be able to step out of my roles, is manifestly unhelpful. The faith in value and condition neutrality of the individual and the state is a common failing of contemporary liberal theory. The account defended here is one of role-relativity and *degrees of increased objectivity*, but it remains an empirical fact that the more valued roles an individual fills, the easier it is for her to see the needs and claims of others from their point of view.

What are the implications of role-relative true interests for the theoretical understanding of the political significance of practical reason? There is a tendency amongst theorists to assume that the evaluation and satisfaction of needs can be accomplished through practical reason in the absence of coercion. In fact, the prevalent conception of practical reason excludes coercion because it understands this evaluative process in terms of voluntary individual action in the *moral* domain. It conceives of practical reason in purely individualised terms, as a series of small-scale interactions in which *individuals* use rational intelligence and insight to appraise their motivations and act practically in the world. This is linked to claims about responsibility and a mechanistic understanding of the separateness of persons; that is, that the only relevant causal elements are those related directly to an individual's choice and action. It is argued that without this understanding of individual, responsible practical reasoning we are in danger of losing an important aspect of being human: the self-respect that comes from knowing that some changes in the world around me come from my actions and my assessments of moral goods without the intervention of others and which are therefore attributable to me as separate from others.[52] However, this kind of approach, call it the moral conception of practical reason, fails to give enough weight to the preconditions for and constraints on individual practical reasoning.[53] The preconditions, means, goals and aspirations that are constitutive of practical reasoning are determined or heavily influenced by an array of institutions, practices and mechanisms.

These causal preconditions, constraints and interconnections are artificially removed from consideration because the predominant moral discourse finds value in a highly abstracted, moral notion of practical reason as sufficient condition for politics and political decision-making. In other words, practical reason, or the individual capability to critically compare, evaluate and rank alleged human goods and ends, is understood in abstraction from what this might involve, that is, an evaluation of the conditions and constraints of practical reasoning, for example, human needs and extant institutions, practices and types of coercion. Moreover, analysis of the existing conditions would leave the theorist of practical reason in no doubt that no amount of practical reason alone will achieve the goals envisaged by its proponents. Practical reason will not be the outcome nor will it alone be sufficient to transform a distorting institution. This is the case because our individual reasoned actions are determined in part by actual conditions – material and coercive constraints and possibilities and the interventions of others – and our individual reasoned actions alone are never sufficient to bring about changes in the world. Thus there are a number of components missing from the moral conception of practical reason.

I propose a broader conception of practical reason that moves beyond the moral conception while retaining its basic element: the critical comparison, evaluation and ranking of alleged human goods and ends. An institutional consequentialism of the kind proposed here will ultimately have to be able to justify its evaluation in terms of these goods and ends; in other words, in terms of how it enhances individuals' abilities in the evaluation and ranking of human goods and ends. That is to say, its main goal is the general enhancement of the practical reason of individuals within any given

---

[52] H. L. A. Hart and A. M. Honoré, *Causation in Law* (Oxford: Clarendon Press, 1985), p. lxxx, cited in K. Graham, *Practical Reasoning in a Social World: How we act together* (Cambridge: Cambridge University Press, 2002), p. 185; see also O. O'Neill, *Constructions of Reason: Explorations of Kant's Practical Philosophy* (Cambridge: Cambridge University Press, 1989); O'Neill, *Towards Justice and Virtue: A constructive account of practical reasoning* (Cambridge: Cambridge University Press, 1996); O'Neill, 'Four models of practical reasoning', in *Bounds of Justice* (Cambridge: Cambridge University Press, 2000), pp. 11–28.

[53] Graham, *Practical Reasoning*.

society. However, it can only achieve this in a way that undermines the claim that practical reason can ensure these goals obtain. This is the case for two reasons. The first is concerned with the practical imperative for the existence of a coercive authority. My account of institutional consequentialism coupled with the census is a procedural means of evaluating true interests that avoids the politically unrealistic assumptions concerning attention to individuals evident both in my original analysis of true interests and in Sen's approach. Communitarians may argue that a desirable level of attention to individuals and their needs is foreseeably accomplishable only within small self-regulating communities, but as I have argued their ideals are both utopian and conservative; that is, they are potentially counterproductive to meeting and developing diverse needs.[54] Now, as has been argued, the main aim of this census-based institutional consequentialism is to propose certain institutional changes where and when they are necessary to improve the conditions under which true interests are evaluated – in other words, to enhance practical reason in the evaluation of true interests. In theory this sort of critique does not necessarily require the scrapping of the suspect institutions but in criticising them its main goal is to persuade the individuals who defend or practise the practices, defend or constitute the institutions (and those that are affected by either or both) to re-orient those with which they are concerned. However, acting on this criticism in practice often will demand the use of a coercive authority. This is the case because suspect institutions often legitimate some highly cherished beliefs, attitudes, needs and roles; and, consequently, consensus over whether (let alone how) to transform the institutions will be achieved only in exceptional cases. Moreover, the kind of force required to elicit the information required in a census might be impossible without the authority of the state.[55] The second reason is that the moral conception of practical reason seems to assume that there is a single endpoint of reason, achievable

[54] An efficient census does not necessarily require a reduction in the sizes of communities or states; in fact it would probably become otiose within small communities. This is important because whatever communitarian thinkers argue we might gain from reducing the size of our political communities will be lost by an increase in the informal rigidity and control that is normally concomitant with a decrease in size. As I argue in my '"Civil Society": Critique and Alternative', and about which I say a little more below (chapter 4, section 7), ideally the coercive authority must coerce an area and group of people large enough and diverse enough to encourage diversity, experiment and change, and small enough for it to be able to be responsive to legitimate avowed needs and interests. However, the actual size can only be decided in context and only once the need-based institutions of participation are in place, which is the case in no existing state. Political theorists must think about how to secure these institutions rather than stipulate from afar the preferred size or demographic make-up of political communities.

[55] In practice this kind of intervention might be abhorrent to some groups in modern liberal societies, despite the fact that it is not unlike the 'intrusion' by the state for reasons of tax collection. An

once and for all. My approach to the evaluation of true interests understands the substantive criteria for any particular contextual evaluation, the particular needs and extant institutions and roles, as being in a state of continual flux. Therefore, the resources, powers and criteria for the ranking of contextual goods, as required by the individual in the constant process of true interest evaluation, will themselves be in constant flux. Obviously, the requirements and objectives instantiated in the general vital and agency needs are criteria that stand above context, but they can be misinterpreted on the ground, both by individuals and by the coercive authority.

It is, therefore, a logical conclusion of this account of true interest evaluation that practical reason alone will not engender the enhanced meeting of needs and the evaluation of true interests unless an entity exists that can *constantly enforce* changes to institutions and role matrices that act counter to these goals. As will be argued below, the only authority that has the *potential* to meet these demands is the modern state. This is the case for two reasons. (1) The modern state is the only existing institution, or collection of institutions and practices, that monopolises legitimate coercion; that is, the modern state is a unique institutional association of rule. (2) The reach and extent of the functions of the modern state display important need evaluative *potentials*, given some important functional and participative adjustments. The modern state is *potentially* able to do two things that require coercion and over which any single government can display degrees of authority. First, it must take the role of ultimate evaluator of institutions and role matrices in order to be able legitimately to transform those institutions and roles that directly or indirectly distort agents' perceptions of true interests. In other words, it must perform the five institution-related evaluative procedures stipulated above. Second, it must evaluate institutions and role matrices in line with the constant requirement to satisfy post-evaluation needs. It has to meet certain objective criteria as regards the evaluation of needs that provide constant means of improving individual practical reason, or in other words individual assessment of true interests.

individual's income, savings and inheritance would have to be taken into consideration as one among many objective criteria in the census, in terms of which her avowed needs, preferences and interests are evaluated. However, this kind of information would only be used to judge the relative weight need-claims deserve; it would not be used to police other aspects of agents' lives. Cf. Robert Nozick, *Anarchy, State and Utopia* (Oxford: Basil Blackwell, 1975). For more on these issues and the subject of paternalism, see chapter 4, section 6.

CHAPTER 4

The state of needs

In this chapter I argue that given modern conditions of politics a coercive authority is a *sine qua non* in the evaluation and meeting of needs as proposed in this political philosophy of needs. I argue that the modern state has the *potential* to be this authority but only if it institutionalises successfully a particular kind of need-based and institution-directed dynamic approach to constant transformation. This kind of political authority would instantiate the sort of need-disclosing procedures and goals outlined here, and constantly transform itself in line with these procedures and goals. I call this kind of transforming, need-disclosing authority a 'state of needs'. Were a modern state to become a state of needs it would become a radically new kind of political authority. This is the case because some of the need-disclosing procedures and goals, for example individual participation in the everyday evaluation of needs and institutions, require fundamental transformations, as will be discussed below. I propose an understanding of this radically new form of coercive authority, the state of needs, in terms of the disclosure, evaluation and transformation of needs, true interests, institutions and need trajectories. Recall that need trajectories are the various different actual and possible paths or trajectories down which the development of needs can progress.

The state of needs would be a constant participant in the disclosure and evaluation of needs, interests, institutions and need trajectories *and* simultaneously the agency that ultimately decides when and how to act on the extant information in order to transform institutions and role matrices, choose trajectories, prioritise needs, and allocate resources in line with these choices and priorities. Although the individual is the final court of appeal in any particular evaluation of true interests, the state of needs ultimately decides and coerces institutional changes, need trajectory choices, and need priority. But the state of needs only chooses need trajectories and controls institutions legitimately given certain participative procedural requirements, which are safeguarded. That is, the procedures of need trajectory evaluation, which involves the prioritisation of need and the transformation of institutions and roles, are only legitimately undertaken once citizens enjoy specified kinds of participative control over the state's functions.

Thus, following a discussion of the modern state and coercion, I stipulate procedural means to improve political participation through the constant transformation of institutions that act against individual participation in the evaluation of true interests. I provide a short *speculative* institutional proposal for how citizens might more efficiently communicate their interests and choices concerning need trajectories to the state, and how they might evaluate their state's actual and potential need-based and institution-directed mechanisms of analysis and transformation. Finally, I defend the claim that these aspects of the state of needs' function problematise the contemporary theoretical understanding of state legitimacy and paternalism, and that my understanding of need sheds new light on these issues.

I   THE STATE

Why do the evaluation, prioritisation and meeting of needs require the constant presence of a single coercive authority? What is coercion and how does it relate to power? What kind of participative control over the state's functions will ensure constant improvements in extant institutions and roles? What is the relationship between a state's authority and the evaluation and satisfaction of needs and true interests? How might this aspect of a state's function be improved? To answer these questions, a prior question must be addressed first: What is the state? Here I say something about the concept of the state, its origins and its modern form and conception. I analyse the idea of the state, draw on Hobbes' account of the necessity for a state, and focus on Weber's account of the actually functioning 'modern state'. I argue that although Weber's analysis rests on a relatively crude conception of coercion and power, it identifies why the modern state is the only institutional structure that has the *potential* to achieve legitimately the goals of evaluating needs and transforming roles and institutions.

In pursuing this argument I do not claim that the present state form, or any existing state, does or is able to evaluate and meet needs as proposed here; my claim is that the modern state has the *potential* to do so *if and only if* it is changed in the manner stipulated here. All existing modern states fall way short of the mark of instantiating the sort of need-disclosing procedures and goals that would characterise states of needs. Hence my distinction between actual states and what I call states of needs. However, despite this fact concerning modern states and despite my distinction, modern states and their histories are important for an understanding of states of needs. This is the case because a state of needs is not a single ideal state or state form, but rather a constantly evolving locus of rule and evaluation that necessarily must develop out of the modern state. Thus this account of the state of needs understood as an 'ideal' coercive authority rests on an understanding of existing states, or state forms. The relation between an ideal state and existing states is fraught with ambiguities. This is no reason to avoid it, however; rather the opposite. This relation between the ideal and the actual is an instance of a common problem concerning the relation between philosophy and history, or between ideal theory and empirical social science, which theorists tend to avoid at their peril.[1] As will become clear, any conception of an ideal coercive authority, and particularly any practical proposal for it to obtain, is necessarily linked conceptually, ethically and even causally to the contemporary form of final coercive authority – the idea of the state, its intellectual history, and actually existing states and their ideological and material histories. Residual ambiguities may remain but that is not necessarily a bad thing.

The concept of the state

The use of the concept 'state' – and its vernacular cognates such as *stato, état, Staat, estado* – in a recognisably modern form came to the fore gradually and only in the *relatively recent* historical past. As Skinner has shown, the term only begins to be used in an abstract way to describe an impersonal form of political authority located in an entity distinct from both rulers and ruled in the late sixteenth and early seventeenth centuries.[2] It is only at this point, due to various social, historical and ideological changes, that the state begins to be understood and conceptualised as separate from both the officials entrusted to exercise its powers, and from the society (or community) over which its powers are exercised. Needless to say, the institutional and conceptual break from older kinds of political association and structures of authority was not a straightforward or clean one. Skinner shows that from the early thirteenth-century Italian Renaissance writers through to Hobbes in the middle of the seventeenth century, there were

---

[1] B. Williams, *Truth and Truthfulness* (Princeton: Princeton University Press, 2002); Williams, 'Why Philosophy Needs History', *London Review of Books* 24. 2 (17 October 2002), pp. 7–9; R. Geuss, *History and Illusion in Politics* (Cambridge: Cambridge University Press, 2001).
[2] Q. Skinner, 'The State', in T. Ball, J. Farr and R. L. Hanson (eds.), *Political Innovation and Conceptual Change* (Cambridge: Cambridge University Press, 1989).

three strands of thought that analysed civil authority in terms different from those that were common within the conceptual apparatus inherited from the ancient and medieval worlds.[3] First, early republican thinkers thought of the state and its institutions as separate from the actual person (or persons, officials) who filled them, and therefore that the state and its property were not their property, but they equated the power of the state with the power of the people that constituted the community. Second, the theorists of divine right did not differentiate between the person (the King and his property) and the state, but argued that the state (the King) and its (his) God-given power and authority formed an entity distinct from the people and their powers and rights. Finally, in the tradition of natural-law absolutism, the state was not only conceptualised as separate from the persons that exercised its powers for a limited period of time, but also understood as an entity that was both phenomenologically and metaphysically separate from the people. Hobbes is the main figure in this third trajectory of thought because he was the most assured and clear about these two kinds of separation, especially in his *Leviathan*. The idea of this famous work is that the figure of the Leviathan is an 'artificial man' that embodies the power and authority of the state, and that the legitimacy of its authority is not conferred by constant consent of the people but by a series of original (hypothetical) contracts that (allegedly) explain our escape from the state of nature.[4] Given that the state of nature is not an actual historical period out of which states have developed but rather the state or condition of existence outside of a state – a state of war of all against all brought on by uncertainty and fear – Hobbes provides a justification for the necessity of the state. His is not an argument about the legitimacy of kinds of states or forms of government but rather an argument for the necessity of state authority, for without the security provided by the authority of the state individuals would have trouble meeting even their most vital needs. In developing this argument,

---

[3] It is a very important (and often forgotten) fact that the ancient and medieval worlds did not have an equivalent term for, or concept of, the state. (The Greeks talked about the πόλις, which had the inherent goal of allowing humans to live the best life possible for them.) This is important for two reasons. First, the fact that there was no single term to describe what we call 'the state' does not indicate simply that conditions were different, but also that this affected the kinds of questions ancient philosophers could ask. Second, the transposition of ancient and medieval ideas into our own time is best tempered by (at least) an acknowledgement of this difference in conditions and its effects on theorisation. (The use of the term 'state' in translation of these texts does not help matters, but because concepts are so flexible, nothing stops us from extending their use backwards.) An acknowledgement of these differences and historical antecedents may create greater clarity in analysis of authority and legitimacy in the modern world and their connection to how earlier thinkers were restricted or enabled by the existence or non-existence of this concept.

[4] T. Hobbes, *Leviathan*, ed. R. Tuck (Cambridge: Cambridge University Press, 1991), esp. chs 13–22.

Hobbes crystallises and emphasises two other aspects of the state that have remained significant for the nature of the modern state: its impersonality and its abstract nature. These have reappeared ever since in discussions over the justification and personality of the state.

The modern state

The relative 'modernity' of the concept of the state and the distinctive means of conceptualising the 'separateness' of the state are important for a number of reasons, but I will focus on two: the need within political associations of a certain level of development and size for a separate coercive authority; and the related issue of how the state's coercive authority *relates* to the evaluation and satisfaction of needs.

Amongst modern theorists of the state, it is Weber who is most helpful in understanding especially the first issue. Needless to say, when Weber speaks of the 'modern state' he is talking about the state (in historical and analytical terms) at the turn of the twentieth century. Weber's definition is functional, in the sense that he defines the state as 'that human community which (*successfully*) lays claim to the *monopoly of legitimate physical violence* within a certain territory, this "territory" being another of the defining characteristics of the state'.[5] It is functional because the state is simply that modern institutional arrangement that has successfully gained control over the threat and use of violence. The modern state is defined by the fact that it, and it alone, can legitimately use physical violence. More exactly, although the use of violence by the state is always present as a real possibility and its threat is therefore often more important than any actual use or display of force, its actual use is the final resort or '*ultima ratio*'.[6] In other words, the *ultima ratio* is a precarious political achievement, nothing more nothing less.

Weber goes on to add two more conditions that a state must satisfy to be a state. The first of these, that is, the second of Weber's three conditions, is touched on at the end of the above quote from Weber: that the state has jurisdiction over a specified geographic area and is only a state if it actually monopolises the legitimate use of violence throughout the specified area.

---

[5] M. Weber, 'The Profession and Vocation of Politics', in *Weber: Political Writings*, ed. P. Lassman and R. Spiers (Cambridge: Cambridge University Press, 1994), pp. 310–11; Weber, *Economy and Society*, ed. G. Roth and C. Wittich (Berkeley: University of California Press, 1978), esp. vol. 1, part I, Ch. i, 1–17 (pp. 54–5 for quote).

[6] Weber, *Economy and Society*, p. 54. Weber is well aware from the start that every state has a tendency to replace the direct use of violence with appeals to legitimacy.

Hence, under Weber's definition, the contemporary Colombian state is not in fact a state since it does not successfully monopolise the legitimate use of violence in all of its territory – at the time of writing, the *Fuerzas Armadas Revolucionarios de Colombia* (FARC) successfully carry out this function within large tracts of Colombia's territory. Weber's third condition is that the rules that constitute the order of the state are *imposed* on all the members of a designated area or populace, for example all those that reside in or enter the specified geographic area. Adherence to the rules of a state is *not* voluntary. If I enter Colombia (or at least that part of Colombia that is controlled by the Colombian state) I am under the jurisdiction of the Colombian state, and I cannot simply decide to adhere to the rules or demands of the United States of America. Similarly, I cannot simply decide to construct my own *independent political* association with its own set of rules within the territorial confines of the British state. These three conditions are actual conditions for modern statehood, and the final condition is particularly important because it shows clearly the inappropriateness of the prevailing current of 'contract theories'. States are not and are not intended to be voluntary associations.[7] Hence, the attempts to legitimise the state by reference to assent, consent, or its negative form, dissent, are at least misguided and at worst illusory.

Weber's analysis is important because he manages to give an account of the modern state as a separate entity, in both senses discussed above, *without* any initial reference to the legitimacy of the state. And he does not rely on dubious metaphysical claims about the teleology of history or human spirit, as is the case, for example, in Hegel's account of the state. This does not of course mean that the state does not need to be legitimate in more elaborate senses or that actual states do not in fact constantly attempt to legitimise themselves. Nor, of course, does it mean that any single specified state is not, therefore, the executive arm of its own ruling class. The latter could (and often is) an empirical fact even when and where the two kinds of separation exist. This is Marx's well-known and important insight. Drives to legitimacy may often be the result of concerns over elite power, as well as the distribution of normative power. Moreover, states can and do exist even when they are not legitimate in any more elaborate sense of the term legitimate. The issue concerning (internal) legitimacy revolves around how the state moves from being in the position of constantly having to use physical violence to existing on its threat alone. (See section 6 below for an account of legitimacy and its different forms.) But, as I see it here,

---

[7] See Dunn, *The Cunning of Unreason: Making Sense of Politics* (London: HarperCollins, 2000), ch. 2.

political associations move beyond being associations to being states when the means to ensuring that people follow the rules of the said association are in the hands of a separate entity that has the monopoly of the use of physical violence. This is Weber's definition, but its origins reach back to Hobbes. The need for an ultimate coercive force is not only necessary in the basic Hobbesian sense, that is, for setting the rules, without which we would tear each other to pieces every time we tried to make a decision (i.e. for reasons of personal survival and security). It is also ultimately the condition for us to be able to follow the rules. As Hobbes shows, it only becomes prudential for me to follow the rules when there is a coercive force in place to ensure that I will not be alone in doing so.

2   THE MODERN STATE, COERCION, AND POWER

In general terms, then, the modern state is an institutional association of rule that is separate from the rulers and the ruled. It, therefore, has its own identity above and beyond those particular elements that constitute the rulers and the ruled. There are a number of important and interesting issues that surround the identity and personality of the modern state – whether it is a corporation (Maitland),[8] or the apotheosis of human spirit (Hegel), or even the managerial elite of one class (Proudhon and Marx) – which I will not tackle here. However, I will argue that the nature and function of the modern state are best understood in the light of the fact that the modern state has the potential to be the state of needs; that is, the site of ultimate coercive authority whose main function and aim is to constantly transform institutions and roles in line with two ever-shifting objectives: the correct evaluation of true interests and the meeting of valued human needs. It does not follow from this that some actually existing modern states achieve 'state of needs' status. The opposite is in fact true. Most actually existing states are nowhere near achieving this goal, and there exists a great deal of variety in attention to needs amongst the large number of extant states. Some states are quite proficient in their disclosure and attention to needs, but this is often for reasons of contingent historical advantage and relative power over markets rather than evidence of their becoming states of needs; while other states are simply pure sites of domination.[9] Yet, however abstract or theoretical it remains, the development and satisfaction of needs

---

[8] D. Runciman, *Pluralism and the Personality of the State* (Cambridge: Cambridge University Press, 1997); and 'Is the State a Corporation?', *Government and Opposition*, 35. 1 (2000), pp. 90–104.

[9] As Dunn claims, states such as contemporary Myanmar 'approximate closely to pure structures of domination'. Dunn, *The Cunning of Unreason*, p. 78.

is fundamental to the form and function of modern states. A clear grasp of coercion provides a means of understanding why this is the case, and thus illuminates related concerns in the state of needs.

Why, it might be asked, do humans associated within large modern states need an external coercive authority? To answer this it is important to be clear about what a coercive authority might be, and in order to do that it is helpful to look more closely at coercion itself. Coercion is distinct from violence and power. Violence is normally descriptive of human action and does not have a significant relation to the 'teleological dimension of human action';[10] that is, it has little to do with the achievement of any particular end. Coercion is different on both counts. It is concerned with doing something, with the actual achieving rather than the 'how' of the doing, and it directly relates to achieving some specific end. We normally speak of 'X coercing Y to do Q'. This can be accomplished in various ways: journalists, political scientists and philosophers most often highlight direct force, terror tactics, or deception.[11] But coercion can occur without violence or direct deception: X can coerce Y to do Q without resorting to these kinds of acts. For example, I may be coerced into buying a fuel-inefficient car if the available options do not include fuel-efficient cars. It might not be in the interest of producers to produce smaller, more fuel-efficient, cars, in which case this kind of car simply is not an object of choice: it is not produced so it does not exist.[12] However, it could not reasonably be claimed that the producers were acting violently in coercing me in this manner. At its most abstract, to be coerced is normally understood as meaning to be left with no alternative but Q. On the ground, though, being 'left with no alternative but Q' normally amounts to being 'left with no *reasonable* alternative but Q'. Hence, one could claim that I do have an alternative to a fuel-inefficient car, I can assemble one myself or import one from somewhere that produces them. But, of course, if none of these are 'reasonable alternatives' I am in fact being coerced without any need for or use of violence or deception. What will count as 'reasonable' will depend on circumstance and one elaborate way of controlling the individuals within a society is achieved by changing what they consider to be 'reasonable' alternatives.[13]

Power is distinct from coercion mainly in that it is at once more general and more focused: it relates to the ability to achieve desired ends, be they

[10] Geuss, *History and Illusion in Politics*, p. 21.
[11] O. O'Neill, 'Which are the offers **you** can't refuse?', in *Bounds of Justice* (Cambridge: Cambridge University Press, 2000), pp. 81–96.
[12] For a case in point (General Motors) and an analysis of its ramifications, see R. Dahl's discussion, in *A Preface to Economic Democracy* (Cambridge: Polity Press, 1985).
[13] Geuss, *History and Illusion in Politics*, p. 22.

general human ends or particular individual goals, within relations of power. The common tendency to think about power in terms of the individual ability to get what one *wants* whatever the obstacles is evident in Weber's analysis.[14] This is misconceived because in laying importance simply on 'getting what one wants' it under-emphasises the relational aspect of power *and* presupposes that individuals involved in a relation of power have fixed and well-articulated wants and preferences. Moreover, it makes the mistake of assuming that their initial preferences will be the same as their all-things-considered preferences in the light of more knowledge about needs in general and within an evaluation of true interest. In the real world, my power to do, achieve or have something will depend on whether it is available, whether it is deemed a valued goal or thing in my society, and on my position in the normative power relations. And these variables are determined by the configuration of practices, institutions and roles.

Power relations and coercive action are pervasive within and between human practices, institutions and roles. And I have argued that coercion necessarily involves human goods and ends because it always has a significant focus on the teleology of human action. Two things follow from the conjunction of these two facts, two things that large tracts of modern political philosophy have neglected. This is especially true of anarchist, communitarian and some liberal positions, which assume that coercion is inherently evil or at least conclude that it is best avoided. First, it is important to start from the fact that power relations and coercive acts are pervasive in modern societies and then to think about the nature of coercion and its control within this context and in terms of specified human goods. I argued that in practice 'X coercing Y to do Q' normally amounts to the leaving of X with no reasonable alternative but Q, and what will count as 'reasonable' will depend on circumstances. Now, the 'circumstances' are the existing institutions, roles and normative power relations that configure the relational power of individuals. Hence, the exercise of coercion is infused by the relational sense of power: power is distinct from coercion, but one can have more or less power to coerce another dependent on a number of variables. Coercion is normally exercised between agents of one form or another, but the power to coerce is not dependent on individual will, strength or guile (or at least not only), but rather on the nature and distribution of normative power and the configuration of roles and institutions. Coercion may operate on the will but it is most successful when the will in question

---

[14] Weber defines power as 'the probability that one actor within a social relationship will be in a position to carry out his own will despite resistance, regardless of the basis on which this probability rests'. Weber, *Economy and Society*, vol. 1, part I, Ch. i, 16, p. 53.

has no other reasonable options beyond the one proposed and when extant norms and power relations legitimise the proposed option or position of the coerced.[15] For example, someone might be able legitmately to coerce me to take a certain job (rather than no job) within the context of the actual criterion of legitimacy, in this case the capitalist wage bargain, but this is only because the contextual normative power relations and institutional configurations legitimise that criterion. My coercer might find that ruled out, illegitimate, were he normatively weaker than me or under distinct normative criteria, power relations and institutions. There is, therefore, a practical imperative to ensure that existing institutions and roles do not foreclose on what is 'reasonable' and that individuals have increased control over the analysis of the criteria of reasonableness and the circumstances themselves. This is achievable via analysis and control of the extant *trajectory of need* and its institutional determinants, for which coercion is an inescapable necessity.

The second thing that follows from the nature of coercion and the pervasiveness of power and coercion is that there is, therefore, a requirement for an ultimate coercive authority to control the pervasive powers and coercions (i.e. coercers) in the light of human goods and under the control of those for whom the goods are goods. More specifically and in terms of my account of the formation and evaluation of need, there is a constant imperative to evaluate between the effects of institutions and roles and if necessary legislate to transform the offending institutions. This is the case because institutions and role matrices, which may be affected by biased normative power differentials, directly or indirectly distort agents' perceptions of true interests. The exercise of everyday coercion is dependent on power relations in general, and normative power relations in particular, and the procedure of true interest evaluation demands the constant rectification of biases in normative power relations. Since normative power disparities are givens at any point in time, there is a requirement for an authority to take account of these power biases in the evaluative process. Moreover, this authority must be sufficiently powerful to be able to take responsibility for the outcomes of these evaluative processes. These kinds of interventions are accomplishable ultimately only through the use of legitimate coercion, which is unique to the modern state. A state's legitimacy is based on authority. The link between legitimacy and various kinds of authority, ultimately in the light of this account of need, will be developed in section 6 below; but for the sake of the argument here note that one important kind of state authority comes

---

[15] Cf. O'Neill, 'Which are the offers **you** can't refuse?', pp. 89ff.

from the fact that it is that unique authority that has the coercive power to transform institutions and roles in line with meeting and developing vital and agency needs. More exactly, it has the *potential* to be that agency that acts to create and implement rules and transform institutions and roles that guide and legitimise human action in line with these need-based goals. Since rules will always be directly connected to the teleology of individual action in context, they need to be informed and legitimised by an account of significant particular needs and their causally significant institutions, practices and roles. Hence, if the state were able legitimately to guide (i.e. create rules conducting) teleological human action it would need to have the ability to assess the value of specified human institutions and actions in terms of actual felt and avowed needs and more general vital and agency needs. In other words, to be the ultimate coercive authority, the state of needs would have to display a degree of competence in the collation and use of information for this task. If it is unable to achieve this performative task it is in danger of being reduced to simply another power within a field of powers.

In sum, then, coercion is pervasive within any structure of power relations; in other words, existing institutions, practices and roles are necessarily constituted by coercion. Given this, there is a practical imperative for an ultimate coercive authority like the state of needs to regulate the extant differentials in the power to coerce in order to engender correct evaluations of true interests. Moreover, as was discussed in the previous chapter, the reality of the evaluation of needs and need-claims is a state of constant political conflict: discursive agreement over which roles and institutions are to be transformed, or even how to go about this transformation, is the exception rather than the rule. This is the case because the evaluation of true interests is ultimately an evaluation of extant felt needs and (possibly) cherished institutions and roles, all in the context of normative power differentials. The coercive authority of the state is a necessary condition for the evaluation and meeting of needs in the face of this constant conflict, but it can only act as legitimate ultimate evaluator if it institutionalises the evaluation of true interests as proposed here rather than through paternalist practices and institutions that either are unable to recognise actually avowed needs or simply disregard them.[16] In the remaining sections I give a speculative account of the state of needs in terms of its function as the ultimate evaluator and guarantor for meeting needs.

---

[16] This does not mean that the particular government concerned 'should' not have recourse to 'expert' opinion over issues that relate to vital and agency needs. But the reality is that there is sometimes just as little chance of agreement in these quarters as there is amongst the preferences of the general populace over needs, institutions and roles. Here I only point out this large problematic area.

3   THE STATE AS ULTIMATE EVALUATOR AND GUARANTOR
FOR MEETING NEEDS

Despite the fact that Weber understands individual power as one's ability to realise one's will even against opposition no matter what the ability depends on, his account of the nature of the modern state brings to light the connection between coercion, the modern state and its involuntariness. The idea that because the modern state involves and requires coercion it must be formed voluntarily (allegedly because we would only voluntarily impose such a thing as coercion upon ourselves) misses two important insights: membership of a modern state is *de facto* not voluntary; and coercion is a necessary antecedent for co-ordinated human action. That coercion is a necessary antecedent or precondition for co-ordinated human action is true even of strict co-ordination, such as is evident in the rules of the road and their enforcement. But it is most obvious in terms of having co-ordinated communal control over the generation and satisfaction of needs, or at least the general trajectory of that dynamic. As I have argued, because human action is always teleological at some level, the decisions about what to coerce people to do must ultimately return to questions of vital and agency needs, that is, to the *ends* of human actions. This is important because it is only on this understanding that the necessary act of state coercion ('necessary' in Hobbes' terms) can be conceived in line with the above full account of coercion: the activity of directing human action by improving or restraining choice or removing or delegitimising (i.e. rendering unreasonable) available alternatives in the light of certain specified means and normative goals.

In more specific and procedural terms, the goals and means that require the use of the state's authority point to a four-fold function for the state of needs that evolves constantly over time. (1) It must evaluate institutions in line with my earlier account of census-based institutional consequentialism (chapter 3, sections 2 and 3) and with the goal of improving the evaluation of true interests. (2) It must use its coercive authority to transform role matrices and ensure that vital needs are met, both in line with the goal of improving participant control over the evaluation of institutions and interests. (3) It must also evaluate and reform institutions that act against the satisfaction of post-evaluation needs, especially vital needs and the means to developing agency needs. (4) It must choose between actual and possible need trajectories, which will determine how its citizens' needs are developed and met (about which more below). As a result, the state of needs would act as guarantor for the meeting of needs in two inter-related senses. The first concerns the production and maintenance of conditions in which the members of society can come to a correct evaluation of their true interests. The second concerns the requirement of having an ultimate evaluator and guarantor for the meeting of needs and the choice of need trajectories. It does not follow from this understanding of the state as final evaluator and guarantor that the state is or ought to be the actual provider of the stipulated valued needs. In many cases and under specific conditions markets might do a more efficient job. Nor does it follow from this that the state is the appropriate final evaluator and guarantor of all needs – think of the need for personal intimacy. With this in mind, how are these four functions or tasks best undertaken?

4 NEED PRIORITY: PRACTICAL NOT THEORETICAL

One very common way of answering this question is to stipulate in theory and practice the basic needs of citizens understood as those basic requirements or means *individuals* need to undertake these four tasks. Needs in these common approaches are understood to be the universal preconditions for citizens to satisfy freely their personal needs, make effective use of their rights, and act on their individual preferences. In chapter 1 I argued that there are a number of problems with these kinds of approaches in terms of their understanding of needs, but there is another subset of related problems that are a consequence of the combination of this theoretical assumption with a defining feature of practical politics: its countless concerns over need priority. In other words, given practical politics, imbalances in normative and material power, and the concomitant constant conflict over values and resources, decisions in politics involve the need to prioritise demands and objective human goods. Political theory in general reacts to this practical imperative for prioritisation in a number of ways. I focus on only two practical matters of priority, but both link directly to central issues within contemporary theoretical attempts at prioritisation and highlight the degree to which current theoretical hierarchies and priorities are a distorted outcome of a common misunderstanding about needs. This then paves the way for a better kind of priority and safeguard based in vital needs and the fundamental requirement of constant citizen participation in the evaluation of needs, institutions and need trajectories. This provides a broad outline for the state of needs as ultimate evaluator and guarantor for disclosing and meeting needs, which is discussed in subsequent sections.

The first practical matter of priority is vital need versus agency need priority, which in different terms (the language and practice of rights) is of central concern in liberal political discourse. And the second practical matter of priority is the idea of intrinsic group needs, which is central to discussions of minority rights and 'identity politics'. These two matters clarify why it is important to think about theoretical priority in terms of the imperative to guide practical choices between possible need trajectories, and why it is a mistake to stipulate hierarchies of particular needs. The state's choice of need trajectory determines the general goals that guide the contextual evaluation of particular institutions. And since the outcomes of institutional evaluations determine individual participation in the evaluation of true interests and the individual capability to satisfy needs, the choice of need trajectory is of paramount importance. Theoretical hierarchies simply negate the importance of this practical participation; they inadvertently take on the role of the dictatorial state.

The issue of the relative priority of vital and agency needs is of crucial importance. It seems morally incontestable that, given a certain amount of resources and a situation in which groups of individuals are in need, say, of food or shelter, the resources should first be directed to meeting these objective vital needs. Thereafter, so the argument goes, surplus resources can be used for less pressing needs. Moreover, this moral concern seems to be supported by a universal fact. Think of the countless examples of individuals and groups whose vital needs are met but whose agency needs are underdeveloped; then try and provide examples of groups and individuals whose agency needs are developed but whose vital needs are not. The reasons for this are obvious. First, if my vital needs go unmet at the very least I function at a bare minimum of material necessity and at worst I am dead. Second, agency need development is significantly causally dependent on the extant kind of procedures and institutions for meeting vital needs. This is clearly the case at one extreme because being forced by necessity to attend incessantly to the meeting of vital needs obstructs the development of agency needs: individuals in this state simply do not have the time or energy to engage in the everyday evaluation of needs that is the motor for agency need development. This basic minimum of the satisfaction of vital needs is a necessary but not sufficient condition for the development of agency needs.

Above the threshold of extreme necessity, however, the situation is more complicated than it first appears. As I have argued, the everyday individual perception and interpretation of vital needs is not self-evidently unproblematic because it involves the evaluation of *particular* manifestations of vital needs. And leaving certain agency needs completely unattended might distort the perception of vital needs within an evaluation of true interests.

For example, my insistence on my need for a car for transport might be the result not only of the fact that the train services have been allowed to deteriorate but also of a lack (or distortion) of my need for intersubjective recognition. I might be motivated in part for reasons of status inspired by extant consumption practices and by my lack of recognition in other areas of my life, like my non-meaningful job. I might, therefore, plough my available resources into meeting needs which, despite being experienced as vital needs, under further evaluation might not emerge as viable candidates of particular manifestations of vital needs. More importantly, depending on the distribution of normative power, I may also be able to control the constant want-need dynamic towards legitimising my private ineluctable need as a public ineluctable need. And a direct consequence of this will be the use or transformation of public services and resources for a distorted end. Hence, because prioritisation for meeting needs is always prioritisation for meeting particular needs, it must involve, first and foremost, a contextual and practically resolvable analysis of both the material conditions under which claims are made and the relative normative power of the different groups concerned. In order for this to be achieved, the existing conditions and levels of agency need development must be analysed prior to the creation of particular vital need priority within public policy.

However, the causal relationship between particular agency and vital needs does not shift the ultimate priority away from vital needs. But it does introduce a condition: that avowed vital needs be evaluated in the light of structural analysis of agency need development – the significant institutions and roles. I call this a *conditional vital need priority*, where the conditionality does not remove the ultimate priority but introduces an evaluative, contextual requirement. This evaluative requirement ensures that vital needs are also periodically evaluated in order to ensure that their required quantity and quality is not simply assumed by the central administration of the state of needs. But the ultimate priority of vital need ensures that legitimate vital needs, or in other words post-evaluation vital needs, are always afforded priority at the end of any particular evaluation of needs. As will be discussed in the next section (section 5), certain safeguards on political participation ensure that in this evaluation everyone's vital needs are disclosed. But these safeguards also ensure that beyond the requirement of meeting vital needs, a certain (determinate) level of practical knowledge of political mechanisms (especially of what needs are and how they arise) is therefore not only fundamental to evaluative self-reflection more generally but also necessary for effective political participation. Moreover, being able to develop one's agency needs is a necessary condition and consequence of more effective political participation than is currently evident even (or especially) in the most liberal and 'open' of societies.[17] Thus the most important questions of priority concern not so much the substance of needs but the procedural requirements for participation in the evaluation of needs, interests and need trajectories.

The conditional vital need priority defended here is not a kind of welfarist evaluation of Pareto optimality. Nor is it the kind of more nuanced 'maximin' rendition of the welfarist intuition that underpins Rawls' difference principle. Rather, it is an evaluation in context of the severity and urgency of vital need demands and an evaluation of which kinds of claims constitute claims of vital needs. Any action to meet the vital need priority will only be completed successfully once everyone's legitimate vital needs have been met. It is not sufficient to argue that at least no one has been made worse off, or that the least advantaged have benefited most. This is the case because some people may have to be made worse off for everyone's vital needs to be met; and because the phrase 'the greatest benefit of the least advantaged members of society' concerns redistribution of theoretically pre-determined 'citizens' needs' rather than real felt needs. As I argued in chapter 1, section 5, Rawls' conception of 'primary goods as citizens' needs' constitutes a misconception of needs, or at least an unrealistic idealisation thereof, which reifies the justice of the status quo at the expense of political participation. Rawls distinguishes citizens' needs from other (human) needs in order to establish a relatively simple, objective, static list of concerns that are or ought to be specific to the political sphere as contrasted with other spheres of human interaction. He maintains that 'the political conception of the person and the idea of primary goods specify a special kind of need for a political conception of justice. Needs in any other sense, along with desires and aspirations, play no role.'[18] This amounts to a spurious distinction between what he calls 'higher-order interests' and other needs, wants, wishes, desires and likings, as if these 'lower', everyday needs and desires did not affect our interpretation and specification of our 'higher', *political* needs and interests.

But this ontological error, or at least complete lack of concern for the causal story of needs and interests, has highly problematic consequences.

---

[17] For some of the causes and consequences of the state of disillusionment, low levels of political participation, and 'disengagement from the processes of the state' in contemporary Western Europe, see I. Wallerstein, 'The Albatross of Racism', *London Review of Books*, 22. 10 (May 2000), p. 11. The situation in the USA is much worse: only 49% of the population voted in the previous presidential elections.

[18] J. Rawls, *Political Liberalism* (New York: Columbia University Press, 1996), p. 189n.

It allows Rawls to argue that 'claims to these goods are counted as appropriate claims'.[19] Thus a normative distinction between primary goods and other goods amounts to a theoretically pre-determined distinction between appropriate claims to need and inappropriate claims to need. Like other purely normative conceptions of needs, this undermines politics as a whole. If the evaluative distinction between 'appropriate' and 'inappropriate' is already provided, what is the point of political participation, evaluation and avowed individual needs and interests? In the Rawlsian case, however, this misconstrual of needs underpins a highly developed blueprint for justice, and thus adds insult to injury. If one assumes, with Rawls, that primary goods are static givens of a political conception of the person, it follows quite neatly from this that the more important principle is not primary goods, or necessity, but freedom. If one assumes that the redistribution of goods will involve the redistribution of static primary goods (understood as unchanging higher-order needs), which by definition do not require evaluation, one's first concern will be to guarantee liberty: redistribution of primary goods is uncomplicated and can easily be secured once freedom is in place. Thus one can give lexical priority to certain rights and liberties (Rawls' first principle of justice), and the principle of redistribution can follow on behind. Hence, needs are not only misunderstood, they are relegated to the second principle within a theory of justice in which the first principle holds lexical priority. Justice as fairness affords lexical priority to the principle that 'each person has an equal claim to a fully adequate scheme of equal basic rights and liberties'.[20]

Conversely, in the political philosophy of needs and participation proposed here, vital needs, not basic rights and liberties, are given priority. And, as the reader will recall from my discussion of vital needs in chapter 1, the idea of vital needs is manifestly full of content; it is not a subcategory of vital needs carefully crafted for a 'reasonable' politics. Moreover, we cannot simply redistribute vital needs as if they were primary goods, resources or commodities. The satisfiers of primary goods are relatively basic but they will take different forms in different contexts, and thus the distribution of resources and means to their acquisition may have to be unequal and cannot be achieved efficiently if redistributed. The existing practices and institutions of distribution must be understood and changed in line with the goals adumbrated here, often in unequal measure. For example, in a global context, in order to meet the vital needs of the African population international institutions must weight their distribution of opportunities,

---

[19] Ibid., p. 180.   [20] Ibid., pp. 5–6.

goods and services to the needs of this population at the cost of those who meet their vital needs with ease in the North. At a more local level the same is required for working-class, immigrant and traditionally oppressed groups in Britain (for example, the black population), as it is for more pressing and obvious historical reasons in the context of the new South Africa. But this kind of affirmative action will only work if it is undertaken at the level of large institutional change aimed at improving the way in which resources, roles and institutions are distributed and organised to meet needs.[21] The vital needs and their priority are not understood in terms of basic rights and liberties because the alleged basic rights and liberties that are normally given priority in liberal political theory must themselves be lowered into the pot of political participation in terms of needs.

Obviously, this emphasis on the priority of participation is in stark contrast to justice-based political theories and philosophies that attempt to safeguard universal substantive human concerns, for example certain basic needs or rights. Rawls' two principles of justice in his account of justice as fairness is an attempt to do just that. In sum, there are two things wrong with this kind of move. First, it assumes certain universal needs and rights and then proceeds to make them inviolable, irrespective of the outcomes of contextual, political evaluation. Second, once it tackles justice in this way, it is forced to prioritise at the level of theory, for justice will invariably contain certain competing concerns. For example, the liberal dilemma amounts to a choice between liberty and equality. In practice, this often involves a trade-off, but in the justice-based accounts that dominate theory today, an ultimate choice and priority is required. Witness Rawls' lexical priority for liberty, his first principle of justice. And, basically, this amounts to one individual's conception of human good and value imposed upon everyone else, disguised in the form of universal means to freedom. Together these two problems undermine the point of politics because they undermine the point of evaluating principles and safeguards in terms of their consequences. A strict justice-based account draws principles of justice from highly abstract universals of human existence and then prioritises them in the light of either abstract moral universals or highly idealised conceptions of human nature, choice or rationality. Need priority is undoubtedly important, but political theory must refrain from proposing hierarchies of principles or hierarchies of particular needs. Given certain general vital need and procedural participative safeguards, the particular priorities will emerge in practice.

---

[21] I discuss this more fully in a text provisionally entitled *States and Markets of Needs*.

This brings me to the second practical matter of priority: group needs and strategic moves. I speak of the development of the agency needs of human individuals throughout this account not because I am dissociating the individual from the group but because I see the need for group recognition as being a matter of strategic importance rather than fundamental necessity for attending to the agency needs of individuals. To return to an earlier example of recognition: for the black Briton to be intersubjectively recognised, two processes have to proceed hand-in-hand; two processes that require group activity and emphasis. The individual working-class black Briton might need improved consciousness of her position as an oppressed member of an oppressed group, in terms (where applicable) of class, gender and race/colour.[22] And also, the members of the privileged groups of the population might need to be shocked into perceiving their *relatively* privileged treatment within their society in order for them to *recognise* their own prejudices and assumptions, manifest in their everyday needs, deeds and words. Hence, agency needs are applicable to individuals *and* groups, but *only* when the recognition, expression and autonomy of the group is a necessary strategic move (or condition) for the recognition, expression and autonomy of its constitutive individuals. In these instances the agency needs of the group might be prioritised over the agency needs of the individuals, but only for short-lived strategic goals, and never over the vital needs of any individuals concerned. Recall from my critique of 'identity politics' that groups do not have a need for recognition themselves, as if they had their own cognitive and ontological properties. Moreover, 'identity politics' shoots itself in the foot by adopting the concept of rights: the entrenchment of a particular right I hold as a black Briton simply enters another right into an already overloaded and well-hierarchised set of rights. It is much less efficient (and more likely to reify identities) than calling for a conceptual and institutional change within which our claims might be better recognised and met.

---

[22] In reality these issues are never as simple as they might seem; generalised oppression is hardly ever simply a race/colour or class or gender issue, but usually mixes of these. For example, the *União dos Negros pela Igualdade* ('The Union of Blacks for Equality'), a political movement in Salvador, Brazil, is quite clear that the fact that people of Afro-Brazilian origin constitute 99% of the poorest (and most under-privileged) people in Northeast Brazil is not explained through race alone, but also by means of class. See the booklet by one of the founding members, Niveldinho Felix, *Raça e Consciência de Classe* (Salvador, BA, Brazil, nd). Note that in Brazilian Portuguese *negro* does not mean the colour black, *preto* denotes that colour; and the originally derogatory term *negro*, with racial rather than colour connotations, is used in everyday speech as a consequence of an original attempt at once to emphasise the ongoing political element and to affirm racial difference as a strategy for change. In fact, people in these movements find it odd, even archaic, that this is not more common outside of Brazil.

In sum, then, the evaluation and meeting of vital needs are a priority, alongside the priority of safeguards of political participation to be discussed in the next section.[23] There is the further requirement of unimpeded access to the four social roles (discussed in chapter 1, section 4, and chapter 3, section 3); and the fact that group agency needs can be prioritised, but only as part of relatively short-lived strategic moves to overcome extant normative power imbalances. However, neither of these priorities demands a hierarchy of extant felt needs at the level of theory, evident in the work of Nussbaum and Doyal and Gough. Nor do they involve a strict priority for any particular means or ends, *à la* Rawls. As I have argued, in strict contradistinction to Rawls' first principle of priority, this account does not prioritise agency needs above vital needs, let alone a specific one – liberty (which for Rawls equates to autonomy). Both of the practical issues discussed in this section identify the danger of assuming that particular needs can be stipulated in theory. In doing so theorists either assume or engender spurious acontextual hierarchies of need that undermine any role for individual preferences *per se*, preferences over needs, and participation in the evaluation of needs. I claim that these kinds of approaches (unintentionally) condone a disregard for felt needs and preferences because they react in an infelicitous theoretical manner to a context-bound practical imperative to prioritise needs. At the level of theory it is more helpful first to *understand* the situation and only then stipulate preferred general need trajectories and concomitant (examples of) institutional changes that might improve participative control over the formation, articulation, recognition and satisfaction of needs.

5 POLITICAL PARTICIPATION: PROCEDURAL AND INSTITUTIONAL PROPOSALS

There are three main forms of democracy: the liberal, constitutional model; the republican model; and the model of direct democracy.[24] They have ideal

---

[23] As I have argued, this is because satisfied vital needs and certain kinds of political participation are necessary conditions for the development and satisfaction of other kinds of needs. However, mere knowledge of these necessary conditions is not in itself a sufficient condition for resolving the present state of affairs, which is characterised by there being no single existing society whose government actually meets these *minima* for all its citizens. Vital needs and political participation in the evaluation of needs may be necessary conditions but there are others: resources, political will and coercion through the medium of law (about which more below).

[24] This is, obviously, a crude summary. 'Democracy' is an ideal, a concept, and a set of institutions that has an ancient pedigree and many forms, the best modern accounts of which can be found in D. Held, *Models of Democracy*, 2nd edn (Cambridge: Polity Press, 1996), and J. Dunn (ed.), *Democracy: The Unfinished Journey 508 BC to AD 1993* (Oxford: Oxford University Press, 1993). The terms 'democracy' and 'democratic' have not always been used and understood in the positive manner characteristic of today. For a long time they were terms of derision and criticism.

theoretical forms and messy practical manifestations, although the republican and direct forms are now thin on the ground. I claim that in practice
the liberal, rights-based constitutional form now has few democratic or participative credentials. It parades rights as a means of securing democratic
participation but that is ultimately an illusion. The actions of particular
governments are supported or suspended by periodic vote, while the everyday decisions that determine the lives of citizens are taken by the elites in
power within a pre-determined structure of rights. Even the governing elites
are far from free to adjust these *meta*-political rights or evaluate social and
political means and possibilities outside of the practice of rights-discourse
and extant rights-based institutions. Liberal constitutional democracy locks
citizens within an iron cage of rights by entrenching historically variable
conditions and goals within (largely) historically invariable legal structures.

The two other alternatives are, however, even more debilitating, but for
different reasons. Accounts of direct participatory and republican democracy are implausible. The republican model stresses individual virtue as
determined by the ability to suspend self-interest and prudence (which are
given free rein in my approach) for the requirements of a public interest or
common good. The direct participatory (or Athenian) model stresses constant public political activity in a deliberative context. Now, if my account
of needs, true interests and their evaluation is true, the core assumptions of
these two approaches are false: first, beyond my argument about the flaws
in claims concerning the suspension of felt need and interest, the idea of
a public interest or common good is misplaced – it assumes wrongly that
there is a single specifiable good at any point in time for all groups and
individuals in society irrespective of their material conditions and relative
normative power;[25] second, deliberation is not as attainable or as successful as proponents of direct deliberative democracy tend to assume. In any
case, both of these approaches are manifestly unhelpful because they make
anachronistic and unrealistic assumptions concerning the daily life of the
modern individual, and concomitantly tend to assume a high degree of
surveillance, or hope to engender it in practice.

In contrast, my account works from the here and now of modern existence and politics and proposes certain procedures for transforming the

---

[25] The idea of the 'common good' and the idea of the 'public interest' are not identical, and the
latter is a much more common modern locution than the former, but they have many historical,
normative and ideological links and similarities. For more on these issues within an account of the
'public interest' that partly escapes my criticism, see R. E. Flathman, *The Public Interest: An Essay
Concerning the Normative Discourse of Politics* (New York: John Wiley & Sons, 1966). I am indebted
to Andrew Gamble for this reference.

state and other institutions across society that might engender and improve participation. The substantive goal is the transformation of those extant institutions and roles that restrict individuals from being heard and heeded in the evaluation of needs and interests. These institutions and roles, however, can be fully analysed only in the context concerned. However, as I have argued, that does not mean that they are relative to the context concerned: vital and agency needs are universal determinants of and guides to individual and political agency. Nor does it mean that some institutions, practices and roles do not actually cover, or at least affect, the whole globe. All that follows is an understanding that the institutions and roles that affect the causal and normative power of individuals will have a lot more to do with localised issues of class, power and privilege than allegedly universal ideas and means such as rights, state neutrality, tolerance and democratic deliberation. However, this point about the importance of contextual understanding does not disallow a speculative outline of some procedural requirements and evaluative processes that follow from my understanding of need.[26] In fact, given that rights-discourse dominates modern democratic practice and theory, my approach to need would be incomplete without a short general sketch of an alternative to these three broad kinds of democracy or participation.[27] This alternative must meet the two main demands of my conceptual account. That is, it must meet the demand that citizens have increased control over the evaluation of true interests and the choice of need trajectories, as well as the related demand that this must be achieved without having to ahistorically reify the needs and power relations of the status quo. In any case, beyond these procedural concerns, it is important to think about how the citizenry might evaluate their state's performance

---

[26] See the main conclusion for a short, contextual application of these speculative proposals to a particular empirical context. For a book-length empirical analysis that makes similar points concerning understanding, though not in terms of need, see B. Flyvbjerg, *Rationality and Power: Democracy in Practice* (Chicago and London: Chicago University Press, 1998).

[27] Although my approach intentionally does not provide a blueprint for 'designing' better institutions, it is directed at providing means of changing certain kinds of institutional structures, especially those that push citizens further and further away from grasping that their needs have origins and consequences beyond themselves. The institution of rights generally, and the right to private property in particular, is the archetypal institution within which needs are defined as being solely the 'property' of individual subjects. As I have argued, this state of affairs is reinforced by the existing want-need dynamic, or, in other words, the actual institutions for articulating need and the extant distinctions between private and public. The fundamental ethical issue – how should we live? – arises at the core of the dynamic and the trajectory of need. If the state of needs, under the control of its citizens, does not evaluate, choose and prioritise between actual and possible need trajectories, other existing institutions will do so in its place, institutions over which the citizens have a great deal less control. For more on how institutional blueprints and 'tinkering' of institutions can often be counterproductive, see C. Offe, 'Institutions in East European Transitions', in R. Goodin (ed.), *The Theory of Institutional Design* (Cambridge: Cambridge University Press, 1998), p. 214.

in transforming institutions in line with its position as ultimate need evaluator and guarantor for the meeting of needs. So, how can citizens increase their control over need and true interest evaluation *and* the evaluation and transformation of institutions?

Speculative procedural and institutional proposals

There are two related procedural requirements and a block of criteria within a separate procedure, which together constitute my alternative two-tiered form of evaluative participation. I will take the procedural requirements first because I argue that they must exist independent of any single government and an assessment of government is not their direct concern. The assessment of government is the separate procedure. It involves an evaluation of government in terms of criteria that relate to my substantive account of true interest and need trajectory evaluation, and of the proficiency of government in following and periodically evaluating the guidelines evident in the two procedural requirements. The two requirements amount to a needs-based procedural constitution: a constitution that is not, and is not understood as being, prior to the state, *meta*-political or the product of some form of social contract. Rather, it is a constitution in the sense of an established, constantly reassessed and dynamic institution whose procedures are directed at responding to needs; that is, a constitution quite unlike the rights-inspired notion of a set of legal guarantees or trumps that are the inalienable property of individuals, which amounts to a kind of *meta*-political ossification of means and ends. As proposed here, a needs-based constitution involves the construction of a set of safeguards for individual political participation in the periodic evaluation of true interests and need trajectories. They do not have to be individual legal guarantees but they must be legally enshrined procedural guarantees.

In line with my account of true interests, in which true interests are contextually and historically specific, evaluated, individual needs, the first requirement is the institution of an annual true interest evaluation. This would make use of the elaborate and frequent census, as discussed in chapter 3, sections 3 and 4, as well as local, regional and global sources of information on more macro-level economic and political institutions and practices. Rotating local level representatives would undertake this true interest evaluation under the leadership of the local state authority. Essentially it would be a means through which local governmental administration could react to articulated and evaluated need, but it must not affect the standing of the existing government. The evaluative process must involve representatives from local areas or streets as well as local business, labour and consumer representatives. The aim would be to reach a decision, a majority decision if necessary, over local true interests in order that the extant local government can ensure that the state and the various markets and market-related institutions respond to post-evaluation needs. In other words, this would not amount simply to the aggregation of individual preferences for political representatives or policies, but constitute an assessment of needs, preferences and interests that relate to political and economic goods.

The second requirement is the institution of a periodic process of need trajectory evaluation and choice. In contrast to the short-term concerns of true interest evaluation, this would involve a relatively protracted communication and evaluation of ideas and possibilities, say over a period of one month once every ten years, that relate to long-term choices. Such choices would involve, for example, broad questions of public policy, such as environmental policy, transport policy, fiscal policy, and even longer-term proposals and ideas concerning very large structural issues, such as forms of production and distribution and kinds of property ownership and inheritance, and possibilities for their institutional re-arrangement or transformation. This might encourage a number of things that are discouraged within liberal constitutional frameworks. First, it would provide citizens with some control over the long term and therefore might persuade them to think beyond their immediate, short-term interests. Second, it might dissociate historically specific events, successes or failures from specific parties, governments or groups. Third, it might encourage citizen groups to take risks, to put forward untried and untested novel proposals for how to evaluate and meet needs more efficiently, safe in the knowledge that a system could be tested for a ten-year period and then, if necessary, discarded. Fourth, it could react to changes in the nature and form of human needs and how they are met. It would be a great deal more flexible than a reified code of rights both because it could be adjusted more easily and because it dissociates the human goods and means under analysis from a notion of individual ownership or entitlement. Needs and trajectories are not things humans could come to think they own or deserve. And, fifth, as a consequence especially of the last two points, it would encourage consequentialist rather than deontological practical reasoning. By testing a number of variants humans can achieve a greater causal understanding of the effects of institutional arrangements on perceiving, articulating, recognising and meeting needs. This enhanced understanding may generate the desire to experiment beyond the status quo.

In both the true interest and need trajectory evaluative procedures there is no assumption or requirement that either the process be deliberative or that the outcome be consensual. Given my understanding of needs under modern conditions, both deliberation and consensus are highly unlikely and, depending on the extant normative power relations, often undesirable. This does not mean that the process is not participative; it is highly participative. These procedures broaden and focus the normal notion of 'political participation': it is understood here as participation in the evaluation of human needs, in the sense of having the means and resources to cognise, meet and criticise needs in everyday contexts and within the two formal procedures outlined above. Hence, this approach to participation does not make the normal mistake of conflating participation with deliberation. Ultimately, because consensus is the exception within both procedures, after the process of collecting information and preference and need avowal is complete, decisions must be made dependent on a majority vote. However, the local arm of the state must be able to adjust the outcome of the final decisions dependent on its appraisal of normative power balances and publicly available evidence of justified need. And it must then justify publicly its decisions in terms of these objective conditions. More exactly, it must decide and justify based on material from the elaborate census – objective conditions of the local populace, their avowed needs and the possible means to increasing future participation. This is especially important when and where there is a split vote, distortions in turnout, or very low turnout.

There is a block of criteria that relates directly to the true interest and need trajectory evaluative procedures. I list them in a relatively generalised form because their substantive concerns, which essentially amount to institutional evaluation and transformation, are necessarily specific to context, to particular institutions and to particular means and ends. These general considerations are also important because they form part of the criteria of electoral evaluation of government. There is no reason why this could not continue to function in a similar way to the way it does in many contemporary liberal democracies and as frequently as it does, but it would be a separate procedure from the two procedures that constitute the needs-based constitution.

There are two parts to the block of criteria. The first focuses on five substantive concerns: (1) the government's efficiency in constantly transforming roles and institutions with the goal of improving the evaluation of true interests and choice of need trajectory, or in other words of undertaking need-based and role-relative institutional consequentialism;

(2) the government's efficiency in transforming role matrices in line with the goal of improving participant control over these two evaluative procedures; (3) the government's proficiency in controlling the distribution of normative power in general and in relation to these procedures in particular; (4) how the government evaluates and reforms institutions that act against the meeting of post-evaluation vital needs and the means to developing agency needs; and (5) the form of control the citizens have over the final choice of general need trajectories. The second part relates to how well government enables the two main procedures stipulated in the need-based constitution and related considerations. For example, each new act of governmental legislation will have to pass through a set of transparent evaluative mechanisms that are accountable in the light of these codified procedures, with the aim of maintaining citizen power over true interest and need trajectory evaluation and monitoring how well government controls and evaluates the meeting of needs. (See below for more on accountability.) Moreover, since the true interest procedure involves local level citizen evaluation of policy outcomes and aspects of implementation, government would need to be assessed for how local government perceives and attends to institution and role configurations in the light of met and unmet local needs. Regional and state representatives can then be assessed for their efficiency in relating these needs to central government and organising state resources and general distribution in the light of them.

Central government's main function would then centre on three institutional configurations that can be evaluated using information from the elaborate and frequent census and macropolitical and -economic analysis: state security, citizen security, and international markets and their effects on meeting needs. These local, regional and international functions are all brought together in government and their evaluation (by government) returns to the broader, constant, evaluative analysis of the society's institutions, practices and role matrices. Institutions, particularly, are therefore under constant critique from government and as a consequence of the two periodic procedures. In sum, the main concern for citizens, and by extension government, is how well government is able to react to the outcomes of its analyses and the two periodic procedures in the broad sense of controlling and transforming practices and institutions that impede citizen participation within the two procedures.

Finally, above and beyond the procedural requirements, there is the vital need safeguard. As I argued in the previous section, individuals' vital needs have conditional policy priority. However, this does not mean that any action or policy must be curtailed or stopped for fear of not meeting vital needs. As was established in my analysis of the causal and cognitive relation between vital and agency needs, even vital needs have to be brought within a consequentialist frame of analysis, evaluation and reasoning. This is especially important where policy is uncertain about outcomes, which accounts for much of policy-making. It is better to take risks than to be ossified through fear of unmet vital needs, but no action or policy can be justified if, given relatively recent experience, it is likely to act against the meeting of vital needs. Above that, priority is determined in relation to the outcome of the contextual true interest evaluative procedure. Take my example of Jack, his car, and Jill and their need for mobility and clean air. First, Jack and Jill's vital needs for mobility and clean air are conditional policy priorities. Second, if Jack's claim for a better motorway acts to reduce Jill's capability to meet either of these vital needs, it must be disregarded, especially when there exists a means or alternative solution, for instance a reliable train service, that meets both of the general vital needs to which their need-claims ultimately reduce. If that causality is not manifestly apparent, then Jack and Jill's true interest claims must be role-modified and analysed in the light of the above account of institutional consequentialism. A publicly funded, evaluated and efficient transport system would meet Jack and Jill's vital needs, but only if it did not have to compete against forms of transport that actively ghettoise groups of individuals in terms of their conditions of needing. The only possible practical means of achieving this kind of goal is for the state to use its coercive force to foster the generation and acceptance of the need to use public transport to meet our need for mobility, even if that means controlling other 'markets' in transport needs.

To sum up, the speculative institutional proposals outlined in this section make certain safeguards instrumental requirements or means within this kind of political philosophy of needs, safeguards which would have to be enshrined in a need-based constitution. These safeguards include the following: first, a conditional priority for meeting vital needs, which would involve safeguarding life in terms of prohibiting capital punishment; second, a number of procedural safeguards related to political participation in the evaluation of true interests and need trajectories. Only once these are secured would various rights and liberties then be assessed in the light of other less primary concerns. If need be these secondary concerns, in terms of rights (say the right to private property) or otherwise, can also be safeguarded at a constitutional level, if only to enable efficient legal functioning. However, they will require periodic evaluation in the light of vital and agency need disclosure, development and satisfaction. A sensible period might be something like once every decade. Moreover, this assessment must be participative in the manner described in the second safeguard noted above. In other words, not only must this evaluation involve all citizens, whether highly trained in legal issues or not, but also it must be given the same status as the other periodic assessment of needs, interests and trajectories.

Accountability

All told there are a number of levels over which the administration of a state of needs can be held accountable: with regard to the evaluation of needs and institutions; in the light of its choice over need trajectories; in terms of its procedural efficiency; and according to whether it enables the meeting of vital (and agency) needs. It would be incumbent on the various levels of government to respond to the various needs, preferences and interests and adjust political and economic institutions accordingly. Thus they could be held accountable not only with regard to their procedural efficiency and transparency but also with regard to how successful they were in re-arranging the institutional framework in line with needs. As I hope is obvious by now, this political philosophy of needs emphasises accountability in terms of consequences of institutional re-arrangement above the oft-heard concern for 'transparency'. In general current literature tends to over-emphasise procedural transparency and accountability, or at least the need for greater trust in present procedures and institutions, at the expense of suggesting possible institutional re-arrangements for generating greater political accountability in terms of the *consequences* of procedures.[28] This is a consequence of the fact that normally accountability is understood in terms determined by the rights-preferences couple, in which politics is understood either as the technical aggregation of individual preferences or the public face and form of individual moral problems. Given my account of needs and institutions, it is more felicitous for political and economic institutions to be held responsible and accountable in light of their consequences on human needs and political agency rather than in light of the intentions or virtues of their constitutive individuals as they attempt to follow extant rules and procedures.

[28] For examples of an over-emphasis on trust and transparency respectively, see O. O'Neill, *A Question of Trust* (Cambridge: Cambridge University Press, 2002); and M. Lane, 'Accountability, Transparency, Legitimacy: the new staples of democratic discourse and their implications for non-elected institutions', unpublished paper presented at the Annual Meeting of the American Political Science Association, 29 August – 1 September 2002.

6 LEGITIMACY AND PATERNALISM

The state of needs' de jure *legitimacy: the* de jure *authority to guide the trajectory of need*

Weber does not cover the kinds of concerns discussed in my account of coercion and its relation to the evaluation and satisfaction of needs, for these concerns relate to *normative* criteria for the legitimacy of a state. Although Weber goes beyond his initial condition of the monopoly of legitimate violence, his final account does not enter into any normative discussion. He argues that beyond and alongside direct constant coercion, the state secretes around itself a moral and legal apparatus of beliefs, rules and practices about what is and is not warranted. In particular, it defines what is 'legitimate' and what is 'illegitimate'. In doing so it appeals to three different kinds of warrant: the authority of rational-legal procedures; traditional authority; and charismatic authority.[29] As I understand the state, coercion and need, the state's legitimacy would involve another element. What could this be called and how does it differ from other kinds of legitimacy?

Legitimacy is another protean term that is used in a number of contexts. For example, in international law, a state is legitimate if it is recognised as a sovereign state; and in international relations theory, actual governments are described as legitimate if they follow their own internal rules of conduct and those set up by inter-national agencies, such as the United Nations. Legitimacy in these senses relates to how an agency conforms to accepted (and usually codified) rules. But there is another sense that relates to more vague rules and norms and centres on what makes the decision, action or entity binding or not. And this latter kind is resolved by thinking about why the agency concerned can give me a directive; i.e., what kind of authority gives it a warrant to be obeyed. Geuss provides a clear taxonomy of five kinds of authority and how they relate to legitimacy. The first is 'epistemic authority', which is gained by my being a skilful practitioner of, or by my having theoretical knowledge of or reliable information concerning, the matter I am directing.[30] The second is what is sometimes called 'natural

---

[29] Weber, *Economy and Society*, p. 215 (for full account see vol. 1, part I, Ch. iii, 1–22, and vol. 11, Chs x–xv); and Weber, 'Profession and Vocation', pp. 311–12.

[30] Some philosophers, especially Plato and Gadamer, have tended to construe political authority in terms of epistemic authority. This is erroneous because political authority is not just bestowed on individuals, groups or states simply by virtue of the fact that they are in possession of knowledge that it might be unwise to ignore. What qualifies an authority as a political authority is that it (also) has a *warrant* of some kind and an *expectation* of being obeyed. Geuss, *History and Illusion in Politics*, pp. 38–9.

authority', which is evident when someone who is not necessarily in a position of authority takes control and gets obeyed in a moment of crisis. The third sense is *de facto* political authority, which is characterised by the simple fact that a group of people monopolise the use of violence and succeed in getting obeyed. The fourth sense is what some people call *de jure* authority; that is, that there is a set of rules that the authority successfully follows that makes it authoritative (and there is normally a concomitant law that prescribes that people should obey the specified authority). Geuss calls this 'descriptive *de jure* authority'. As he points out, although many philosophers have been content with these four kinds of authority, there is another kind of *de jure* authority:

> X has authority (in this sense) if he has a warrant that is not legally correct or conforms to *some* set of rules, but which will stand up to some further moral scrutiny that could be brought to bear on it, that is, X has '*de jure* authority' if X has a warrant that 'ought to' be obeyed, where the 'ought' is relative to some more or less free-standing moral judgement we make.[31]

Geuss calls this 'normative *de jure* authority'.

Understood under this classification, Weber's account of legitimacy is an example of descriptive *de jure* legitimacy. It is not, therefore, I would argue, a full account of legitimacy. It provides a set of significant conditions but it falls short of the final hurdle. It is this final hurdle and how it relates to coercion and needs with which I am ultimately concerned here. I add, therefore, a fourth condition (to supplement Weber's three conditions) that must be filled by a state for it to be a legitimate state. In general terms, it must monopolise the ultimate decision (or ultimate evaluative structure) with regard to disputes over need-claims and interests, and it must retain the required means to evaluate and change those institutions whose function it is to meet post-evaluation vital needs and the means to developing agency needs. In particular, because of the strict requirement of participation in the two main procedures of true interest and need trajectory evaluation, the state's legitimacy will be dependent on how well it institutes the procedures, reacts to the outcomes of evaluation, and transforms institutions to ensure continued participation. If the state loses the monopoly of control over these tasks, it loses the associated 'normative *de jure* authority' that comes from successfully carrying out these tasks. More specifically, however, the conditions centre on two separate issues. The first issue is the manner in which evaluation takes place: it holds that if ultimate control is allowed to slip out of the control of the state, it loses the aspect of its legitimacy

---

[31] Ibid., p. 41.

that comes from being the authority over information and conflict about extant institutions, practices and roles and how they relate to extant needs, need trajectories and the two periodic procedures. The second issue is the authority to determine the trajectory of needs in line with the citizens' demands and claims *vis-à-vis* the institutional conditions for a fully functioning life for all and in line with the basic requirement of participation within the two procedures. There is, in other words, an epistemic, a normative and a performative aspect to this fourth condition. Hence, all told, my conception of *de jure* authority, call it the '*de jure* authority to guide the trajectory of need', is ultimately grounded in my analysis of needs and the participative approach to true interest and need trajectory evaluation. As I have argued, these emerge out of both necessity and morality. This therefore qualifies Geuss's 'normative *de jure* authority', authority which rests on any moral warrant, because a state under my conception could have the *de jure* authority to guide the trajectory of need and still fail to meet other moral criteria we could mount against it. All of the above does not, of course, negate the obvious fact that Weber's three conditions have to be filled for my fourth condition to obtain. Hence, all four conditions are necessary conditions for the legitimacy of the modern state.

It follows from my account of need and the state of needs that a fundamental condition for the state to retain legitimacy is that it acquire the legislative means to ensure that vital needs are met, and that all citizens are able to take a meaningful part in the valued social roles and the two periodic procedures of evaluation. This is a significant and demanding task, which flies in the face of the current dogmatic faith in the 'slim' state. The contemporary concern with and justification of a slim state that acts to impose as little regulation on the institutions of the 'free' market as is possible is nothing more than a consequence of the growth in normative power of one section of society, a section which has (ingenuously) managed to co-opt the governments of most states in a process that may end in the destruction of their state's normative *de jure* legitimacy. Nevertheless, it is a highly significant empirical fact that some modern states are able to retain authority and descriptive *de jure* legitimacy under these conditions. Why? If they stick to their own rules of conduct and are in the fortunate position of controlling and benefiting from various institutions, practices and relations that hold significant causal power within the international capitalist economy, they can in effect meet most of these need-based demands *without* the constant coercive intervention of the state. However, the same cannot be said for other (more numerous) weaker, poorer and less historically fortunate states on the globe. It is here that we see the real effects of unmet needs on state legitimacy; it is also here that we see the political fallout that results from long periods of consistently unmet needs. There are numerous obvious examples of this amongst the poorest and weakest of modern states, but the effects of unmet needs on state legitimacy is perhaps brought into sharpest relief amongst 'middle income' states, for example South Africa (during and after apartheid) and Brazil. The legitimacy of these otherwise legitimate, relatively strong states is constantly undermined by their inability to act as ultimate guarantors and evaluators of their citizens' needs. More often than not any political moves in the right direction are stillborn in the face of scarce resources and the financial instability brought about by unregulated global financial markets. This lack of legitimacy and financial stability is a direct consequence of these states' historically contingent weakness, or lack of power, in the face of the real centres of power in the international political economy: the United States of America (USA), the European Union (EU), Japan, the World Trade Organisation (WTO), the International Monetary Fund (IMF), the World Bank, and the North Atlantic Treaty Organisation (NATO).[32]

In sum, the meeting of needs, and the need for a coercive authority to achieve this, are to be valued not only in themselves as valuable human goods, but also because they are both necessary conditions for improving the circumstances under which humans participate politically. That is, by suggesting ways of improving the conditions under which we evaluate our true interests, a politics of needs of this kind provides new opportunities for us to have greater interpretive control over the origins, nature and significance of our needs. And every increase in normative power as regards needs translates directly into greater individual participative control over how the state acts with regard to humans and their needs.

Paternalism

One of the problems with liberal political theory is that it emerges from a principled allergy to *all* forms of paternalism. Its indiscriminate exclusion

---

[32] There is a tendency amongst critical commentators to assume that real power lies with multinational corporations (MNC's), but I maintain that this under-estimates a glaring historical truth: the above-listed political states and institutions, in particular the powerful North Atlantic member states of the WTO, defend the interests of MNC's and other concentrations of global capital through a combination of legal and military support. And they do so because their interests tend to coincide with the interests of the MNC's, a large proportion of which have their national bases in one or more of these powerful states. See my 'Needs, States, and Markets: democratic sovereignty against imperialism', *Theoria*, 102 (December 2003). And, as the example of national oil companies highlights, these states themselves are large and important economic players with concomitant interests. See Lane, 'Accountability, Transparency, Legitimacy'.

of any hint of paternalism marks a failure to acknowledge the reality of human dependence. And, as I have argued in the context of practical reason, liberal theory thus promotes a fantasy of human independence that, when realised in practice, ensures that important human needs go unrecognised and unmet. Moreover, this principled exclusion and its consequent fantasy shroud a great irony: modern liberal political theory begins from an anti-paternalist premise and theory and ends up proposing and supporting paternalist practices and institutions. Its main premise is that a properly instituted set of rights will safeguard vital interests and freedom of choice, but given its main assumptions concerning theoretical blueprints it engenders paternalism in practice. This is the case for two reasons that I have discussed already. First, modern liberal political theory tends to opt for the safety of justice as against the risk of democracy, thereby reifying certain human goods at the expense of practical, political evaluation. Second, it reduces political action to a species of individual action and argues that a paternalist act is one in which an individual or institution exercises decision-making power to confer benefits or prevent harm for another individual or group of individuals regardless of the latter's informed consent.[33] This seems to forget not only that *liberal* representative democracies would not function were they unable to do as much, but also that politics ultimately involves collective rather than individual action.

The liberal assumption that political action is legitimate only when it is non-paternalist emerges from a naïve view of politics and an impoverished conception of paternalism. Paternalism involves not only the direct exercise of power or authority on a single individual's choice, decision or action regardless of informed consent, but also broad decisions over possible paths of development, or need trajectories, that directly and indirectly affect these choices, decisions and actions. And these are not the same thing. The direct exercise of decision-making power by one institution or individual over another individual's evaluation of his true interests irrespective of the latter individual's informed consent is not equivalent to a central authority exercising decision-making power over the choice of possible future need trajectories. For one thing, as has already been discussed, the latter will not involve the direct coercion of action and choice but rather the indirect removal or provision of choice that normally involves being 'left with no *reasonable* alternative but Q'. Moreover, the choice of need trajectories can involve various kinds of participative frameworks or a complete lack of participation, which will involve different kinds and degrees of paternalism.

---

[33] J. Feinberg, *Harm to Self* (New York: Oxford University Press, 1986); R. Sartorius (ed.), *Paternalism* (Minneapolis: University of Minnesota Press, 1983).

My main concern has been to identify and suggest means of transforming the institutions that hold greatest determining power in this constant process of indirect coercion that determines need trajectories; but it does not follow from this that this kind of paternalism is abhorrent or not necessary, rather the opposite. In my conception of participation within a state of needs, *this* kind of paternalism is both legitimate and necessary, but only if it involves the ultimate decisions over need trajectories and general needs, and only after a stipulated period and kind of participation.

Having said this, the liberal assumptions and concerns over paternalism are reactions to an important intuition about the virtues of certain guarantees against paternalism. I argue that my political philosophy of needs provides four important ways of safeguarding against paternalism, or in other words, four important ways in which anti-paternalism is guaranteed. First, it focuses on *felt* needs, both in understanding needs and within proposals for constant attention to them, and thus guarantees that this approach *begins* from and generates anti-paternalism with regard to needs. Second, although the evaluation of an individual's true interest must involve others as well as objective accounts of vital and agency needs, in this account the individual's 'true interest' is always particular to context and time and is always subject-relative at the end of any single process of evaluation. Third, the normative goals of the theory as a whole are posited in order to improve the participative power individuals have over the evaluation of their needs and over their government's actions and choices with regard to need trajectories. Fourth, this account is not developed as a universal blueprint for action and institutional construction. Rather, it is developed as a kind of filter that works to undermine needs, interests, institutions and roles that are counterproductive to the meeting of vital and agency needs, while providing theoretical support for true interests and certain kinds of need trajectories, and their associated institutions and roles, as well as safeguards for vital needs and political participation. But it does not follow from these four guarantees that a state of needs cannot ultimately decide upon trajectories of needs; in fact these guarantees require states of needs to make these kinds of decisions. Thus, although this whole approach to needs aims to generate autonomy and anti-paternalist political institutions it is sensitive to different kinds and qualities of paternalism, and holds that not all forms of paternalism are equally objectionable. In fact, I take it to be important that this philosophy of needs permits us to identify forms of paternalism that are not only benign but also necessary to human functioning.[34]

---

[34] I am indebted to an anonymous Cambridge University Press reader for this and a number of other helpful points.

7 STATES OF NEEDS

I argued in the previous chapter that an analysis of true interests, that aims both to enhance individual participative power and to retain an objective account of human goods, requires a substantively rich and need-based critical analysis of extant institutions, practices and roles in a way that is not achieved by the contemporary wave of 'civil society' theorists. (My stronger claim was that the concept, and especially their use of it, is positively detrimental to that goal.) In this chapter I have defended the claim that a first and very significant step in that direction is an understanding of the state of needs as the coercive site of ultimate need evaluation. This conception of the state pinpoints three main functions for the state that all focus on the goal of improving the individual evaluation of true interests and control over the evaluation of the more general need trajectories, and thereby the power of individuals to participate in the generation and satisfaction of their needs. As I pointed out, in any single evaluation of true interests the individual is the last, ultimate court of appeal; but in the less frequent evaluation of institutions, roles and need trajectories the state of needs must make the final, ultimate decision, without contravening the vital need and participative safeguards. More specifically, the legitimate state of needs must institutionalise procedural means through which it is able to act as ultimate evaluator of: (a) institutions in the five ways constitutive of institutional consequentialism; (b) institutions and roles with regard to their efficiency in satisfying post-evaluation needs; and (c) actual and possible trajectories of need.

The issue of need trajectory evaluation is particularly important for three reasons. First, it identifies the vital distinction between short-term and long-term interests in politics and shows that amongst other things a single coercive authority is a *sine qua non* of the evaluation and choice of long-term interests and goals. Second, the accountability and legitimacy of a state of needs must be assessed in the light of the consequences of its representatives' choices with regard to institutional re-arrangement and possible need trajectories; mere 'transparency' is insufficient and often illusory. Third, the state's role in the choice of need trajectories highlights the fact that not all forms of paternalism are necessarily abhorrent or opposed to human functioning and freedom. However, all of the above three procedural means must be institutionalised *within* the confines of the stipulated procedural requirements of a need-based constitution, which include the two safeguards.

The reader will have noticed that I have said nothing about the optimal or preferred size of states of needs or for that matter anything about their territorial, geographical, or demographic make-up. This silence has been intentional. Amongst other things, the distinction I make between states of needs and modern states is a means of dissociating the justification for the state from justifications for cultural, racial, linguistic or national homogeneity. And, in particular, it is a means of undermining claims based on existing 'identities', for normally these 'identities' are the consequence of current, historically contingent, state formations and borders. In other words, instituting a state of needs is one way of removing the 'nation' from the 'nation-state'. In order to meet the demands and safeguards of vital need satisfaction and participation in the evaluation of needs and institutions – that is, in order for modern states to become states of needs – they may have to change their size or transform extant 'national' boundaries. This may involve as well a radical transformation of immigration laws.[35] Ideally the coercive authority must coerce an area and group of people large enough and diverse enough to encourage diversity, experiment and change, and small enough for it to be able to be responsive to legitimate avowed needs and interests. This latter reason is one amongst a number of reasons why the state of needs cannot be a single global authority, some actually existing *global* authority, say the United Nations (UN), the World Bank or one large super-state, or any possible single global authority.[36] However, the actual size and other related concerns can only be decided in context and only once the need-based institutions of participation are in place within the current confines of existing states, which is the case in no extant modern state. Political theorists must think about how to secure these institutions, and concomitantly the state of needs, rather than stipulate from afar the preferred size or demographic make-up of political communities. It may follow from this that some modern states may have to become larger, while others may have to be made smaller, but we cannot be sure until these institutions are in place. But one thing is certain. Whatever communitarian thinkers hope to gain from reducing the size of our political communities will be lost by an increase in the informal rigidity and control that is normally concomitant with a decrease in size. The political philosophy of needs defended in this book could be expanded beyond the confines

---

[35] However, I maintain that free migration is not a panacea for all our existing problems, for not only does it assume a possible 'free market' in labour, but also it fails to identify the effects of this alleged freedom on weaker, poorer, less 'attractive' states – a massive 'brain-drain' – and thus removes the incentives for states to provide free formal education from which they may benefit in the future. It removes the point of investing in education and training: if there is a good chance that one's child will emigrate and work somewhere else, one's state will be tempted to question whether it should invest in her or his education.

[36] For all the reasons and a defence of this claim, see my '"Civil Society": Critique and Alternative', in S. Halperin and G. Laxer (eds.), *Global Civil Society and Its Limits* (London: Palgrave, 2003), section IV.

of a state of needs to inform global concerns and institutions (although, as I have said, it does not support the idea of a single global authority), but it does not and cannot condone the appeal to small homogeneous communities as the basis for political identity and sovereignty. If anything, as I have alluded to in my discussions of 'identity politics', my account of the disclosure and evaluation of needs, institutions and roles is intended as a means of generating greater diversity of needs, interests, outlooks and associations, and thus removing the point of making recourse to national, ethnic or racial justification, stereotype or prejudice.

Thus the state of needs is in no way equivalent to the nation-state. But this is not the only practical or theoretical state form against which it can be marked out. The state of needs is not equivalent to the ancient kind of association that gives a state-like authority a strict teleology inherently related to human happiness. Nor is the state of needs that Hegelian entity that finally reconciles agents to their world by providing meaning in that world. And it is clearly quite unlike the liberal notion of the state as the neutral entity that acts free from power relations in the maintenance of justice. Rather, in the account defended here the legitimate state of needs is the state that fulfils the interconnected function of guaranteeing the conditions for constantly improved true interest evaluation, the meeting of vital needs, and the development of agency need. In doing so it may engender consent. But this is an important by-product rather than a condition of state legitimacy and authority. Consent does not provide any ultimate means of assessing the legitimacy of a state. This is the case because, amongst other things, consent can be engendered as a consequence of many other reasons, such as capitalist growth and consumption opportunities, even where and when the state is not legitimate in any of the senses discussed here. I argued that this kind of statist account is more likely to *increase* the power of individuals in the assessment and control over their lives than accounts of direct participatory democracy or civic republican models.[37] And I provided a short speculative, procedural account of a possible alternative to rights-based constitutional democracy. But the effectiveness of this solution is only verifiable through empirical application. In the main conclusion I provide a speculative analysis of what might follow from its application in a particular empirical case and context.

[37] My account understands democratic participation as a process of participation in the evaluation of need rather than simple consent or dissent (or contestability). For a recent republican approach to democratic involvement in terms of 'contestability', see P. Petit, *Republicanism: A Theory of Freedom and Government* (Oxford: Oxford University Press, 1999).

Conclusion

The goal of this political philosophy of needs was to develop and defend a theoretical conception that moves beyond the dominant rights-preferences couple and better articulates the material and ethical concerns of political theory and practice. Given the state of modern need theory and the impoverishment in political thought brought about by this couple, I focused most of my attention and energy on clarifying the nature and formation of needs and the actual and possible means of disclosing and evaluating needs.

There are five main conclusions to the political philosophy of needs developed in this book.

(a) *The Nature of Needs* Felt needs are motivational forces that can take the form of drives or goals. Needs are distinguishable from wants and interests not because their lack of satisfaction creates lack or objective harm but because their satisfaction, lack of satisfaction, distortion or trajectory of development have direct, specifiable consequences on human functioning. Vital needs and agency needs together constitute the *general* necessary conditions for minimal human functioning and the individual and political agency that is characteristic of full human functioning. Social needs are *particular* manifestations of the general needs and of wants that have become legitimised as ineluctable.

(b) *The Formation of Needs* There is an identifiable causal relationship between the perception and interpretation of the general vital and agency needs and the extant nature and trajectory of particular needs. That is, the perception, interpretation and subsequent recognition and meeting of vital and agency needs are determined by the extant distinction between wants and (social) needs. And this distinction is determined by the existing means of satisfying wants and needs and of articulating, recognising and meeting need. Hence, I emphasise the importance of the existing mechanisms within which these processes occur, for example the production of knowledge, beliefs, conventions and rules and the production and consumption of commodities; and the causal significance of the institutions, practices and roles that constitute and determine these mechanisms, for instance the institution of private property, welfare state and market-related institutions, and rights-based constitutions.

(c) *The Distortion of Needs* The perception of vital and agency needs can be distorted in a number of different ways by and within an array of different mechanisms. I discussed the causal and cognitive importance of normative power differentials, substitute gratification, the possibility effect and the endowment effect. Together these mechanisms, differentials and effects demonstrate the depth of significance and the pervasive nature of the formation and trajectory of particular needs in the perception and interpretation of vital and agency needs. Moreover, they reveal that groups and individuals can be oppressed in terms of need as a result of their socially determined relative power to affect norms, have need-claims recognised as such, and meet needs. This finding shifts the focus from how to engender deliberative consensus over need to how to improve the conditions under which need is generated, perceived and met.

(d) *The Evaluation of True Interests* As a consequence of the above analyses I then developed a conceptual apparatus that enables an improvement in need perception and satisfaction. It is based on my account of need but uses a specifically contextual notion of true interests that relates to particular acts of evaluation. True interests are post-reflective and role-dependent vital or agency needs, or satisfiers thereof, of a particular person in a particular time and place. A statement of true interest can be evaluated in the light of the person's objective conditions, for example, her material situation and extant roles, as revealed by a more elaborate and frequent census (in the sense developed in the third chapter). Within resource restrictions social policy must attend to all avowed true interests dependent on the outcome of this assessment; but, because true interest avowal is determined by existing institutions and roles, a full evaluation of true interests must also involve an analysis and critique of extant institutions and roles in the light of how they affect the distribution of met need and normative power. My account of institutional consequentialism coupled with a more elaborate and frequent census is one possible means of achieving this.

(e) *Meeting Needs* I argued that these goals, which are underpinned by the goal of meeting vital need and developing agency need within valued social roles, do not obtain as a consequence of 'civil society', practical reason or deliberation. They require a single coercive authority whose legitimacy is determined by how well it functions as the ultimate need evaluator and guarantor; that is, with regard to how well it transforms the conditions under which true interests are evaluated and post-evaluation vital and agency needs are satisfied. I argued that, above and beyond the participative procedure for true interest evaluation, my approach to need in general and institutional consequentialism in particular requires the successful institutionalisation of a participative procedure for choosing long-term need trajectories. I maintained that the modern state is the only authority that has the *potential* to be what I call the state of needs, but only if it institutes the political evaluation of true interests and need trajectories proposed in my account of a flexible, participative and needs-based constitution. This constitution safeguards a priority on vital need satisfaction and political participation in the disclosure and evaluation of needs and interests. This final proposal is novel because it is based on a distinctive conception of participation, and it clarifies why participation in the evaluation of human needs is both a good in itself and an instrumental good. It is constitutive of the development of individual agency, or rather one subset of agency needs, autonomy, and it is an instrumental condition for meeting real human needs in large societies.

I   WHAT NEEDS TO BE DONE? THE CASE OF SOUTH AFRICA

Institutions are important and they can be evaluated and changed. In what follows I provide a concrete proposal for transforming an existing institution, the South African Constitution of 1996. Using the example of land reform and the property clause, I show how and why the constitution in its present form acts against some of its stated goals and how these problems could be overcome if it were transformed along the lines of my earlier speculative proposals. The main goal is to increase participative power and decrease normative power differentials in the generation, disclosure, evaluation and meeting of needs in the South African context.

South Africa has only recently emerged out of nearly half a century of authoritarian rule founded on racist ideas, policies and constitutions.[1] These apartheid ideas and laws legitimised and secured a racially skewed

[1] South Africa has a long history of drafting and modifying constitutions. Natal (now the province of KwaZulu-Natal) received its first constitution in 1856. A large number of regional constitutions followed. Then, in 1908, a constitutional convention was held, which resulted in the British Parliament passing an act that established the Union of South Africa in 1910. This constitution lasted until 1983 but not without a number of modifications. M. Newitt, 'Introduction', in M. Bennun and M. Newitt (eds.), *Negotiating Justice: A New Constitution for South Africa* (Exeter: University of Exeter Press, 1995), pp. 10–11.

system of land ownership and economic and political participation that ensured a relatively cheap, constant labour force for white business and farming interests. Freedom of ownership, movement, residence, association, expression and many other civil and political liberties were the privileges of whites only. However, the institutions and practices that characterised and legitimised these conditions have their origins in an era that pre-dates apartheid. They stretch far back into the colonial period, with their roots in the original activities of eighteenth- and nineteenth-century Dutch and British settlers and the laws they enacted, or in terms of specific policy at least back to 1828.[2] Most of this 'activity' amounted to struggle over land, and gradually first the Dutch and then the British colonisers forcefully occupied most of what is now South Africa. This control was legally ratified, and the subsequent forced removals of Africans were legitimised, by the 1913 Natives Land Act, thirty-five years before the legal institutionalisation of apartheid in 1948. This land act reserved 7 per cent (increased to 13.6 per cent in 1936) of South Africa's land for 'native reserves' and prohibited Africans from buying land elsewhere.[3] The 1913 Land Act was defended under the new racial ideology of 'segregation' but had as much to do with the preservation of a large pool of cheap labour.[4] The combination of these restrictions on land ownership in 'white' areas, the subsequent massive overcrowding in the 'reserves', and the support for communal tenure in the traditional system led very quickly to an abandonment of attempts at securing individual land tenure by and for Africans. The consequence of these and other policies, such as the Group Areas Act, was an institutional arrangement in which the distribution of goods, services and land ownership left the needs of most South Africans either unmet or distorted. The distortions are evident throughout this polarised and divided society.

During and following the end of apartheid, there was a now well-documented period of negotiation in which this history was thick in the air. Most of those involved in negotiations felt the real, pressing need to address,

---

[2] See R. Davenport and C. Saunders, *South Africa: A Modern History* (5th edn) (London: Macmillan, 2000), chs 7 and 8. Racist policy in South Africa has a longer history than most people realise. For example, ordinance 49/1828 required black people to carry passes for entry into the Cape Colony and a pass was required before they could seek employment. A. Caiger, 'The Protection of Property in South Africa', in Bennun and Newitt, *Negotiating Justice*, pp. 113–40, at p. 113n.

[3] R. Hall and G. Williams, 'Land Reform in South Africa: Problems and Prospects' (unpublished paper, developed from paper presented at a workshop on the Politics of Land Reform in the New South Africa, Development Studies Institute (DESTIN), London School of Economics, June 2000), p. 11. I am indebted to Scott Drimie for bringing this paper to my attention.

[4] It was recommended by the Lagden Commission of 1903–5 and later reinforced and intensified through Hertzog's 1936 Native Trust legislation and the Bantu 'homeland' policy from 1955. Davenport and Saunders, *South Africa*, pp. 192, 588–90.

and find means of redressing, the legacy of colonialism and apartheid. In the negotiations themselves, the focus was on practical issues, such as the handover of rule and the shape of future rule and government. Three fora of discussion and debate over the content and form of the latter culminated in a new constitution. The first two fora led to the drafting of the 1993 interim constitution and the third led to the final 1996 constitution.[5] This constitution is a groundbreaking legal document, both in terms of what it attempts as a constitution and in terms of what it hopes to achieve in the context of South Africa. Its main aim is to provide a set of entrenched rights, safeguards or guarantees, for all South Africans irrespective of race, colour, sex or creed, while at the same time stipulating goals, means and broad directives to remedy and redress the injustices of the past. Moreover, in stark contrast to earlier South African constitutions it is linked explicitly and frequently to international law in general and to human rights in particular. For example, the main preamble states that the freely elected representatives adopted the constitution to 'heal the divisions of the past and establish a society based on democratic values, social justice and fundamental human rights'.[6] The document is simultaneously of strict constitutional form and full of history and political goals and aspirations. Even the Bill of Rights, an elaborate fourteen-page second chapter, makes constant reference to the injustices of the past, both in the rights clauses themselves and in the limitation clauses.

[5] The constitutional process that began very soon after the unbanning of political opposition in South Africa on 2 February 1990 involved three distinct fora and periods. First, the Convention for a Democratic South Africa (CODESA) forum was established in December 1991 and lasted until May 1992. Second, the Multi-Party Negotiating Process (MPNP) in Kempton Park ran between March and November 1993 and saw the transitional process through to the creation of an Interim Constitution on 17 November 1993 and South Africa's first democratic elections on 27 April 1994. And, finally, the forum of the Constitutional Assembly discussions led to the certification of the final constitution on 6 September 1996. For full discussions of the first two fora and their context, see Bennun and Newitt, *Negotiating Justice*; T. Marcus, K. Eales and A. Wildschut, *Down to Earth: Land Demand in the New South Africa* (Durban: Indicator Press, 1996), part 3; D. van Wyk, J. Dugard, B. de Villiers and D. Davis (eds.), *Rights and Constitutionalism: The New South African Legal Order* (Oxford: Clarendon Press, 1996). For insights into the third forum, see 'Certification of the Constitution of the Republic of South Africa, 1996', heard on 1–5 and 8–11 July 1996 and decided on 6 September 1996, at http://www.concourt.gov.za/judgements/1996/const.html; and the various Judicial Service Commission Interviews, at http://www.concourt.gov.za/interviews.

[6] Preamble to the *Constitution of the Republic of South Africa* (Pretoria: Government Printers, 1996); also available at http://www.polity.org.za/govdocs/constitution/saconst.html. The constitution makes constant reference to human rights and the requirement, when necessary, to use international law to inform the process of constitutional interpretation. Moreover, chapter nine stipulates that a human rights commission be formed as a fundamental means of 'supporting constitutional democracy'. For a legal analysis of how the constitution is linked in form and content with international law and the doctrine of human rights, and the degree to which this is novel, see J. Dugard, 'International Law and the South African Constitution', *European Journal of International Law*, 8. 1 (1997).

This concern for the past within a future-oriented document is most manifest in clause 25 of the Bill of Rights, the property clause. For this and a number of more obvious ideological reasons, 'the property clause was a bone of contention right from the outset'.[7] At the start of negotiations, there was some consideration, for example by the African National Congress (ANC), over whether a property clause might be left out of the Bill of Rights altogether.[8] However, the ANC at least were soon persuaded otherwise by arguments put forward by a coterie of liberal South African judges and by a claim that its exclusion would severely hamper foreign investment.[9] Very soon the question became not whether to omit a property clause from the Bill of Rights, but how to accommodate both a right to property and a directive to address historical disadvantage created by apartheid laws and policies. In the final constitution, the clause seems to go some way down the path of meeting both demands. Nowhere does it actually state that individuals have 'rights in property' or 'rights to property', and in the subclause on compensation for expropriated land, 25(2), there is a directive to balance individual interest and public interest, where the latter is defined as 'including the nation's commitment to land reform'.[10] In fact, eight of the nine subclauses either discuss means of securing insecure land tenure or propose considerations for the expropriation of land for redistribution as determined by need or for the restitution of rights lost as a consequence

---

[7] L. M. Du Plessis, 'A background to drafting the chapter on fundamental rights', in *Birth of a Constitution*, ed. by B. de Villiers (Kenwyn, South Africa: Juta & Co, 1994), p. 97.

[8] The ANC Freedom Charter, adopted at the Congress of the People at Kliptown, Johannesburg, on 25 and 26 June 1955 and used in its original form at the beginning of the 1990s' constitutional process, states that '[r]estriction of land ownership on a racial basis shall be ended, and all the land *redivided* amongst those who work it, to banish famine and land hunger', and '[a]ll shall have the right to *occupy* land wherever they choose'. A. Luthuli, *Let My People Go* (London: Collins, 1962), p. 213 (my emphases), from Caiger, 'Protection of Property', in Bennun and Newitt (eds.), *Negotiating Justice*, pp. 124–5. These provisions are not reconcilable with the protection of property as part of first-generation rights, i.e. with a right to private property. For more evidence, see A. J. van der Walt, 'Property Rights, Land Rights, and Environmental Rights', in van Wyk et al. (eds.), *Rights and Constitutionalism*, p. 481.

[9] The restrictions imposed by powerful international trade and 'development' organisations have become starkly apparent again of late: despite serious internal criticism, the ANC government recently adopted with few changes a World Bank proposal for land redistribution. For more on the effects of World Bank foreign investment orientation on the government and its land reform policy, see Hall and Williams, 'Land Reform in South Africa', pp. 3–5, and note 13 below.

[10] Needless to note, property is not reducible to land. There are other kinds of property, for example, fixed, personal, capital, etc., and this is constitutionally acknowledged in the property clause – 'property is not limited to land', 25(4). However, land and land reform dominate the property clause. This is the case because they are the most pressing practical concerns and ways of redressing the historical wrongs of unequal rights to land and property ownership. I focus on land reform for these reasons, but I take it to be only one instance of a need to reassess property ownership and the property clause in South Africa and beyond.

of the 1913 Land Act. In line, then, with the situation on the ground, the constitution stipulates three areas of concern, and there are now as a result three branches of land reform: the restitution of land rights for those who lost their rights as a result of the 1913 Land Act; land redistribution to meet vital housing and subsistence needs and to broaden the base of commercial agriculture; and the recognition of tenure for farm dwellers and others who have insecure tenure, due either to past racially discriminatory policies or allegedly 'traditional' forms of communal ownership. (I will not comment further on the issue of traditional ownership, but it and its constitutional safeguard must be reassessed as stipulated here. In many respects traditional communal ownership is even more detrimental to meeting needs than entrenched rights to land.)

However, these positive aspects of the clause are offset by a number of drawbacks, whose consequences are now clearly evident in the extremely poor delivery on land reform up to the present. The constitution lists a number of things that have to be taken into consideration during decisions over expropriation and compensation. There are five listed under subclause 3, i.e. 25(3), but two are of most significance here: (a) 'the history of the acquisition and use of the property'; and (b) 'the market value of the property'. Over the last seven years these practical considerations have complicated, hindered and in most cases directly blocked the process of land reform. Even claims for the restitution of those land rights that were annulled or expropriated by the 1913 act have been difficult to process, and in the few cases that have been processed most of the claimants have received cash payments.[11] The consequences of the 1913 act are relatively well-documented land evictions that continued right up until 1991, but this is only one, admittedly highly significant, moment in the history of colonial land occupation in South Africa. In the light of the long history of continual colonial land evictions summarised above, this rights-based approach should reach back to at least 1828. The historical and legal complications of such a move are mind-boggling.[12] Moreover, the stipulation to consider the market value of the property has now become a policy, especially in

---

[11] Since 1994, only 3,916 of the 63,455 restitution claims lodged have been settled. Hall and Williams, 'Land Reform in South Africa', p. 6. Only 162 of the claimants have received land, the rest cash payments. And, according to A. Mngxitama (Land Rights Coordinator for the National Land Committee), 'South Africa: land reform blocked', p. 2 at http://jinx.sistm.unsw.edu.au/~greenlft/2000/406/406p25.htm, it could take up to 63 years to deal with the claims load.

[12] It does not follow from this that historical analysis of past injustices is unnecessary, for it is indispensable in persuading ex-colonial powers to provide financial support for the process of land reform. But that would require broad historical research rather than countless investigations of individual cases.

the area of land redistribution, and the state simply does not have enough funds even to begin this process.[13]

But the source of the problem does not lie in the substance of these inevitably complicated practical considerations, or the failings of the ANC government and its policies.[14] Although the ANC government has failed to help matters much and in some cases blunder has followed blunder, the real problem is the constitution. In this case the devil is not in the detail, but rather in the framework. The underlying reason for this lack of delivery is that the property clause is part of an entrenched Bill of Rights in a rights-based constitution. Clause 7 of the constitution states that the Bill of Rights 'enshrines the rights of all people in our country', and that 'the state must respect, protect, promote and fulfil the rights in the Bill of Rights'. In the light of South Africa's history, the property clause obviously aims to safeguard the right of *access* to property, and to aid equal access by providing directives for land reform, rather than safeguard extant property rights and their exercise. However, it in fact achieves the opposite: rather than establishing a means of changing the existing property arrangements it entrenches them. This is the case because, however many subclauses and limitation clauses follow the right, the property right, by virtue of its being a right, has a default priority. This is the case for three reasons, which all relate to the nature of modern rights and rights-discourse and the South African context. The first emerges from the fact that because rights already exist (normally as privileges) prior to constitutionally enshrined equal rights to access or entitlement, the new rights-claims or rights-bearers have to confront a status quo that uses the same language of rights. The second centres on the ontological form of rights, especially the fact that rights are understood as properties of persons. The third concerns the problem of entrenching means and ideals in the same form (as rights).

Rights-based constitutions tend to entrench the extant arrangements of land ownership because those with land – in this case white South Africans, who constitute 13 per cent of population and own 87 per cent of land – have a head start: they have already a right of ownership over a portion of the land to which the constitution gives them a right of access. As regards land redistribution, therefore, it is incumbent upon government to collect information, find evidence and develop arguments for evicting current

---

[13] If the state had to procure the funds for what has become known as the 'willing buyer, willing seller' policy, land reform would take a very long time indeed. This policy is not the answer to the problem. A. Mngxitama, 'South Africa: land reform blocked', p. 3.

[14] These are the reasons put forward by most commentators. For examples, see Hall and Williams, 'Land Reform in South Africa', and A. Mngxitama, 'South Africa: land reform blocked'.

landowners. They have to set aside massive financial resources in order to compensate at or near market rates and provide the capital for new farmers to become commercially viable.[15] As regards the restitution of land rights, the onus is on the individual or community to lodge the claim and provide the supporting evidence. And most of the individuals and communities concerned have few means and poor educational resources. Moreover, because these rights have only 'vertical' and not 'horizontal' application, i.e., rights cannot be claimed between individuals, redistribution and restitution alike are legally achievable only via government action. Hence, those who have the right over property have a three-fold advantage: (a) they are usually better educated and more financially secure than the claimants; (b) their right is of the same form as other inalienable rights in the Bill of Rights; and (c) they have the luxury of sitting on their hands, of not having to prove their right (or need). The government, on the other hand, must be proactive and it must convince the courts in each and every instance that the case in question requires application of the public interest (land reform) *exception* as opposed to the individual right *default*. This takes time and money, although it will provide significant numbers of judges and advocates with a secure job for a long time to come. It also adds legitimacy to an already overloaded and over-bureaucratised administrative structure of countless courts and procedures.

The second reason why rights-based structures hinder change is because, within a discourse of rights, the right to an object or an outcome becomes the property (or at least the entitlement) of the bearer of the right. This is the case because rights are understood as inalienable elements of human nature. And because human nature is not static and is heavily influenced by the contextual or hegemonic institutional arrangements and practices, these institutions and practices come to define the rights-bearers. That is, as things stand, to be a person, to be a human, is to have rights and to have rights is to own or be entitled to certain goods, objects, powers and properties. These goods, objects, powers and properties are heavily fashioned by a contextual domestic or imported status quo, or they can be

---

[15] In fact, these market and resource restrictions have forced the government into favouring claims from those claimants who are able to put forward substantial amounts of their own capital. And this has been reinforced by a World Bank argument that seems to conceive of land reform purely in terms of encouraging commercial agriculture, and the creation of a black commercial farming class, rather than meeting the vital needs of the rural poor. Obviously, the requirement to meet the needs of the rural poor must be balanced with the need for efficient commercial agriculture, but the combination of constitutionally enforced market constraints and rights-based evaluation and World Bank ideology has ensured that segregation based on race has quickly become segregation based on class. Hall and Williams, 'Land Reform in South Africa'.

a combination of both. And amongst other things the domestic or imported status quo may be distorted, or the import may not fit the domestic context. In the case of South Africa there is an unfortunate mix of both problems: an allegedly universal human rights structure that misfits a distorted status quo. Yet, however distorted or forced the defining arrangements, since the right is inalienable and the bearer of the right is understood as having sovereignty over himself, each limitation on a right is a strict exception that requires careful attention. Hence, in the case of land reform for example, every case becomes an analysis of the rights-bearer and his property: 'the history and acquisition of the property'. Essentially what each case amounts to is a highly individualised conflict of existing right (or ownership) versus original right, right of tenure, or right of access (property right claim). The evaluative permutations and requisite historical evidence and discussion are both highly complicated and often inconclusive, but they are inescapable so long as rights are the main basis upon which evaluation rests.

These problems are not peculiar to the question of property; they have arisen and will continue to arise in questions relating to all the other roughly thirty-five rights that constitute the Bill of Rights. The rights of association, expression, human dignity, equality, freedom and security of the person, trade, occupation and profession, do and will favour the most advantaged in the status quo, which in the case of South Africa is a status quo very much still tainted and structured by apartheid. This is because the organisation of political guarantees, means and goals in terms of rights and rights-based constitutions must (mistakenly) assume an equality of resources, access and information. In other words rights-based constitutions make a condition, a means, out of an ideal (equality) and claim that the condition exists because the right exists. As I have argued in the main body of the work, this illusory move is made possible because the rights-discourse assumes static universal conditions or means to certain (implicitly) valued ends, while formulating the set of aspirations or ends in the form of rights. Thus the third reason rights-based constitutions entrench the status quo is because, by making everything a right, they not only reify extant conditions but also artificially impose equal value on conditions and goals.

The government is, therefore, unable to enforce the directives or achieve the goals stipulated in the constitution for two reasons. (1) The constitution unintentionally ossifies the positive rights of the status quo, like various kinds of existing property rights and the social relations and inequalities they guarantee and entrench. These can then be utilised by individuals in ways that act against the aspirational rights: because they are given the same ontological form and moral value, they appear as a conflict over rights, which are then resolved within a formal judicial framework. (2) Values and goals and the means to their achievement, which are essentially contextual and political questions, are universalised and de-politicised.[16] The political and ethical values and goals that are adumbrated in the constitution are thus shorn of their political and ethical nature: they are given a 'natural' character within a *meta*-political institution, the constitution, especially where and when that constitution is linked to the doctrine of human rights. A rights-based constitution stacks the odds against government-driven change because it reifies historically variable conditions and means within an historically invariable legal code. The constitutional goals are therefore hamstrung by the constitution itself. The main political institution eclipses the main political practice of evaluation; and evaluation is removed to the sterile confines of an unaccountable chamber. Consequently, the crucial part of the constitution that deals with important means and goals related to property, whose possession and use is fundamental to meeting needs, is severely constrained by the constitution itself. And this is as true of any other state on the globe as it is of South Africa. Change under all constitutions is the exception rather than the rule and South Africa is not unique in requiring change. Alongside human rights, this characteristic of liberal constitutional democracy is the great tragic irony of our age.

There are a number of proposed solutions to this problem. But all of them take the basic problem to be a question of what or what not to include in the constitution, or parts thereof, or they take it to be a difficulty that is specific to the right to property.[17] That is, they do not see the problem as having its source in the idea of rights but as a problem with particular kinds of rights and what to do with them within the framework of a rights-based constitution. I maintain that these moves resolve little. In fact, they shroud the problem behind yet more technicalities while missing the source of the problem. Given my account of the source of the difficulty, I want to propose

---

[16] This is a typical move amongst the liberal tradition in general and liberal legal philosophy and practice in particular. It is no accident that many of the drafters of both constitutions and a number of constitutional court judges, e.g., Hugh Corder, Dennis Davis, John Dugard, E. Mureinik, are influenced by the work of Rawls and Dworkin. See Judicial Service Commission Interviews, http://www.concourt.gov.za/interviews.

[17] For example, see D. Davis, 'The case against the inclusion of socio-economic demands in a Bill of Rights except as directive principles', *South African Journal of Human Rights*, 8 (1992); and, for the case against including property rights in the Bill of Rights, see A. J. van der Walt, 'Developments that may Change the Institution of Private Ownership so as to meet the Needs of a Non-racial Society in South Africa', *Stellenbosch Law Review*, 1 (1990), and 'The Fragmentation of Land Rights', *South African Journal of Human Rights*, 8 (1992). For overviews of the different positions, see van der Walt, 'Property Rights', in van Wyk et al. (eds.), *Rights and Constitutionalism*; and Caiger. 'Protection of Property', in Bennun and Newitt (eds.), *Negotiating Justice*.

the following for the South African constitution. First, the problem is not with a constitution *per se* but with its form and formulation in its rights-based variety. An immutable form of constitution that formulates its guarantees and goals in terms of rights doubly reinforces against change. Both of these restraining characteristics must be overcome. Second, the inclusion of values and aspirations in this kind of apolitical structure in the same form as other requirements is counterproductive. Hence, rather than following the prevailing hegemony of (human) rights-based constitutions, the South African constitution could concretise procedures that safeguard the means to ensuring needs-based institutional critique and guarantees to transform institutions in line with meeting post-evaluation needs. This would involve guaranteeing the satisfaction of vital needs and a level of participation that would demand the institutionalisation of the two procedures summarised at the end of the fourth chapter. These would secure the required level of political participation in the periodic evaluation of needs, interests and need trajectories. South Africa could seize this exciting and unusual historical juncture and develop a constitution that at once secured the means and ends of participation in the evaluation of interests and needs, and that stipulated a full set of goals and aspirations for change. Moreover, if the recommendations developed in the text are followed, periodic reappraisals of the two procedures *and* the stipulated aspirations would need to be instituted. The substantive issues are only achievable if the aspirations and goals are conceptualised as needs, and if the procedures are enshrined in terms of rules for periodic political participation. Neither must be understood in terms of rights nor be fixed and inflexible. The procedural rules can be coercively, legally enforced opportunities. It is important that they be understood as opportunities rather than obligations, for even in the case of vital need priority individuals should have the choice to opt out.[18]

This will return the evaluative processes, considerations and decisions to the truly political, legislative arena because the constitution would only safeguard the rules of the procedures, and because the real processes of

---

[18] If not, an obligation-based approach may reinforce the manifold problems evident in human rights based legal evaluation. Prevailing laws and policy on voluntary assisted euthanasia are a good example of the current problem. Human rights can be used to defend *and* oppose voluntary assisted euthanasia, but if interpretation of the doctrine keeps to the letter of the doctrine, which claims to enshrine inviolable individual rights of humans irrespective of their preferences, then it will oppose it. Hence, as in the recent Diane Pretty case in Britain, someone who is unable to commit suicide but would like to end their life for reasons of severe pain, or otherwise, will be forced to live when they want to die. However, if the human rights doctrine is given a different interpretation, it could be used to allow choice in this matter. See A. C. Grayling, 'A Good Death', *Guardian*, 27 October 2001 for an heroic attempt. Unfortunately, however, because it is a human *rights* doctrine it normally engenders the former slant and hence verdict.

true interest and need trajectory evaluation will involve government action both in the process itself and as the main agent of ultimate decision-making. The premium will be on change and risk rather than the status quo and safeguards. Moreover, substantive issues, such as land reform and property ownership, will be understood and evaluated in terms of need. And property ownership under the logic of need avoids all three hindrances to achieving land reform. It will not require long and expensive historical analysis of rights-claims because land reform will amount to redistribution in line with post-evaluation, legitimate need rather than the restitution of historical rights. It will not favour the status quo because all land will be evaluated equally in terms of the demands of redistribution according to vital need satisfaction and of redistribution for developing a viable and effective commercial agricultural sector. Finally, in determining *possession* in line with need, it would disassociate property from private persons and their properties and achievements. Land could be possessed or owned for private consumption, use, and exchange, and this could be safeguarded in terms of rights, but these rights must not be understood or treated as *inalienable* individual rights. Rather, they would be rights to use and exchange that would be assessed periodically in line with needs. This would also be true of other forms of property that generate needs and their satisfiers; in other words, all existing forms of private property excluding items of personal property. Given that single individuals would never have the inalienable right to land (and other forms of need-related institutions of property), it follows that land would not be inheritable.

Finally, I ought to stress two points. First, I am not arguing that my solution will resolve all the problems of political evaluation, implementation and conflict, but it will, at least, return an inherently political process to its truly political, rather than rigidly legal, court of evaluation. Accountable and publicly elected representatives must control evaluative procedures and decisions. There will be consequences and problems of this shift to which I as a theorist (or any other theorist) may not be able to provide answers. Some of these problems and concerns can only be dealt with on the ground. As I have said before, this is not a coherentist approach to political theory. In contrast to a Platonist or a Kantian, I maintain that political theory cannot provide a full theoretical answer to the whole range of political problems; political theory cannot replace the practice of politics. Second, despite my emphasis on the modern state, and in this conclusion the South African state, there is no reason whatsoever why we should not ascribe the same force to needs in the larger context of international problems in the evaluation and meeting of needs. States of needs do not have to leave unchanged the framework set by modern states. And the concerns over how to think about constitutions in particular do not need to be restricted to state constitutions. Obviously, if extended this kind of analysis will have to focus first on doctrines such as the hegemonic doctrine of human rights, about which, unfortunately, I can say no more in this context. These considerations have received insufficient theoretical attention. They require extensive empirical study and theoretical analysis, especially in terms of the ideological, political and material histories and consequences of current, international, legal and economic institutions and practices.

As I have argued, needs, institutions, roles and the general trajectory of need are, or at least ought to be, the central concern of politics. This is the case for the simple reason that politics is ultimately about control over the things that are valuable to humans, and thus by implication the means to this control, in particular the forms of rule that secure it. That we function and how well we function are indisputably of value to all humans and since the development and satisfaction of needs determines these two concerns, they are central to politics. Now, if humans are to increase their power over these concerns we (us humans) must at least try to understand and if necessary transform the determinants of the nature, formation, articulation, recognition and meeting of needs. In this book I have pinpointed what I maintain are the main general mechanisms of doing so, and in this concluding chapter I have provided an example of one institutional culprit that requires urgent attention. The more aware we become of this task and the more we position it in its true social and political (rather than natural and moralising) context, the better will be our grasp of politics and how to improve its practice. If we begin by thinking about politics as concerned with the constant collective choice between actual and possible need trajectories, we may improve our chances of being able to choose our needs rather than have them determine our choices.

Bibliography

Adorno, T. W., *Minima Moralia*, London: Verso, 1978.

Negative Dialectics, London: Routledge, 1990.

Adorno, T. W. and Horkheimer, M., *Dialectic of Enlightenment*, London: Verso, 1979.

Althusser, L., *For Marx*, trans. B. Brewster, Harmondsworth: Penguin, 1977.

Anderson, P., 'Antinomies of Antonio Gramsci', *New Left Review*, 100 (1976–7).

Appiah, K. A., 'Race, Culture, Identity: Misunderstood Connections', in K. A. Appiah and A. Gutmann (eds.), *Color Consciousness: The Political Morality of Race*, Princeton: Princeton University Press, 1996.

Arato, A., 'Civil Society Against the State: Poland 1980–1', *Telos*, 47 (1981).

'Empire vs. Civil Society: Poland 1981–2', *Telos*, 50 (1981–2).

Arato, A. and Cohen, J., 'Social Movements, Civil Society, and the Problems of Sovereignty', *Praxis International*, 4. 3 (1984).

Aristotle, *The Nicomachean Ethics*, trans. and intro. D. Ross, Oxford: Oxford University Press, 1980.

The Politics, ed. S. Everson, Cambridge: Cambridge University Press, 1988.

Eudemian Ethics: books I, II and VIII, trans. M. Woods, 2nd edn, Oxford: Clarendon Press, 1992.

Armitage, D., *The Ideological Origins of the British Empire*, Cambridge: Cambridge University Press, 2000.

Arneson, R., 'Equality and Equality of Opportunity for Welfare', *Philosophical Studies*, 56 (1989).

Arrow, K. J., *Social Choice and Individual Values*, 2nd edn, New Haven: Yale University Press, 1963 (1st edn 1952).

'Some Ordinalist Notes on Rawls' Theory of Justice', *Journal of Philosophy* (1973).

Augustine, *The City of God against the Pagans*, ed. R. W. Dyson, Cambridge: Cambridge University Press, 1998.

Ball, T., Farr, J. and Hanson, R. L. (eds.), *Political Innovation and Conceptual Change*, Cambridge: Cambridge University Press, 1989.

Barry, B., *Political Argument*, London: Routledge, 1965.

'The Public Interest', in A. Quinton (ed.), *Political Philosophy*, Oxford: Oxford University Press, 1967.

'Justice and the Common Good', in A. Quinton (ed.), *Political Philosophy*, Oxford: Oxford University Press, 1967.

Benhabib, S. (ed.), *Democracy and Difference: Contesting the Boundaries of the Political*, Princeton: Princeton University Press, 1996.

Benn, S. I., '"Interests" in Politics', *Proceedings of the Aristotelian Society* (New Series), 9.

Benn, S. I. and Peters, R. S., *Social Principles and the Democratic State*, London: Allen & Unwin, 1959.

Bennun, M. and Newitt, M. (eds.), *Negotiating Justice: A New Constitution for South Africa*, Exeter: University of Exeter Press, 1995.

Bentham, J., *Anarchical Fallacies*, in J. Waldron (ed.), *'Nonsense Upon Stilts': Bentham, Burke, and Marx on the Rights of Man*, London: Methuen, 1987.

Berlin, I., *Four Essays on Liberty*, Oxford: Oxford University Press, 1969.

Berry, C. J., *Hume, Hegel and Human Nature*, The Hague: M. Nijhoff, 1982.

  The Idea of Luxury, Cambridge: Cambridge University Press, 1994.

Bond, P., *Elite Transition: From Apartheid to Neoliberalism in South Africa*, London: Pluto, 2000.

Braybrooke, D., *Meeting Needs*, Princeton: Princeton University Press, 1987.

  Moral Objectives, Rules, and the Forms of Social Change, Toronto and London: Toronto University Press, 1998.

Brett, A. S., *Liberty, Right and Nature: Individual rights in later scholastic thought*, Cambridge: Cambridge University Press, 1997.

Brock, G. (ed.), *Necessary Goods: Our Responsibilities to Meet Others' Needs*, Oxford: Rowman and Littlefield, 1998.

Bull, M., 'Slavery and the Multiple Self', *New Left Review*, 231 (Sept./Oct. 1998).

Caiger, A., 'The Protection of Property In South Africa', in M. Bennun and M. Newitt (eds.), *Negotiating Justice: A New Constitution for South Africa*, Exeter: Exeter University Press, 1995.

Carver, T., 'Marx's 1857 Introduction', *Economy and Society*, 9. 2 (1980).

Castoriadis, C., *The Imaginary Institution of Society*, trans. K. Blamey, Cambridge: Polity Press, 1987.

Cohen, G. A., *Karl Marx's Theory of History: A Defence*, Oxford: Clarendon Press, 1978.

  'On the Currency of Egalitarian Justice', *Ethics*, 99 (1989).

  'Equality of What? On Welfare, Goods and Capabilities', *Recherches économiques de Louvain*, 56 (1990).

  'Incentives, Inequality and Community', in G. Petersen (ed.), *The Tanner Lectures on Human Values*, vol. XIII, Salt Lake City: University of Utah Press, 1992.

  'Equality of What? On Welfare, Resources and Capabilities', in M. C. Nussbaum and A. K. Sen (eds.), *The Quality of Life*, Oxford: Clarendon Press, 1993.

  Self-Ownership, Freedom and Equality, Cambridge: Cambridge University Press, 1995.

Cohen, J. L., *Class and Civil Society: The Limits of Marxian Critical Theory*, Amherst: University of Massachusetts Press, 1982.

Cohen, J. L. and Arato, A., *Civil Society and Political Theory*, Cambridge, MA: MIT Press, 1992.

Connolly, W., 'On "Interests" in Politics', *Politics and Society*, 2. 4 (Summer 1972).

'Legitimacy and Modernity', in W. Connolly (ed.), *Legitimacy and the State*, New York: New York University Press, 1984.

Copp, D., Roemer, J. and Hampton J., *The Idea of Democracy*, Cambridge: Cambridge University Press, 1993.

Cunningham, F., *The Real World of Democracy Revisited*, New Jersey: Humanities, 1994.

Dagger, R., 'Rights', in T. Ball, J. Farr and R. L. Hanson (eds.), *Political Innovation and Conceptual Change*, Cambridge: Cambridge University Press, 1989.

Dahl, R. A., *A Preface to Economic Democracy*, Cambridge: Polity Press, 1985.

Dasgupta, P., *An Inquiry into Well-Being and Destitution*, Oxford: Clarendon Press, 1993.

Davenport, R. and Saunders, C., *South Africa: A Modern History*, 5th edn, London: Macmillan, 2000.

Davidson, D., *Essays on Actions and Events*, Oxford: Clarendon Press, 1980.

Inquiries into Truth and Interpretation, Oxford: Clarendon Press, 1984.

'Judging Interpersonal Interests', in J. Elster and A. Hylland (eds.), *Foundations of Social Choice Theory*, Cambridge: Cambridge University Press, 1986.

Davis, D., 'The case against the inclusion of socio-economic demands in a Bill of Rights except as directive principles', *South African Journal of Human Rights*, 8 (1992).

Dewey, J., *Human Nature and Conduct*, London: Allen and Unwin, 1922.

The Public and its Problems, New York: Holt, 1927.

'Theory of Valuation', in *Int. Encycl. Unified Sci.*, 2. 4., Chicago: University of Chicago Press, 1939.

Doyal, L., 'Thinking about Human Need', *New Left Review*, 201 (Sept./Oct. 1993).

Doyal, L. and Gough, I., *A Theory of Human Need*, London: Macmillan, 1991.

Dugard, J., 'International Law and the South African Constitution', *European Journal of International Law*, 8. 1 (1997).

Duncan, G., *Marx and Mill*, Cambridge: Cambridge University Press, 1973.

Dunn, J., *Western Political Theory in the Face of the Future*, Cambridge: Cambridge University Press, 1979.

The History of Political Theory and Other Essays, Cambridge: Cambridge University Press, 1996.

'The Contemporary Political Significance of John Locke's Conception of Civil Society', *Iyyun, The Jerusalem Philosophical Quarterly*, 45 (1996).

'Public and Private: Normative map and political and social battleground', paper presented at conference on 'Asian and Western Conceptions of Public and Private', Cambridge, September 1999.

The Cunning of Unreason: Making Sense of Politics, London: HarperCollins, 2000.

Dunn, J. (ed.), *Democracy: The Unfinished Journey 508 BC to AD 1993*, Oxford: Oxford University Press, 1993.

Du Plessis, L. M., 'A background to drafting the chapter on fundamental rights', in B. de Villiers (ed.), *Birth of a Constitution*, Kenwyn, South Africa: Juta & Co., 1994.

Dworkin, R., *Taking Rights Seriously*, London: Duckworth, 1977, repr. 1991.

'What is Equality? Part 2: Equality of Resources', *Philosophy and Public Affairs*, 10 (1981).

Law's Empire, Cambridge, MA: Harvard University Press, 1986.

Elster, J., *Ulysses and the Sirens: Studies in Rationality and Irrationality*, Cambridge: Cambridge University Press, 1979.

Sour Grapes: Studies in the subversion of rationality, Cambridge: Cambridge University Press, 1983.

'Weakness of Will and the Free-Rider Problem', *Economics and Philosophy*, 1 (1985).

'The Market and the Forum: Three varieties of political theory', in J. Elster and A. Hylland (eds.), *Foundations of Social Choice Theory*, Cambridge: Cambridge University Press, 1986.

Alchemies of the Mind: Rationality and the Emotions, Cambridge: Cambridge University Press, 1999.

Elster, J. and Hylland, A. (eds.), *Foundations of Social Choice Theory*, Cambridge: Cambridge University Press, 1986.

Elster, J. and Moene, K. Ove (eds.), *Alternatives to Capitalism*, Cambridge: Cambridge University Press, 1989.

Elster, J. and Skog, O.-J. (eds.), *Getting Hooked: Rationality and addiction*, Cambridge: Cambridge University Press, 1999.

Elster, J. and Slagstad, R. (eds.), *Constitutionalism and Democracy*, Cambridge: Cambridge University Press, 1987.

Emmerich, Z., 'The Form and Force of an Argument', unpublished paper, Cambridge, 2001.

Engels, F., *Outlines of a Critique of Political Economy*, in *Karl Marx Frederick Engels Collected Works Vol. 3 (MECW 3)*, London: Lawrence & Wishart, 1975.

Fay, M., 'The 1844 Economic and Philosophic Manuscripts of Karl Marx: A Critical Commentary and Interpretation', PhD thesis, University of California, Berkeley, 1979.

'The Influence of Adam Smith on Marx's Theory of Alienation', *Science and Society*, 47 (1983–4).

Fehér, F., Heller, A. and Márkus, G., *The Dictatorship Over Needs*, Oxford: Basil Blackwell, 1983.

Feinberg, J., 'Harm and Self-Interest', in P. M. S. Hacker and J. Raz (eds.), *Law, Morality and Society: Essays in Honour of H. L. A. Hart*, Oxford: Clarendon Press, 1977.

Rights, Justice and the Bounds of Liberty, Princeton: Princeton University Press, 1980.

Harm to Self, New York: Oxford University Press, 1986.

Felix, N., *Raça e Consciência de Classe*, Salvador, BA, Brazil, nd.

Festinger, L., *A Theory of Cognitive Dissonance*, Stanford: Stanford University Press, 1957.

Feuerbach, L., *Preliminary Theses on the Reform of Philosophy* (1842), in *The Fiery Brook: Selected Writings of Ludwig Feuerbach*, trans. Z. Hanfi, Garden City, NY: Anchor Books, 1972.

Principles of the Philosophy of the Future (1843), in *The Fiery Brook: Selected Writings of Ludwig Feuerbach*, trans. Z. Hanfi, Garden City, NY: Anchor Books, 1972.

Finnis, J., *Natural Law and Natural Rights*, Oxford: Clarendon Press, 1980.

Fitzgerald, R. (ed.), *Human Needs and Politics*, Oxford: Pergamon, 1977.

Flathman, R. E., *The Public Interest: An Essay Concerning the Normative Discourse of Politics*, New York: John Wiley & Sons, 1966.

Fleischman, E., 'The role of the individual in pre-revolutionary society: Stirner, Marx, and Hegel', in Z. A. Pelczynski (ed.), *Hegel's Political Philosophy: Problems and Perspectives*, Cambridge: Cambridge University Press, 1971.

Flew, A., *The Politics of Procrustes*, London: Temple Smith, 1981.

Flyvbjerg, B., *Rationality and Power: Democracy in Practice*, Chicago and London: Chicago University Press, 1998.

Foucault, M., *Surveiller et punir*, Paris: Gallimard, 1975.

Power/Knowledge: selected interviews and other writings 1972–77, ed. and trans. C. Gordon, Brighton: Harvester, 1980.

Fraser, I., *Hegel and Marx: The concept of need*, Edinburgh: Edinburgh University Press, 1998.

Fraser, N., 'Talking about Needs: Interpretive Contests as Political Conflicts in Welfare-State Societies', *Ethics*, 99. 2 (1989).

Unruly Practices: Power, Discourse and Gender in Contemporary Social Theory, Cambridge: Polity Press, 1989.

'From Redistribution to Recognition? Dilemmas of Justice in a "'Post-Socialist'" Age', in *Justice Interruptus*, London and New York: Routledge, 1997.

'Rethinking Recognition', *New Left Review*, 3 (May/June 2000).

Frazer, E. and Lacey, N., 'MacIntyre, Feminism and the Concept of Practice', in J. Horton and S. Mendus (eds.), *After MacIntyre: Critical Perspectives on the Work of Alasdair MacIntyre*, Cambridge: Polity Press, 1994.

Freyre, G., *The Masters and the Slaves*, trans. S. Putnam, New York: Knopf, 1963.

Gamble, A., *Hayek: The Iron Cage of Liberty*, Cambridge: Polity Press, 1996.

Politics and Fate, Cambridge: Polity Press, 2000.

Gellner, E., *Conditions of Liberty: Civil Society and Its Rivals*, London: Penguin, 1996.

Geras, N., *Marx and Human Nature: Refutation of a Legend*, London: Verso, 1983.

Geuss, R., *The Idea of a Critical Theory*, Cambridge: Cambridge University Press, 1981.

'Freedom as an Ideal', *The Aristotelian Society*, Supplementary Vol. 69 (1995).

Der Freiheitsbegriff im Liberalismus und bei Marx', in J. Nida-Rümelin and W. Vossenkuhl (eds.), *Ethische und politische Freiheit*, Berlin: Walter de Gruyter, 1998.

Morality, Culture, and History, Cambridge: Cambridge University Press, 1999.

'Virtue and the Good Life', *Arion*, 8. 1 (2000).

History and Illusion in Politics, Cambridge: Cambridge University Press, 2001.
Public Goods, Private Goods, Princeton: Princeton University Press, 2001.
'Liberalism and Its Discontents', *Political Theory*, 30. 3 (2002).
'Happiness and Politics', *Arion*, 10. 1 (2002).
Gibbard, A., 'Interpersonal Comparisons: Preference, Good, and the Intrinsic Reward of a Life', in J. Elster and A. Hylland (eds.), *Foundations of Social Choice Theory*, Cambridge: Cambridge University Press, 1986.
Giner, S., 'The Withering Away of Civil Society', *Praxis International*, 5. 3 (1985).
'Civil Society and Its Future', in J. A. Hall (ed.), *Civil Society: Theory, History, Comparison*, Cambridge: Polity Press, 1995.
Glaser, D., 'Civil Society and Its Limits: The Case of South Africa', *Strathclyde Papers on Government and Politics*, 105 (1995).
Goodin, R., 'Vulnerabilities and Responsibilities: An Ethical Defense of the Welfare State', in G. Brock (ed.), *Necessary Goods: Our Responsibilities to Meet Others' Needs*, Oxford: Rowman and Littlefield, 1998.
Goodin, R. (ed.), *The Theory of Institutional Design*, Cambridge: Cambridge University Press, 1998.
Graham, K., *Practical Reasoning in a Social World: How we act together*, Cambridge: Cambridge University Press, 2002.
Gramsci, A., *Selections from the Prison Notebooks*, ed. and trans. Q. Hoare and G. Nowell Smith, London: Lawrence & Wishart, 1971.
Pre-Prison Writings, ed. R. Bellamy, trans. V. Cox, Cambridge: Cambridge University Press, 1994.
Grayling, A. C., 'A Good Death', *Guardian*, 27 October 2001.
Griffin, J. P., *Well-Being: Its meaning, measurement and moral importance*, Oxford: Clarendon Press, 1986.
'Consequentialism', in T. Honderich (ed.), *The Oxford Companion to Philosophy*, Oxford: Oxford University Press, 1995.
Gutmann, A. (ed.), *Multiculturalism: Examining the politics of recognition*, Princeton: Princeton University Press, 1994.
Habermas, J., *Knowledge and Human Interests*, Boston, MA: Beacon Press, 1971.
Legitimation Crisis, trans. T. McCarthy, Cambridge: Polity Press, 1988 [1979].
Theory of Communicative Action, Vol. 1: Reason and the Rationalization of Society, trans. T. McCarthy, Boston, MA: Beacon Press, 1984.
Theory of Communicative Action, Vol. 2, Lifeworld and System: A Critique of Functionalist Reason, trans. T. McCarthy, Boston, MA: Beacon Press, 1987.
Between Facts and Norms: Contributions to a Discourse Theory of Law and Democracy, trans. W. Rehg, Cambridge: Polity Press, 1996.
Hall, J. A., *Powers and Liberties: The Causes and Consequences of the Rise of the West*, Oxford: Basil Blackwell, 1984.
Hall, J. A. (ed.), *Civil Society: Theory, History, Comparison*, Cambridge: Polity Press, 1995.
Hall, R. and Williams, G., 'Land Reform in South Africa: Problems and Prospects', unpublished paper, developed from paper presented at a workshop on the Politics of Land Reform in the New South Africa, Development Studies Institute (DESTIN), London School of Economics, June 2000.

Halperin, S. and Laxer, G. (eds.), *Global Civil Society and Its Limits*, London: Palgrave, 2003.

Hamilton, L. A., 'A Theory of True Interests in the Work of Amartya Sen', *Government and Opposition*, 34. 4 (1999).

'"Civil Society": Critique and Alternative', in S. Halperin and G. Laxer (eds.), *Global Civil Society and Its Limits*, London: Palgrave, 2003.

'Needs, States, and Markets: democratic sovereignty against imperialism', *Theoria*, 102 (December 2003).

Hardimon, M., *Hegel's Social Philosophy: The project of reconciliation*, Cambridge: Cambridge University Press, 1994.

Harrison, R., *Democracy*, London and New York: Routledge, 1993.

Hart, H. L. A., 'Are There Any Natural Rights?', *The Philosophical Review*, 64. 2 (April 1955).

Hart, H. L. A. and Honoré, A. M., *Causation in Law*, Oxford: Clarendon Press, 1985.

Hausmann, D. M. and McPherson, M. S., *Economic Analysis and Moral Philosophy*, Cambridge: Cambridge University Press, 1996.

Hawthorn, G., 'Max Weber' (British Academy Master Mind Lectures), London, 1998.

'Liberalism since the Cold War: An enemy to itself?', *Review of International Studies*, 24, special issue (1999).

Hayek, F. A. (ed.), *The Constitution of Liberty*, London: Routledge, 1960.

Collectivist Economic Planning: Critical Studies on the Possibility of Socialism, Clifton, NJ: Augustus M. Kelley, 1975.

Hearn, J., 'Foreign Aid, Democratisation and Civil Society in Africa: A Study of South Africa, Ghana and Uganda', *Institute of Development Studies Discussion Paper*, 368 (March 1999).

Hegel, G. W. F., *The Logic of Hegel*, trans. W. Wallace, Oxford: Clarendon Press, 1892.

The Science of Logic, trans. A. V. Miller, London: Allen and Unwin, 1969.

Hegel's Phenomenology of Spirit, trans. A. V. Miller, with analysis and foreword by J. N. Findlay, Oxford: Oxford University Press, 1977.

System of Ethical Life and First Philosophy of Spirit, trans. H. S. Harris and T. M. Knox, Albany, NY: State University of New York, 1979.

Hegel and the Human Spirit: A Translation of the Jena Lectures on the Philosophy of Right (1805–6) with Commentary, ed. and trans. L. Rauch, Detroit: Wayne State University Press, 1983.

Elements of the Philosophy of Right, ed. A. W. Wood, trans. H. B. Nisbet, Cambridge: Cambridge University Press, 1991.

Heilbroner, R., *The Worldly Philosophers*, London: Penguin, 1991.

Held, D., *Models of Democracy*, 2nd edn, Cambridge: Polity Press, 1996.

Held, D. et al., *Global Transformations*, Cambridge: Polity Press, 1999.

Heller, A., *The Theory of Need in Marx*, London: Allison and Busby, 1976.

'Can "True" and "False" Needs be Posited?', in K. Lederer (ed.), *Human Needs: A Contribution to the Current Debate*, Cambridge, MA: Gunn and Hain, 1980.

Hirschman, A. O., *The Passions and the Interests: Political Arguments for Capitalism before Its Triumph* (20th anniversary edn), Princeton: Princeton University Press, 1997 [1977].

Hobbes, T., *Leviathan*, ed. R. Tuck, Cambridge: Cambridge University Press, 1991.

Hohfeld, W., *Fundamental Legal Conceptions as Applied in Judicial Reasoning*, Westport, CT: Greenwood Press, 1978.

Hollis, M., *The Cunning of Reason*, Cambridge: Cambridge University Press, 1987.
'Freedom in Good Spirits', *The Aristotelian Society* (1995 supplement).

Honneth, A., *The Struggle for Recognition: The Moral Grammar of Social Conflicts*, Cambridge: Polity Press, 1995.
'Democracy as Reflexive Cooperation: John Dewey and the Theory of Democracy Today', trans. J. M. M. Farrell, *Political Theory*, 26. 6 (1998).

Hont, I., 'Liberty, Equality, Prudence', *The Times Higher Education Supplement*, 9 October 1992.

Hont, I. and Ignatieff, M. (eds.), *Wealth and Virtue*, Cambridge: Cambridge University Press, 1983.

Horton, J. and Mendus, S. (eds.), *After MacIntyre: Critical Perspectives on the Work of Alasdair MacIntyre*, Cambridge: Polity Press, 1994.

Humboldt, W. von, *Ideen zu einem Versuch, die Grenzen der Wirksamkeit des Staates zu bestimmen*, Stuttgart: Reclam, 1967.

Hume, D., *An Inquiry Concerning Human Understanding* [1748], ed. C. Hendel, Indianapolis: Library of Liberal Arts, 1955.
A Treatise of Human Nature, 2nd edn, ed. L. A. Selby-Bigge, Oxford: Clarendon Press, 1978 [1st edn 1888, orig. edn 1739–40].
Political Essays, ed. K. Haakonssen, Cambridge: Cambridge University Press, 1994.

Huntingdon, S. P., *Political Order in Changing Societies*, New Haven: Yale University Press, 1968.

Hurley, S. L., 'Cognitivism in Political Philosophy', in *Well-Being and Morality: Essays in Honour of James Griffin*, Oxford: Oxford University Press, 2000.

Husami, Z. I., 'Marx on Distributive Justice', in M. Cohen, T. Nagel and T. Scanlon (eds.), *Marx, Justice and History*, Princeton: Princeton University Press, 1980.

James, C. L. R., *Notes on Dialectics*, London: Allison and Busby, 1980.

Kain, P. J., *Marx and Ethics*, Oxford: Clarendon Press, 1988.

Kant, I., *Critique of Pure Reason*, trans. and ed. P. Guyer and A. W. Wood, Cambridge: Cambridge University Press, 1998.

Keane, J., *Democracy and Civil Society*, London: Verso, 1988.
Civil Society and the State, London: Verso, 1988.

Kneale, M., *The English Passengers*, London: Penguin, 2001.

Kojève, A., *Introduction to the Reading of Hegel*, trans. J. Nichols, New York: Basic Books, 1969.

Laclau, E. and Mouffe, C., *Hegemony and Socialist Strategy: Towards a Radical Democratic Politics*, London: Verso, 1985.

Lane, M., 'Accountability, Transparency, Legitimacy: the new staples of democratic discourse and their implications for non-elected institutions', unpublished paper given at Annual Meeting of the American Political Science Association (APSA), 29 August – 1 September 2002.

Lawson, T., *Economics and Reality*, London and New York: Routledge, 1997.

Lear, J., *Love and Its Place in Nature: A Philosophical Interpretation of Freudian Psychoanalysis*, New Haven: Yale University Press, 1990.

Lederer, K. (ed.), *Human Needs: A Contribution to the Current Debate*, Cambridge, MA: Gunn and Hain, 1980.

Lehning, P. B., 'Toward a Multicultural Civil Society: The Role of Social Capital and Democratic Citizenship', *Government and Opposition*, 33. 1 (1998).

Locke, J., *Two Treatises of Government*, ed. P. Laslett, Cambridge: Cambridge University Press, 1988.

Lukács, G., *History and Class Consciousness: Studies in Marxist Dialectics*, London: Merlin Press, 1971.

Lukes, S., *Power: A Radical View*, London: Macmillan, 1974.

Luthuli, A., *Let My People Go*, London: Collins, 1962.

Lyons, D., 'Rights, Claimants, and Beneficiaries', *American Philosophical Quarterly*, 6. 3 (1969).

MacIntyre, A., *After Virtue: A Study in Moral Theory*, London: Duckworth, 1981.

Whose Justice? Which Rationality?, London: Duckworth, 1988.

Mackie, J., *Ethics: Inventing Right and Wrong*, Harmondsworth: Penguin, 1977.

Macpherson, C. B., *The Real World of Democracy*, Oxford: Oxford University Press, 1972.

The Life and Times of Liberal Democracy, Oxford: Oxford University Press, 1977.

Mandeville, B., *The Fable of the Bees, or Private Vices, Publick Benefits*, 2 vols., with commentary by F. B. Kaye (1924), Indianapolis: Liberty Fund, 1988 – an exact photographic reproduction of the edition published by Oxford University Press in 1924.

Mann, M., *The Sources of Social Power*, 2 vols., Cambridge: Cambridge University Press, 1986–92.

Marcus, T., Eales, K. and Wildschut, A., *Down to Earth: Land Demand in the New South Africa*, Durban: Indicator Press, 1996.

Marcuse, H., *An Essay on Liberation*, Boston, MA: Beacon Press, 1969.

Counter-Revolution and Revolt, Boston, MA: Beacon Press, 1972.

Marx, K., *Theories of Surplus Value*, ed. K. Kautsky, London: Lawrence & Wishart, 1951.

Oeuvres, 3 vols., Paris: Gallimard, 1965–82.

Critique of Hegel's 'Philosophy of Right', ed. J. O'Malley, Cambridge: Cambridge University Press, 1970.

Grundrisse, trans. M. Nicolaus, Harmondsworth: Penguin, 1973.

'Comments on James Mill, Élémens D'Économie Politique (1844)', in *Karl Marx Frederick Engels Collected Works Vol. 3 (MECW 3)*, London: Lawrence & Wishart, 1975.

Economic and Philosophic Manuscripts of 1844, in *Karl Marx Frederick Engels Collected Works Vol. 3 (MECW 3)*, London: Lawrence & Wishart, 1975.

'[Theses on Feuerbach]', in *Karl Marx Frederick Engels Collected Works Vol. 5 (MECW 5)*, London: Lawrence & Wishart, 1975.

'The German Ideology', in *Karl Marx Frederick Engels Collected Works Vol. 5 (MECW 5)*, London: Lawrence & Wishart, 1975.

Notes on Adolf Wagner, in *Karl Marx Texts on Method*, ed. T. Carver, Oxford: Oxford University Press, 1975.

The Poverty of Philosophy, in *Karl Marx Frederick Engels Collected Works Vol. 6 (MECW 6)*, London: Lawrence & Wishart, 1976.

Capital, 3 vols., intro. E. Mandel, trans. D. Fernbach, Harmondsworth: Penguin, 1976–8.

The Holy Family, in *Karl Marx: Selected Writings*, ed. D. Mclellan, Oxford: Oxford University Press, 1977.

Theses on Feuerbach, in *Karl Marx: Selected Writings,* ed. D. Mclellan, Oxford: Oxford University Press, 1977.

Karl Marx: Selected Writings, ed. D. Mclellan, Oxford: Oxford University Press, 1977.

Economic and Philosophical Manuscripts (1844), in *Karl Marx Early Writings*, intro. L. Colletti, London: Penguin, 1992.

Early Political Writings, ed. J. O'Malley, Cambridge: Cambridge University Press, 1994.

The Civil War in France, in *Marx: Later Political Writings*, ed. T. Carver, Cambridge: Cambridge University Press, 1996.

Critique of the Gotha Programme, in *Marx: Later Political Writings*, ed. T. Carver, Cambridge: Cambridge University Press, 1996.

Marx: Later Political Writings, ed. T. Carver, Cambridge: Cambridge University Press, 1996.

Marx, K. and Engels, F., *Selected Correspondence*, Moscow: Foreign Languages Publishing, 1956.

The Communist Manifesto, intro. A. J. P. Taylor, Harmondsworth: Penguin, 1967.

Correspondence, in *Karl Marx Frederick Engels Collected Works Vol. 38 (MECW 38)*, London: Lawrence & Wishart, 1976.

The Communist Manifesto, intro. G. Stedman Jones, London: Penguin, 2002.

Maslow, A. H., *Towards a Psychology of Being*, 2nd edn, New York: Van Nostrand Reinhold, 1968.

Motivation and Personality, 2nd edn, New York: Harper and Row, 1970.

Mbeki, T., *Africa: The Time Has Come* (Selected Speeches), Cape Town/ Johannesburg: Tafelburg/Mafube, 1998.

McInnes, N., 'The Politics of Needs — or, Who Needs Politics?', in R. Fitzgerald (ed.), *Human Needs and Politics*, Oxford: Pergamon, 1977.

Mclellan, D., *The Young Hegelians and Karl Marx*, Aldershot: Gregg Revivals, 1993.

McMurrin, S. M. (ed.), *Liberty, Equality, and Law: Selected Tanner Lectures on Moral Philosophy*, Cambridge: Cambridge University Press, 1987.

Meadwell, H., 'Post-Marxism, No Friend of Civil Society', in J. A. Hall (ed.), *Civil Society: Theory, History, Comparison*, Cambridge: Polity Press, 1995.

Meiksens Wood, E., *Democracy Against Capitalism*, Cambridge: Cambridge University Press, 1998.

Mészáros, I., *Marx's Theory of Alienation*, London: Merlin Press, 1982.

Mill, J. S., *The Subjection of Women*, intro. M. Warnock, London: Everyman, 1992. *On Liberty and Other Essays*, ed. and intro. J. Gray, Oxford: Oxford University Press, 1998.

Miller, D., 'Virtues, Practices and Justice', in J. Horton and S. Mendus (eds.), *After MacIntyre: Critical Perspectives on the Work of Alasdair MacIntyre*, Cambridge: Polity Press, 1994.

Mitchell, J., *Mad Men & Medusas: Reclaiming Hysteria and the Effect of Sibling Relations on the Human Condition*, London: Allen Lane and Penguin, 2000.

Mngxitama, A., 'South Africa: land reform blocked', at http://jinx.sistm. unsw.edu.au/~greenlft/2000/406/406p25.htm

Montesquieu, C., *The Spirit of the Laws*, trans. and ed. A. M. Cohler, B. C. Miller and H. S. Stone, Cambridge: Cambridge University Press, 1989.

Mouzelis, N., 'Modernity, Late Development and Civil Society', in J. A. Hall (ed.), *Civil Society: Theory, History, Comparison*, Cambridge: Polity Press, 1995.

Nagel, T., *The View From Nowhere*, Oxford: Oxford University Press, 1986.

Neocleous, M., *Administering Civil Society: Towards a Theory of State Power*, London: Macmillan, 1996.

Newitt, M., *A History of Mozambique*, London: Hurst, 1995.

Nietzsche, F., *On the Genealogy of Morality*, ed. K. Ansell-Pearson, trans. D. Diethe, Cambridge: Cambridge University Press, 1994. *The Birth of Tragedy and Other Writings*, ed. R. Geuss and R. Speirs, trans. R. Speirs, Cambridge: Cambridge University Press, 1999.

Noyes, C. R., *The Institution of Property*, New York: Longmans, 1936.

Nozick, R., *Anarchy, State and Utopia*, Oxford: Basil Blackwell, 1975.

Nussbaum, M. C., 'Nature, Function and Capability: Aristotle on Political Distribution', *Oxford Studies in Ancient Philosophy* (1988 supplementary volume). 'Aristotelian Social Democracy', in B. Douglas and G. Mara (eds.), *Liberalism and the Good*, New York and London: Routledge, 1990. 'Aristotle on Human Nature and the Foundation of Ethics', in J. Altham and R. Harrison (eds.), *World, Mind, and Ethics: Essays in the Ethical Philosophy of Bernard Williams*, Cambridge: Cambridge University Press, 1990. 'Non-Relative Virtues: An Aristotelian Approach', in M. C. Nussbaum and A. K. Sen (eds.), *The Quality of Life*, Oxford: Clarendon Press, 1993. 'Public Philosophy and International Feminism', *Ethics*, 108. 4 (July 1998). *Sex and Social Justice*, Oxford: Clarendon Press, 1999. *Women and Human Development: The Capabilities Approach*, Cambridge: Cambridge University Press, 2000.

Nussbaum, M. C. and Sen, A. K., 'Internal Criticism and Indian Rationalist Traditions', in M. Krausz (ed.), *Relativism: Interpretation and Confrontation*, Notre Dame: University of Notre Dame Press, 1989.

Nussbaum, M. C. and Sen, A. K. (eds.), *The Quality of Life*, Oxford: Clarendon Press, 1993.

Oakeshott, M., *Human Conduct*, Oxford: Clarendon Press, 1975.

Rationalism in Politics and Other Essays, Indianapolis: Liberty Press, 1991.

Offe, C., 'Institutions in East European Transitions', in R. Goodin (ed.), *The Theory of Institutional Design*, Cambridge: Cambridge University Press, 1998.

O'Neill, O., *Constructions of Reason: Explorations of Kant's Practical Philosophy*, Cambridge: Cambridge University Press, 1989.

Towards Justice and Virtue: A constructive account of practical reasoning, Cambridge: Cambridge University Press, 1996.

'Rights, Obligations, and Needs', in G. Brock (ed.), *Necessary Goods: Our Responsibilities to Meet Others' Needs*, Oxford: Rowman and Littlefield, 1998.

Bounds of Justice, Cambridge: Cambridge University Press, 2000.

A Question of Trust, Cambridge: Cambridge University Press, 2002.

Oxhorn, P., 'From Controlled Inclusion to Coerced Marginalization: The Struggle for Civil Society in Latin America', in J. A. Hall (ed.), *Civil Society: Theory, History, Comparison*, Cambridge: Polity Press, 1995.

Pagden, A., *Lords of All the World: Ideologies of Empire in Spain, Britain and France, c.1500−c.1800*, New Haven and London: Yale University Press, 1995.

Pateman, C., *Participation and Democratic Theory*, Cambridge: Cambridge University Press, 1970.

Patrick, M., 'Liberalism, Rights, and Recognition', *Philosophy and Social Criticism*, 26 (2000).

Petit, P., *Republicanism: A Theory of Freedom and Government*, Oxford: Oxford University Press, 1999.

Plant, R., 'Hegel and Political Economy', *New Left Review*, 103 & 104 (1977).

'Needs, Agency and Rights', in C. Sampford and D. J. Gilligan (eds.), *Law, Rights and the Welfare State*, London: Croom Helm, 1986.

Plato, *Republic*, trans. B. Jowett, 2nd edn rev. and corr., Oxford: Clarendon Press, 1881.

Republic, trans. and intro. D. Lee, Harmondsworth: Penguin, 1974.

Primus, R. A., *The American Language of Rights*, Cambridge: Cambridge University Press, 1999.

Proudhon, P.-J., *Système des Contradictions Économiques ou Philosophie de la Misère*, Paris and Geneva: Slatkine, 1982 [1846].

What is Property?, trans. and ed. D. R. Kelley and B. G. Smith, Cambridge: Cambridge University Press, 1994.

Théorie de la Propriété, Paris: Éditions l'Harmattan, 1997.

Putnam, H., *The Many Faces of Realism*, LaSalle, IL: Open Court, 1987.

'Objectivity and the Science-Ethics Distinction', in M. C. Nussbaum and A. K. Sen (eds.), *The Quality of Life*, Oxford: Clarendon Press, 1993.

Rawls, J., *A Theory of Justice*, Oxford: Oxford University Press, 1973.

'Social Unity and Primary Goods', in A. K. Sen and B. Williams (eds.), *Utilitarianism and Beyond*, Cambridge: Cambridge University Press, 1982.

'Priority of Right and Ideas of the Good', *Philosophy and Public Affairs*, 17 (1988).
Political Liberalism, New York: Columbia University Press, 1996.

Raz, J., *The Morality of Freedom*, Oxford: Oxford University Press, 1986.

Rist, G., 'Basic questions about basic human needs', in K. Lederer (ed.), *Human Needs*, Cambridge, MA: Gunn and Hain, 1980.

Roemer, J., 'An Historical Materialist Alternative to Welfarism', in J. Elster and A. Hylland (eds.), *Foundations of Social Choice Theory*, Cambridge: Cambridge University Press, 1986.

Rorty, R., *Objectivity, Relativism and Truth Vol. 1*, Cambridge: Cambridge University Press, 1991.

Rousseau, J.-J., *The Discourses and Other Early Political Writings*, ed. and trans. V. Gourevitch, Cambridge: Cambridge University Press, 1997.
The Social Contract and other late political writings, ed. and trans. V. Gourevitch, Cambridge: Cambridge University Press, 1997.

Runciman, D., *Pluralism and the Personality of the State*, Cambridge: Cambridge University Press, 1997.
'Is the State a Corporation?', *Government and Opposition*, 35. 1 (2000).

Ryan, A., *Property and Political Theory*, Oxford: Blackwell, 1984.

Ryan, A. (ed.), *The Idea of Freedom: Essays in honour of Isaiah Berlin*, Oxford: Oxford University Press, 1979.

Sagovsky, N., 'Who Needs What? Minimum Income Standards and the Ethics of Adequacy', unpublished paper presented at Cambridge conference on poverty, April 2000.

Sartorius, R. (ed.), *Paternalism*, Minneapolis: University of Minnesota Press, 1983.

Sayers, S., *Marxism and Human Nature*, London and New York: Routledge, 1998.

Scanlon, T., 'Preference and Urgency', *The Journal of Philosophy*, 72. 19 (1975).
'Value, Desire and the Quality of Life', in M. C. Nussbaum and A. K. Sen (eds.), *The Quality of Life*, Oxford: Clarendon Press, 1993.

Schatzki, T. R., *Social Practices: A Wittgensteinian Approach to Human Activity and The Social*, Cambridge: Cambridge University Press, 1996.

Schatzki, T. R., Knorr, C. K. and Savigny, E. von (eds.), *The Practice Turn in Contemporary Theory*, London and New York: Routledge, 2001.

Seligman, A. B., *The Idea of Civil Society*, Princeton: Princeton University Press, 1992.
'Animadversions upon Civil Society and Civic Virtue in the Last Decade of the Twentieth Century', in J. A. Hall (ed.), *Civil Society: Theory, History, Comparison*, Cambridge: Polity Press, 1995.

Sellar, A., 'Should the Feminist Philosopher Stay at Home?', in K. Lennon and M. Whitford (eds.), *Knowing the Difference: Feminist Perspectives in Epistemology*, London and New York: Routledge, 1994.

Sen, A. K., *Collective Choice and Social Welfare*, San Francisco: Holden-Day, 1970.
'Choice Functions and Revealed Preference', *Review of Economic Studies*, 38 (1971).
'Behaviour and the Concept of Preference', *Economica*, 40 (1973).

'Rational Fools: A Critique of the Behavioral Foundations of Economic Theory', *Philosophy and Public Affairs*, 6 (1976–7).

Poverty and Famines: An Essay on Entitlement and Deprivation, Oxford: Oxford University Press, 1981. (Originally, 'Starvation and Exchange Entitlement: a general approach and its application to the Great Bengal Famine', *Cambridge Journal of Economics*, 1 [1977].)

'Rights and Agency', *Philosophy and Public Affairs*, 11 (1982).

'Accounts, Actions and Values: Objectivity of Social Science', in C. Lloyd (ed.), *Social Theory and Political Practice*, Oxford: Clarendon Press, 1983.

'Well-Being, Agency, and Freedom: The Dewey Lectures 1984', *The Journal of Philosophy*, 82. 4 (1985).

Commodities and Capabilities, Amsterdam and Oxford: North-Holland, 1985.

'The Equality of What?' [1979], in S. M. McMurrin (ed.), *Liberty, Equality, and Law*, Cambridge: Cambridge University Press, 1987.

On Ethics and Economics, Oxford: Basil Blackwell, 1987.

The Standard of Living, 1985 Tanner Lectures at Cambridge, with contributions by K. Hart, R. Kanbur, J. Muellbauer and B. Williams, ed. G. Hawthorn, Cambridge: Cambridge University Press, 1987.

'Justice: Means versus Freedoms', *Philosophy and Public Affairs*, 19 (1990).

'Welfare, freedom and social choice. A reply', *Recherches économiques de Louvain*, 56 (1990).

'Welfare, Preference and Freedom', *Journal of Econometrics*, 50 (1991).

Inequality Reexamined, Oxford: Clarendon Press, 1992.

'Capability and Well-Being', in M. C. Nussbaum and A. K. Sen, *The Quality of Life*, Oxford: Clarendon Press, 1993.

'Positional Objectivity', *Philosophy and Public Affairs*, 22 (1993).

'Markets and freedoms: Achievements and limitations of the market mechanism in promoting individual freedoms', *Oxford Economic Papers*, 45 (1993).

'Freedoms and Needs: An argument for the primacy of political rights', *The New Republic*, January 10 & 17 (1994).

'Rationality and Social Choice', *American Economic Review*, 85 (1995).

Reason Before Identity, The 1998 Romanes Lecture, Oxford: Oxford University Press, 1999.

Development as Freedom, Oxford: Oxford University Press, 1999.

Shils, E., 'The Virtue of Civil Society', *Government and Opposition*, 26. 1 (1991).

Short, C., MP, 'NGO's in a Global Future', speech given at Birmingham University on 13 January 1999.

Skinner, Q., 'The State', in T. Ball, J. Farr and R. L. Hanson (eds.), *Political Innovation and Conceptual Change*, Cambridge: Cambridge University Press, 1989.

Smith, A., *An Inquiry into the Nature and Causes of the Wealth of Nations*, 2 vols., ed. A. S. Skinner and R. Meek, Indianapolis: Liberty Classics, 1981.

The Theory of Moral Sentiments (6th edn, 1790), ed. A. Macfie and D. Steuart, Indianapolis: Liberty Classics, 1982.

Lectures on Jurisprudence, ed. R. Meek, D. Raphael and P. Stein, Indianapolis: Liberty Classics 1982.

Soper, K., *On Human Needs: Open and Closed Theories in a Marxist Perspective*, Brighton: Harvester, 1981.

'A Theory of Human Need', *New Left Review*, 197 (1993).

Springborg, P., 'Karl Marx on Human Needs', in R. Fitzgerald (ed.), *Human Needs and Politics*, Oxford: Pergamon, 1977.

Stein, L. von, *The History of the Social Movement in France, 1789–1850*, intro., ed. and trans. K. Bauer-Mengelberg, Totowa, NJ: Bedminster, 1964.

Stewart, F., *Basic Needs in Developing Countries*, Baltimore: Johns Hopkins University Press, 1985.

Stirner, M., *The Ego and Its Own*, Cambridge: Cambridge University Press, 1995.

Streeten, P., 'Basic Needs: Some Unsettled Questions', *World Development*, 12 (1984).

Sunstein, C. R., 'Democracy and Shifting Preferences', in D. Copp, J. Roemer and J. Hampton (eds.), *The Idea of Democracy*, Cambridge: Cambridge University Press, 1993.

Taylor, C., *Sources of the Self: The Making of the Modern Identity*, Cambridge, MA: Harvard University Press, 1989.

'Explanation and Practical Reason', in M. C. Nussbaum and A. K. Sen (eds.), *The Quality of Life*, Oxford: Clarendon Press, 1993.

'The Politics of Recognition', in A. Gutmann (ed.), *Multiculturalism: Examining the politics of recognition*, Princeton: Princeton University Press, 1994.

Philosophical Arguments, Cambridge, MA: Harvard University Press, 1995.

Tester, K., *Civil Society*, London and New York: Routledge, 1992.

Thomson, G., *Needs*, London and New York: Routledge, 1987.

Tuck, R., *Natural Rights Theories: Their origin and development*, Cambridge: Cambridge University Press, 1979.

'The Dangers of Natural Rights', *Harvard Journal of Law & Public Policy*, 20. 3 (1997).

The Rights of War and Peace: Political Thought and the International Order from Grotius to Kant, Oxford: Oxford University Press, 1999.

Tully, J., *A Discourse on Property: John Locke and his adversaries*, Cambridge: Cambridge University Press, 1980.

Turner, S. (ed.), *The Cambridge Companion to Weber*, Cambridge: Cambridge University Press, 2000.

Veblen, T., *The Theory of the Leisure Class*, Boston: Houghton Mifflin, 1973 [1899].

Venable, V., *Human Nature: The Marxian View*, New York: Knopf, 1945.

Villiers, B. de (ed.), *Birth of a Constitution*, Kenwyn, South Africa: Juta & Co., 1994.

Waldron, J., *The Right to Private Property*, Oxford: Clarendon Press, 1988.

Waldron, J. (ed.), *Theories of Rights*, Oxford: Oxford University Press, 1984.

'Nonsense Upon Stilts': Bentham, Burke, and Marx on the Rights of Man, London: Methuen, 1987.

Walicki, A., *Marxism and the Leap to the Kingdom of Freedom: The Rise and Fall of the Communist Utopia*, Stanford: Stanford University Press, 1995.

Wallerstein, I., 'The Albatross of Racism', *London Review of Books*, 22. 10 (May 2000).

Walton, A. S., 'Economy, Utility and Community in Hegel's Theory of Civil Society', in Z. A. Pelczynski (ed.), *The State and Civil Society*, Cambridge: Cambridge University Press, 1984.

Walt, A. J. van der, 'Developments that may Change the Institution of Private Ownership so as to meet the Needs of a Non-racial Society in South Africa', *Stellenbosch Law Review*, 1 (1990).

'The Fragmentation of Land Rights', *South African Journal of Human Rights*, 8 (1992).

'Property Rights, Land Rights, and Environmental Rights', in D. van Wyk, J. Dugard, B. de Villiers and D. Davis (eds.), *Rights and Constitutionalism: The New South African Legal Order*, Oxford: Clarendon Press, 1996.

Walzer, M., 'The Idea of Civil Society', *Dissent* 38. 2 (Spring 1991).

Waszek, N., *The Scottish Enlightenment and Hegel's Account of 'Civil Society'*, Dordrecht and Boston: Kluwer Academic Publishers, 1988.

Weber, M., *Economy and Society*, ed. G. Roth and C. Wittich, 2 vols., Berkeley: University of California Press, 1978.

'The Profession and Vocation of Politics', in *Weber: Political Writings*, ed. P. Lassman and R. Spiers, Cambridge: Cambridge University Press, 1994.

White, A. R., *Modal Thinking*, Oxford: Basil Blackwell, 1975.

Wiggins, D., *Needs, Values, Truth: Essays in the Philosophy of Value*, 3rd edn, Oxford: Clarendon Press, 1998.

Wildt, A., *Autonomie und Anerkennung: Hegels Moralitätskritik im Lichte seiner Fichte-Rezeption*, Stuttgart: Klett-Cotta, 1982.

Williams, B., *Moral Luck*, Cambridge: Cambridge University Press, 1981.

Truth and Truthfulness, Princeton: Princeton University Press, 2002.

'Why Philosophy Needs History', *London Review of Books* 24. 2 (17 October 2002).

Wisner, B., *Power and Need in Africa: Basic Human Needs and Development Policies*, London: Earthscan, 1988.

Wolin, R., 'Review of Jean L. Cohen and Andrew Arato, *Civil Society and Political Theory*. Cambridge: MIT Press, 1992', *Theory and Society*, 22. 4 (1993).

Wollstonecraft, M., *A Vindication of the Rights of Woman*, intro. M. Warnock, London: Everyman, 1992.

Wood, A. W., 'Marx on Right and Justice: A Reply to Husami', in M. Cohen, T. Nagel and T. Scanlon (eds.), *Marx, Justice and History*, Princeton: Princeton University Press, 1980.

Wyk, D. van, Dugard, J., Villiers, B. de and Davis, D. (eds.), *Rights and Constitutionalism: The New South African Legal Order*, Oxford: Clarendon Press, 1996.

Young, I. M., *Justice and the Politics of Difference*, Princeton: Princeton University Press, 1990.

WEBSITES

The Constitution of the Republic of South Africa, Pretoria: Government Printers, 1996, also at http://www.polity.org.za/govdocs/constitution/saconst.html
'Certification of the Constitution of the Republic of South Africa, 1996', at http://www.concourt.gov.za/judgements/1996const.html
Judicial Service Commission Interviews, at http://www.concourt.gov.za/interviews
'South Africa: land reform blocked', A. Mngxitama, at http://jinx.sistm.unsw. edu.au/~greenlft/2000/406/406p25.htm

Index